£4.99

TWISTED SISTERS

ROCKWELL PRESS

TWISTED SISTERS

Women, Crime and Deviance
in Scotland Since 1400

Edited by
Yvonne Galloway Brown and Rona Ferguson

TUCKWELL PRESS

First published in Great Britain in 2002 by
Tuckwell Press Ltd
The Mill House
Phantassie
East Linton
East Lothian, Scotland

ISBN 1 86232 295 3

British Library Cataloguing-in-Publication Data
A catalogue entry is available on request
from the British Library

Typeset by Palimpsest Book Production Limited,
Polmont, Stirlingshire
Printed by Bell and Bain Ltd, Glasgow

For our mums
Hilda and Effie

Contents

List of Contributors

Lynn Abrams teaches modern history at Glasgow University. She has published widely in the fields of European women's history and Scottish social history. Her most recent publications include *The Orphan Country: Children of Scotland's Broken Homes, 1845 to the Present* (1998) and *The Making of Modern Woman: Europe 1789–1918* (2002). She is currently working on a book on women in Shetland.

Yvonne Galloway Brown is employed at Glasgow Caledonian University where she teaches modern history on a part-time basis. She is the membership secretary/website co-ordinator of the Scottish Women's History Network and is an elected member of the steering group of the Women's History Network (UK). Her current research interests are Scottish women and the Second World War. Recent publications include 'Women, 1770s onwards', in Michael Lynch (ed.), *Oxford Companion to Scottish History* (2001).

Gordon DesBrisay is Associate Professor of History at the University of Saskatchewan. He is a contributor to the forthcoming *New History of Aberdeen, 1100–1800*, and his recent articles include 'Wet Nurses and Unwed Mothers in Seventeenth-Century Scotland', in E. Ewan and M. Meikle, (eds.), *Women in Scotland, c.1100-c.1750* (1999).

Elizabeth Ewan is Associate Professor of History/Scottish Studies at the University of Guelph, Ontario, Canada. Her publications include *Townlife in Fourteenth-Century Scotland* (1990), *Women in Scotland, c.1100-c.1750*, co-edited with Maureen Meikle (1999), and articles on Scottish urban and women's history.

Rona Ferguson is Research Assistant in the Centre for Contemporary History, Glasgow Caledonian University. Amongst other things she has published from a recent oral history study of district nursing in Scotland. She is currently working in the history of medical social work, also using oral testimony, funded by the Wellcome Trust.

Dr Anne-Marie Kilday is a Senior Lecturer in History at Oxford Brookes University. Her research interests and publications involve the spheres of gender and crime in Britain during the eighteenth and nineteenth centuries.

Andrea Knox is a Lecturer in History at the University of Northumbria at Newcastle. She has published papers on the themes of female criminality in sixteenth- and seventeenth-century Ireland and Scotland, female criminal networks and female migration to Spain during the early-modern period.

Catriona M.M. Macdonald is Senior Lecturer in History at Glasgow Caledonian University. She is editor of *Unionist Scotland, 1800–1997* (1998), the joint editor of *Scotland and the Great War* (1999) with E.W. McFarland and author of *The Radical Thread* (2000). Her main research interests lie in the social, political and cultural history of late modern Scotland.

Hugh V. McLachlan is a Reader in the Division of Sociology and Social Policy at Glasgow Caledonian University. He has published numerous papers in sociology, philosophy of the social sciences and applied philosophy, particularly in relation to medical ethics, in which area he has written about, for instance, surrogate motherhood, embryology and abortion. He is joint compiler, along with C. J. Larner and C.H. Lee, of *A Source-book of Scottish Witchcraft* (Glasgow University, 1977).

Kimm Perkins is a PhD research student in the Scottish History Department, University of Glasgow. Her thesis topic is 'Religious Women and Their Communities in Medieval Scotland, c.1100–1560', and she is currently looking at the Scottish material relating to women, held in the Vatican records. Other research interests include: medieval women; monasticism; saints' lives; medieval marriage and family; canon law; history of the British Isles; early-modern women; and prosopographical studies.

Kim Swales is a Professor in the Department of Economics at the University of Strathclyde and Research Director of the Fraser of Allander Institute. Together with Hugh McLachlan he has written papers on Scottish witchcraft persecution, Scottish historical crime and crime waves.

Acknowledgements

For the initial motivation to produce this book we wish to thank all those who came along to the Scottish Women's History Network Conference, *Twisted Sisters*, at Glasgow Caledonian University in October 2000 and made it such a success. We wish to acknowledge Norman Aitkinson at Angus Archives, Cultural Services for allowing us to reproduce details of Helen Guthrie (taken from the *Revealing Women Exhibition*) and artist Barbara Robertson for allowing us to use the image for our cover. Special thanks also to our colleague Hugh McLachlan for his unfailing encouragement and unique sense of humour. Thanks also to Beth Ingpen for indexing the volume. We also wish to acknowledge Naomi Brown and Scott Hutton who assisted with the smooth running of the Conference on the day. Finally, we wish to express our appreciation to all of the contributors.

Twisted Sisters: Women, Crime and Deviance in Scotland Since 1400

Yvonne Galloway Brown and Rona Ferguson

Scottish women's history is a lively field with much research currently spurred on by the recent renaissance and reinvigoration of the Scottish Women's History Network.[1] Indeed, this collection of essays arose from a Scottish Women's History Network conference, *Twisted Sisters*, hosted by Glasgow Caledonian University in Autumn 2000. Spanning the medieval period to modernity, the essays examine women's involvement in crime and deviance in both the private and public spheres of Scottish society. They document a new perspective on female behaviour which challenges the received view of women as restrained by the conventions of their time. This collection, therefore, hopes to make a significant contribution to Scottish women's historiography.

Scottish women's history developed relatively late in comparison with most other western countries, including, ironically, the rest of the UK. Breitenbach *et al* have stated that the current state of research on women in Scotland suggests an environment that is arid, if not actively hostile.[2] Moreover, they suggest that our knowledge and understanding of women in Scotland suffer a double disadvantage of marginalisation within a male-dominated Scotland, as well as marginalisation within an English-dominated Britain.[3] Just as Scotland's history as a whole has been romanticised, the life of Scottish women in history has been misrepresented by its few romanticised heroines:

> Scotland has few female icons . . . and those that she has, such as Mary Stuart and Flora Macdonald, appear romantic and doomed as participants in history's lost causes . . . the heroes and villains of our popular histories, with the exception of Mary, are invariably male, and alternatives only replace kings, lairds and politicians with the equally male dominated roster of the Red Clyde Heroes.[4]

There are many reasons we could suggest for this rather late start, but the most obvious (and problematic) reason is that Scottish history has, until recently, been dominated by labour history. Labour history in Scotland is a relatively mature discipline, but it has been, predominantly, a history of *men* rather than *women*, whether in the labour market, trade union movement or as political agitators. Moreover, it has tended to focus in and around the industrial central belt. Scotland's history, at the beginning of the twenty-first century, is a history that still, unfortunately, tells only a partial, patriarchal version of the past.[5]

The first two significant works on Scottish women's history appeared almost twenty years ago: Christina Larner's *Enemies of God*[6] and Rosalind Marshall's *Virgins and Viragos: A History of Women in Scotland 1080–1980*.[7] These works showed to a wider audience that Scottish women did indeed have a history (a point largely previously ignored by social historians of Scotland's past). In the early 1990s, two collections of essays edited by Eleanor Gordon and Esther Breitenbach were published: *The World is Ill-Divided: Women's Work in Scotland in the Nineteenth and Early Twentieth Centuries* and *Out of Bounds: Women in Scottish Society 1800–1945*.[8] These are regarded by many as the 'turning-point' for Scottish women's historiography. Since that time, a number of monographs have appeared on a variety of aspects of Scottish women's past with the focus remaining mainly on the modern period and on single issues, such as Elspeth King and Leah Leneman's respective works on the Scottish Suffragette Movement,[9] Linda Mahood's work on prostitution[10] and Leah Leneman and Rosalind Mitchison's two books on sexuality in both rural and urban societies.[11]

Whilst the subject of Scottish women's past has been addressed by a number of historians in recent years, much more research into a further diverse range of areas relating to Scottish women's unique experiences still remains to be researched and published, particularly in the timespan covered by this collection. Little to date, however, has been published on women in Scotland in the medieval or early modern periods, with the notable exceptions of Elizabeth Sanderson's book on women and work in eighteenth-century Edinburgh[12] and Deborah Symond's work on ballads and infanticide in early modern Scotland.[13] Elspeth King's *Hidden History of Glasgow's Women: The Thenew Factor*, is also worthy of mention as it charts in some detail the history of Glasgow women from the medieval to the modern period.[14] Most recently, there appeared the publication of an edited collection of essays by Elizabeth Ewan and Maureen Meikle, *Women in Scotland c. 1110–1750*.[15] This collection is a welcome addition to the historiography of Scottish women which addresses many important themes including nunneries, consumption and marriage. In the same year, a further edited collection, *Gendering Scottish History: An International Approach*,[16] addressed a wide range of issues from an international perspective. However, both these works reinforce, to a large extent, the idea of a society in which women's traditional roles are upheld; women are represented as essentially passive and restrained. No attention is given in either of these volumes to the themes and issues of crime or deviance.

Many of the papers in this collection concede that Scottish society was indeed one in which women suffered under unequal opportunity and justice. That they were incarcerated within traditional definitions of womanhood bound by culture, state and church cannot easily be disputed, but as Foucault, in a rather different context noted, 'the prison cannot fail to produce delinquents'.[17] In this book, each chapter opens us to ways in which women resisted repression in a culture capable of viewing them as 'twisted by definition'. This collection seeks to celebrate the actions of women that allowed them to be seen as immoral, rebellious or criminal and to portray such deviancy as positive resistance and a force for change. In the context of early Scottish society their actions can be seen here in political radicalism (Knox and Craig), piety unbalanced in the face of ambition (Perkins), manipulation in public scandal (Macdonald), the conjuring of 'new' truth (McLachlan and Swales), subversion of parochial restrictions (Ewan) and brutality in their execution of the most heinous and unfeminine crime (Kilday and Abrams). Women's response to the status quo was not always so overt or so passionate, but nonetheless, effective. In DesBrisay's account of Jean Stevin, for example, we see that even in the acceptance of punishment women could engender in their judges a quiet reassessment of guilt. In short, the chapters here will show women as powerful actors whether on the national or domestic stage.

The collection begins with a chapter by Andrea Knox who examines female criminality, violence and aggression in the early modern period. Knox discusses the effect of English colonial authority and the resistance to such influence from women in Ireland and Scotland. She reveals Scottish and Irish women's connections and networks, together with national identity and conflict, but with a 'twist', as she discusses the activities of Irish and Scottish women in resisting the policies and culture of the incoming English and Scots in Ireland. Knox reveals, moreover, that there was a strong Highland connection with links between Irish female rebels and many Scottish women from the clans, such as Agnes Campbell and her daughter Finola O'Donnell who, through marriage, became Irish rebels themselves, bringing hundreds of Scottish mercenary troops with them to Ireland as their dowries. These women were cited as the cause of rebellion and as the instructors of all Scots in Ireland, and their role in facilitating female spy networks is scrutinised in detail by Knox in this chapter. Many early modern historians have tended to omit the actions and perceptions of women from this period. Knox, however, reveals that a high degree of female-initiated criminal and subversive activities did take place and draws from examples of the many networks between Irish and Scottish women for comparative analysis of such deviant behaviour.

Maggie Craig continues the political theme with an essay examining women's involvement in the '45 Rising. As she points out, this is an area which is all too often overlooked by historians, with the exception perhaps of the Flora MacDonald cult. Craig reveals the considerable support offered to the Jacobite cause by the many women who raised regiments, gathered together horses and supplies, acted as spies and passed on information, nursed the wounded and helped prisoners to escape. Many of these women actively chose to participate, running the risks involved because of their own political convictions, often in direct opposition to the menfolk of their families. Craig also shows that many women undoubtedly exercised a considerable influence on the men around them by means of their wealth – aristocratic women clearly had wide-ranging political and economic clout (unlike their working-class counterparts who were viewed by the authorities as problematic, to be disposed of as quickly and efficiently as possible). The idea of the 'fair sex' as one of the chief civilising forces in a potentially brutish life runs through much eighteenth-century writing, and Craig suggests that Flora MacDonald may continue to be heralded as the 'Highland Heroine' because she continued to correspond to this 'ideal'. She did not have strong political convictions, unlike the majority of the women discussed in this chapter, who, for too long, have been silenced by historical forces and Highland mythology.

However, women's deviancy was not always as blatant as the military aggression of rebels. In Kimm Perkins' exploration of women's rise to the role of prioress in Cistercian religious houses we see how, even in monasticism, women were not always benign. As one of the few life choices open to women, the status of prioress gave women a power unequalled in ordinary life. Working from ecclesiastical records, Perkins details how the ambitions of women were fought out in power struggles to gain the 'fruits of the offices' as prioress. As she points out, much work on the records remains to be done, but from her revealing insight we see that medieval women could be fiercely competitive and persistently litigious. In battles for position they repeatedly brought their female opponents into disrepute. Any notion of sisterly love within the apparently pious walls of the medieval convent are shattered as Perkins outlines the sometimes prolonged struggles for personal advancement.

Any consideration of women in the early modern period is in complete without the mention of witchcraft. However, Hugh McLachlan and Kim Swales provide a different perspective by focusing on the interpretation of the witchcraft trial. By looking at one particular trial, that of Christian Shaw who later came to be known as 'The Bargarran Impostor', they focus on the way such a narrative account of the case could have been created. Beginning with a fascinating philosophical discussion on the nature of language and taking account of the postmodern perspective, they lay out distinctions between *truth* and *meaning*, and *truth* and *truthfulness*. From this the authors establish two basic premises on which their re-assessment of Christian Shaw is founded: that 'the meaning of language derives from its use and social context' and that 'not all "narratives" are equally true'. After a detailed examination of Shaw's case through the *Narrative*, McLachlan and Swales reject the notion of trickery or mental illness. By looking at the production of the *Narrative*, the intentions of those who wrote it and the context of belief in which it appeared, the authors confer a certain innocence on Christian Shaw.

Catriona Macdonald's chapter takes us just beyond the margins of the early modern period in an examination of the morally questionable behaviour of Queen Caroline. Virtually ignored by her husband, the Queen adopted a libertine lifestyle which excited the nation's interest in both moral and political judgement. Macdonald discusses the affair as an event not just of public scandal or gossip but a focus for 'cultural self-appraisal'. The author highlights the relationship between the individual behaviour of the Queen and the appropriation of the story by the media of the day. Viewed by Macdonald to be 'as much a literary phenomenon' as an event, the Queen Caroline affair was to a large extent created by its commentators. Despite her impropriety, Queen Caroline's behaviour was used to argue for the responsibility of husbands as much as the proper role of the dutiful wife. Reformers appropriated Caroline's cause, twisting its moral dubiety to highlight the unconstitutional nature of the King's actions and question his reliability as monarch. Referred to by one of her contemporaries as the 'Bedlam Bitch' and by Macdonald as a woman 'at odds with the moral ideal', the Queen was written into history in the service of both political reformers and moral commentators. While Caroline's behaviour as a woman characterises her as a *twisted sister* in a moral sense, the malleability of her story sees her twisted by others to fit the shape of their own causes.

Deviancy, in its many forms, clearly is a theme which runs through the first section of this collection. Part Two, on the other hand, turns its attention to crime and punishment, commencing with Elizabeth Ewan's chapter which discusses women and daily life in a number of late medieval Scottish towns. Ewan draws upon burgh court records to examine the lives of ordinary women – how they earned a living, cared for their families and formed social bonds within their communities. The author shows that tension between crime and culture was played out in several areas. Throughout the period many women were involved in buying and selling, and a number faced prosecution for unfair trading practices fraud and theft, as well as disputes over credit. Unmarried women who lived alone, while earning a living, aroused the suspicion of authorities, who assumed they were engaged in prostitution. Ewan shows that the official attitudes to prostitution, for a number of reasons, hardened during the sixteenth century, and so what had previously been a legal way of earning a living became a crime. Another area of tension lay in the informal bonds of aid and sociability which women formed with each other, for example helping out neighbours and relatives in times of plague. However, this could result in infringement of the strict plague regulations which attempted to control the movement of people and goods, and severe punishment, even execution, was often the end result. Songs and stories were also often viewed as subversive by authorities worried about social stability, and women were often prosecuted for words which were said in jest or momentary anger as part of the rough and ready urban culture. Ewan suggests that throughout the late medieval period, when attitudes toward financially independent women were altering, perhaps one of the ways to enforce new ideas was increasingly to redefine women's culture as crime.

'Twisted by definition' is how Gordon DesBrisay describes the women of a society obsessed with sin and 'Godly discipline', claiming that for the better part of two hundred years 'the great Calvinist war on sin was the single most distinctive feature of Scottish life'. Using examples of domestic servants convicted of sexual misconduct by state and church, he breaks with the idea of godly discipline in Scotland as gender-blind. He portrays seventeenth-century Scottish society as one that supported a 'whole constellation of restrictive practices' for women that brought many of them before civic and kirk authorities. His account of the rape and punishment of Jean Stevin gets to the heart of a punitive system founded on guilt or innocence through circumstance rather than agency. The system of punishment for sexual sins as meted out to men and women betrayed inherent contradictions. While guilt was conferred by consideration of the sin regardless of agency, the mitigation of punishment which sometimes followed was based on consideration of personal culpability. Despite her professed guilt and even her acceptance of punishment, the case of Jean Stevin exemplifies the confused standards of godly discipline and its treatment of women.

Anne-Marie Kilday examines the incidence and nature of the crime of infanticide or 'maternal murder' in eighteenth-century Scotland. Kilday provides an analysis of the legislative changes which reflected the erratic nature of opinion in Scotland, and indeed Britain as a whole, towards this type of offence in the early modern period and, moreover, provides evidence of the actual act of infanticide itself. Just as Andrea Knox adopted a comparative approach, so too does Kilday. Her Anglo-Scottish analysis investigates the incidence rate of infanticide, the characteristics of the women accused, and the methods used to carry out the offences. Attention is given to the disturbing suggestion that Scottish women committed infanticide in a far more violent and barbarous manner than their English counterparts. Kilday offers suggestions for the rationale behind this apparently gruesome and maternally 'abnormal' activity in an attempt not only to explain this particular anomaly, but also to try to understand why women committed acts of murder against their new-born children. Kilday's chapter sheds new light on the various intricacies of this crime with specific reference to the hitherto unexamined *Scottish* experience of child-killing in the early modern period which provides a clearer *British* picture of this most perplexing, disturbing but fascinating crime.

Infanticide, however, is not a crime confined to the early modern period as we discover in Lynn Abrams' chapter on child murder in late modern Shetland – a relatively isolated community in terms of both geography and insularity from modernising influences in this period. Abrams points out that Shetland was 'a place where pre-modern beliefs and practices arguably survived longer than anywhere else in Britain'. Indeed, it was the kirk session which acted as the primary disciplinary body, 'and thus women under suspicion of child murder were still subject to the observation and intervention of kirk elders and their supporters as a means of maintaining control over all women'. Throughout the nineteenth century, women living on this group of islands far outnumbered men, a statistic which we find had profound consequences for relations between the sexes. As Abrams notes, 'in a marriage market that favoured men, it was in the interests of Shetland men to maintain control over their womenfolk'. This imbalance, however, took the form of a high proportion of women who never married, a significant number of widows and the poverty attendant on unmarried women in the community. Abrams informs us that between 1699 and 1920, only forty cases of alleged child murder or concealment of pregnancy survive in Shetland's records. Furthermore, only seventeen women were tried in the sheriff court and only three of these are known to have served jail sentences – the lengthiest being fifteen months. Thus, the author notes that the crime of child murder, or the alternative and lesser charge of concealment of pregnancy, appears to have been an extremely rare occurrence in Shetland. Abrams focuses on material drawn from thirty-nine of these cases – almost all of whom were young and unmarried. Through use of specific case studies, the author gives the reader an insight into the plight of the unmarried mother in such a community and, moreover, she assesses the changing nature of community (and legal) attitudes towards mothers of illegitimate babies. In Shetland, where women were less likely to find a husband compared with anywhere else in the British Isles and where women's economic position in a society dominated by crofting and fishing was precarious, the crime of infanticide is used by Abrams as a window onto the specific material and cultural conditions of women. Historians of both the early modern and late modern periods have tended to interpret infanticide as either the desperate act of the shamed pregnant woman or the outcome of a woman's marginal economic status within a community. Abrams notes that these factors were indeed present in Shetland but suggests that, in view of these circumstances, it was surprising that so few women were indicted for child murder, and indeed provides more intangible (and thought-provoking) motives for this most uniquely female of crimes on these 'most female of islands'.

This collection offers many new perspectives on and interpretations of women in Scottish society from 1400 to the present, examining crime, deviancy and punishment in their many forms. Whereas history has tended to place women in male social structures, it becomes clear that these structures had many limitations. Women could not be ignored or kept down, but rather, they themselves reacted to situations to effect positive change whether by trading illegally or by murdering their children. Women's social structures may have differed from those of their male counterparts but they are no less important, and thus merit the special attention given to them in this collection which addresses many aspects of women's lives from the medieval to late modern periods in the interesting, informative and lively manner that women's history so rightly deserves. In this volume we seek to complement the work of historians of Scottish women's experiences to date and, hopefully, to expand the debate beyond traditional 'womanly roles' into new areas of investigation.

NOTES

1. For more details, log on to the Scottish Women's History Network website at: http://swhn.gcal.ac.uk.
2. Breitenbach E., Brown A. & Myers F., 'Understanding Women in Scotland', *Feminist Review*, No. 48 (Spring 1998), 44–65, 49.
3. *Ibid.*, 62.
4. *Ibid.*, 45.
5. For further discussion, see, for example, J. Hendry, 'Snug in the Asylum of Taciturnity: Women's History in Scotland', in Donnachie & Whatley (eds.), *The Manufacture of Scottish History* (Edinburgh, 1992), 125–142.
6. Christina Larner, *Enemies of God: the witch-hunt in Scotland* London, 1981).
7. Rosalind Marshall, *Virgins and Viragos: A History of Women in Scotland 1080–1980* (London, 1983).

8. Eleanor Gordon & Esther Breitenbach (eds.), *The World is Ill-Divided: Women's Work in Scotland in the nineteenth and early twentieth centuries* (Edinburgh, 1990) and Gordon & Breitenbach (eds.), *Out of Bounds: Women in Scottish Society 1800–1945* (Edinburgh, 1992).

9. Elspeth King, *Scottish Women's Suffragette Movement* (Glasgow Museums, 1978), Leah Leneman, *A Guid Cause: The Women's Suffragette Movement in Scotland* (Aberdeen, 1991) and Leneman, *The Scottish Suffragettes* (Edinburgh, 2000).

10. Mahood L., *The Magdalenes: Prostitution in the Nineteenth Century* (London, 1990).

11. Leneman L. & Mitchison R., *Sin in the City: sexuality & social control in urban Scotland, 1660–1780* (Edinburgh, 1998) and Leneman & Mitchison, *Girls in trouble: sexuality & social control in rural Scotland 1660–1780* (Edinburgh, 1998).

12. Elizabeth Sanderson, *Women and Work in Eighteenth-Century Edinburgh* (Basingstoke, 1996).

13. Deborah Symond, *Weep Not for Me: Women, Ballads and Infanticide in early Modern Scotland* (Penn. State Press, 1997).

14. Elspeth King, *The Hidden History of Glasgow's Women: The Thenew Factor* (Edinburgh, 1993).

15. Elizabeth Ewan & Maureen Meikle, *Women in Scotland c.100-c. 1750* (East Linton, 1999).

16. Terry Brotherstone, Deborah Simonton & Oonagh Walsh, *Gendering Scottish History: An International Approach* (Glasgow, 1999).

17. Michael Foucault, *Discipline and Punish* (New York, 1979), cited in P. Rabinow (ed.), *The Foucault Reader* (London, 1984), 227.

PART ONE

Twisting Virtue: Women and Deviancy

'Barbarous and Pestiferous Women': Female Criminality, Violence and Aggression in Sixteenth- and Seventeenth-Century Scotland and Ireland

Andrea Knox

Female criminality, violence and aggression in the early modern period have been the focus of several recent studies.[1] The work of Gowing and Jansen on female crime in early modern England has highlighted both treasonable words and the language of insult as areas of particular focus for early modern authorities.[2] This kind of scholarship is a departure from early studies of crime which often conflated areas like theft and moral crimes such as adultery, and was governed by modern conceptions of 'serious crime' such as burglary, robbery, rape and murder.[3] Studies which focus on specifically female crimes have recently moved from these 'serious' areas where women were more often the victims, or accomplices, to crimes which women perpetrated. Female crime in the early modern period came to be increasingly defined as verbal, disruptive and rebellious. From litigation over sexual insults to the relatively small number of English women tried for treasonable words, oral political resistance became a focus for English authorities. This concern deepened in relation to Scottish and Irish women, as colonial and governmental considerations dominated the relationships between the three countries during the sixteenth and seventeenth centuries. The background of specific tensions of the period offers an explanation for the concentrated focus upon female disorder. The growing influence of the Reformation and the accompanying ideas of familial control helped to shape the ways in which Scottish, Irish and English societies came to be organised.[4] The growing power structures in early modern societies sought to regulate and order the lives of the population at every level of society. Courts in England and lowland Scotland began to deal more commonly with the unruly words of women, from the scolds and gossips through to the seditious and treasonable words of women. Scholars who have argued for the use of litigation together with women's testimonies have shown women's use of legal agency.[5] Whilst

these studies have broadened the focus of the history of female criminality
in the early modern period, both European and American scholars have
tended to centre on the experience of English and continental women.
Scottish and Irish female criminality and subversion have been omitted
from the European context of female experience.[6] One of the reasons for
this is the nature of sources relating to female criminality. The limited
number of convictions of Scottish and Irish women in contrast to men,
and in contrast to English women, has meant that Scottish and Irish female
subversion has not been considered of historic interest. Moreover, with
English presence in Ireland expanding from the sixteenth century onwards,
official records represent a history based on external observations of Irish
women. In Scotland the influence of the reformers and the growth of early
modern capitalism in the lowlands placed a new emphasis on the role of
women, and the potential misdeeds of women. Scottish studies of crime
in the early modern period have focused upon the Scottish witch-hunt;
however, less attention has been paid to the role of Scottish women
involved in criminal networks, especially those who worked with Irish
women during the various periods of rebellion.[7]

This chapter will address aspects of Irish and Scottish female criminality and subversion throughout the early modern period, particularly
the organised networked links between Irish and Scottish women, with
the shared aim of resisting English colonial authority. Whilst historians
of early modern Scotland and Ireland have, until recently, emphasised
the lack of shared identity before the seventeenth century, the work
of MacCurtain and O'Dowd on Irish women, and Ewan and Meikle
on Scottish women, has provided a considerable insight into women's
lives.[8] Female networks between the women of Scotland and of Ireland
appear throughout the sixteenth and seventeenth centuries. Extant sources
reveal the widespread involvement of women in criminal and subversive
behaviour which came to be defined as criminal, and women's active
political roles in the numerous periods of rebellion against the English.

Ireland in the sixteenth and seventeenth centuries was subject to major
invasion and settlement. Tudor foreign policy towards Ireland attempted
to introduce an English model of government, and during the reign of
Elizabeth I, attempts were made to introduce the protestant religion.
During the sixteenth century both Ireland and Scotland were the regular
focus of European catholic plots. This led the Tudor monarchs to invade
Ireland with a double agenda: to prevent European invasion, and to subdue
a country in which it had always appeared difficult to exercise any
influence. Henry VIII had unsuccessfully invaded Scotland and France
in the 1540s, and the failure of these interventions precipitated Scottish
and French intervention in Ireland. The English monarchy and officials

then began to enter Ireland and impose colonial settlement and govern-ment. Officials operated increasingly aggressive policies, with English and some Scottish Presbyterian officials moving into positions of judicial and magisterial power. The English officials in Ireland were quick to cite Irish women as rebellious and influential in opposition to English rule. Irish women were involved in diplomacy, spying and raising troops and munitions against the English, and therefore became a focus of criticism, blame and expulsion from Ireland when land was increasingly given over to English settlers. Ireland was the only country in Europe to successfully reject a state-imposed religion in the sixteenth and seventeenth centuries. This did not prevent the wholesale expulsion of chieftain families involved in open rebellion against the settlers. Ireland did not experience a complete reformation, but instead most of Ireland experienced a persistence of traditional culture that enabled Irish women and men to resist external pressures to reform.

During Elizabeth's reign, power in England was shifting from the localities to central government. This was facilitated by the judiciary. Local magistrates were named by the Lord Chancellor and remained under the close scrutiny of, and were directly answerable to, the monarch. Many of these magistrates were from the aristocracy.[9] This pattern was repeated throughout plantation towns in Ireland. This centralisation was repeated in lowland Scotland, although with accountability to local powers, or the Kirk in church courts, particularly after the Reformation.[10] Within Ireland regional administrations placed by Elizabeth were designed to provide more effective government and control areas remote from Dublin.[11]

Scotland had a separate legal code, a different social structure and an aggressive protestant church. However, English suspicions about Cath-olic plots in Scotland continued throughout the period. The influence of the Reformation in Scotland was viewed by the English monarchy as a holding process. The inhabitants of highland Scotland, however, were viewed with suspicion by English officials. Until the period of the highland clearances, the links between Scottish and Irish women were the subject of a considerable level of scrutiny. English attitudes to Scottish and Irish women contrasted starkly with those towards English women. English views of Scottish and Irish women concentrated on racial and gender prejudices, and specifically defined them as rebellious and disorderly, with a particular talent for leading Scottish and Irish men into rebellion.[12] Working against this was an internal environment within Ireland where women were not perceived as a threat to the existing social order. At a time when English men criminalised and indeed demonised women, the Irish did not follow, nor, more importantly, did Irish women simply become victims of anglocentric views of female criminality and disorderly behaviour. In Scotland female criminality and disorder became a particular internal focus of the reformers and also a concern of the English government and monarchy. The highland clans appear to have been more reluctant to demonise their women. Although the ideology of the Kirk was emphasising the importance of conformity, the highland clan system and resistance to English rule prevented the level of conformity that was desired. Ireland had a distinct culture, and factors such as region, status and sept membership cut across gender experience. Septs were dynastic lineages, which included landholding, and were based on kinship, shared names and shared ancestors. However, they included the children named by women as belonging to the sept. There was no need to prove paternity. These were views which were alien to the English. The Scottish clan system was based on ties of blood, linking members in an indissoluble relationship. Connections through land and close relationship to other branches were also part of the system. Sometimes, as with the Irish septs, a common ancestor was invented. A distinct difference lay in the notions of paternity and legitimacy, however. In Ireland it was not necessary to prove legitimacy in order to be acknowledged as the offspring of a sept leader. Women and girls had rights of inheritance in Ireland. In Scotland, as in Ireland, the clan supported its leaders with military service. This included women, which amazed and horrified the English.

The legal system in Ireland which prevailed until colonisation was the system of Brehon law. Brehon law had existed for centuries and was quite distinct from other European legal systems. Brehon law was the customary secular law of Gaelic Ireland. The Brehons were the traditional lawyers of the Gaelic learned class. Within Brehon law women held property rights, were able to inherit, were able to maintain their own property and land, and were able to divorce without the judgement of the church. Within this secular tradition women had high status and social prominence. Both Cosgrove and Simms maintain that the broad principles concerning women's position in regard to marriage, property and legal guardianship remained constant between the thirteenth and sixteenth centuries.[13] Nicholls has noted that Irish women had, by European standards, considerable rights to hold and acquire property independently of their husbands or fathers.[14] Irish women were also accepted as independent witnesses in court, and sept women frequently acted as political agents for their husbands and families as well as arbiters in disputes over property.[15] Irish women were also granted generous rights for divorce; these included a sexually unsatisfactory husband, sterility, impotence, homosexuality, and if homosexuality had been concealed, then substantial compensation was due to the wife. Divorce was also permissible on the grounds of hatred, a husband who was a vagrant, or property-less. If there had been physical abuse within the marriage, women were protected by the law. The legal texts relating to this were positive in respect of women.[16] The burden of proof was not upon the wife to prove a husband had been violent, instead the burden was upon him to prove he had not resorted to violence. This would appear to be different from other European legal traditions, and particularly English legal tradition where women found it increasingly difficult to sue a husband for violent behaviour.[17] Recent work by Graham has shown how Scottish women used the courts of the Reformed Kirk to defend their interests, and to seek protection from domestic abuse.[18] Scottish women were in a more defensive legal position than Irish women. Irish wives had legal protection against husbands' slander or calumny. A husband who revealed sexual secrets about his wife could be divorced, and the wife had to be compensated for breach of privacy. Other grounds for divorce were madness, incurable illness, and hidden identity, including hiding the fact of being a priest. Although canonists and jurists often disagreed over the status and privileges of lay nuns, resulting in some conflicting legal texts, women still appear to have practised many legal rights which allowed them considerable power in public life, as well as within their family and sept groups. Patterson's work on the reaction of the Irish learned class to the Tudor conquest of Ireland and the attempts to change the shape of Irish law throws up the variation of elite responses to growing English rule.[19] Brehon law preserved partible inheritance rather than primogeniture, not only for sons but for daughters also. Inheritance in Scotland was through the male line. Coutts has noted that Scottish wives and widows were not as legally constrained as theory might suggest, although all women were inferior in law, and could not be witnesses in civil cases in the supreme court.[20] It would appear that Brehon law afforded women a legal footing not held elsewhere.

During the middle decades of the sixteenth century incoming English officials condemned Irish dynasties for failure to regularise the transmission of lordship through primogeniture and bastardy rules.[21] However, the strong native traditions of partible inheritance continued. Haderman contends that even though the common law of England was imposed upon Ireland in 1603 with the intention of destroying native Brehon law, the resulting outstanding legal anomalies meant that in practice many customs continued.[22] This point has been applied to highland Scotland, although preserving independent customs does not mean placing women on an equal legal footing. Stiubhart has maintained that the culture of highland Scotland was more strongly imbued with patriarchal ideology than Ireland.[23]

Partible inheritance was formally declared illegal in 1606, but was continued in areas not overtaken by English plantation. Throughout the sixteenth century a changing legal system flourished. The balance between Gaelic Brehon and English institutions lasted until the mid-sixteenth century as Tudor governments initially showed caution towards the Gaelic lordships. After the mid-sixteenth century, plans were broached to dispossess the Irish aristocracy in several regions, replacing them with English planters. MacCurtain has detailed the increasing interest the Tudor monarchy and governments showed in Irish matrimony and the legal rights of women.[24] The broader context of the Reformation and Counter-Reformation led directly to the reform of doctrine, faith, morals and the following reform of marriage into a formal ecclesiastical institution. MacCurtain maintains that this process was delayed in Ireland, and enforcing registration of marriages proved to be an extremely slow process.[25] Successive Irish parliaments in Dublin, acting on behalf of the Tudors, passed a number of pieces of legislation pertaining to marriage, inheritance and legitimacy. Acts that prevented closely related family members from marrying, and solemnising marriage, were passed in 1537 and 1540 respectively. Another major concern was that in Gaelic society marriage among landholding families was often a political alliance and could be dissolved at any time. This presented a problem for the incoming English colonials in that it spawned a great number of politically powerful women who could act independently upon divorce, and had powerful alliances within their septs. Unlike English elite wives who were put aside after divorce or annulment, Irish wives continued to exercise public power. O'Dowd has pointed to the use of multiple political alliances as a tactical political weapon both against other powerful families within Ireland, and later as allied groups against the English.[26] In this way women were still connected to a powerful sept, and were able to participate directly in resistance to early English colonial rule. A number of Scottish women were participants in these septs.

Most of lowland Scotland accepted the Reformation, whilst Ireland resisted. One of the results of this was that Scottish and Irish Gaeldom were increasingly divided by religion. The deeply rooted opposition to the Reformation by the Catholic hierarchy in Ireland and the majority of the population meant that the social and legal, as well as the religious, influences of the Reformation were diluted. Those who remained Catholic in Scotland found allies in Ireland, and this was reciprocated. This meant that alliances existed along religious as well as political lines. These developments in politics and religion led to the emergence of new senses of Irish and Scottish identity despite the fracturing of Scottish and Irish Gaeldom that Dawson clearly identifies at the end of the sixteenth century.[27] This fracture was largely caused by the 5th earl of Argyll, whose support for a Gaelic Reformation meant that by 1600 Scotland was increasingly Calvinist.[28] The result was that old alliances were breaking down, but other alliances had been developing. One of the major influences of the Reformation upon Scotland and Ireland was that it disrupted existing ideas of national identity, and introduced new religious differences. The divide between Catholic and Protestant meant that there was a new unity among Catholic communities, especially those within developing Protestant countries. The Scottish and Irish who did not conform to the ideas of the Reformation found themselves under suspicion.

Throughout the sixteenth century English law was imposed upon Ireland, with the result that by the early seventeenth century it extended to most of Ireland.[29] One aim was to criminalise many of the activities of women on a par with the function of law in England and lowland Scotland. The surviving legal source material I have used in relation to cases of female criminality is derived from indictments against women which specify charges and also provide comments by the recorder as to the nature of the crime. Surviving legal records offer a wide geographical scope, and exist for both secular and religious courts. Many of the legal records survive from the English-dominated towns, including Dublin, Cork, Kinsale and Youghal, which all had English-based civic authority models and English garrisons. The Clonmell Assize records from County Tipperary in the rural south also survive. Dublin was governed by English officials, as was Youghal near the coastline in County Cork. Sir Walter Raleigh had been mayor in Youghal, and had introduced the growing of potatoes as opposed to the previous system of multi-cropping.[30] The Mayors of Youghal were all English. Detailed deposition collections from the north survive from Antrim and Armagh, which were both governed by Scottish Presbyterians after 1603. In western Ireland, particularly in the province of Connaught and County Clare, where the Irish were driven during the settlement of plantation communities, Brehon traditions continued to be practised after 1603, and even infiltrated English ideas. The depositions from the 1641 rebellion also reveal a high degree of female involvement. These records reveal the links between Scottish and Irish women. Throughout the sixteenth and seventeenth centuries the relationship between women was significant in terms of political resistance. The suspicions attaching to Irish and Scottish women centred on the fact that they negotiated with each other, and that they had connections with France, Spain and the Vatican. There was a constant fear of invasion in England.

The wealth of records shows a high degree of female involvement in crime, and a high degree of female-initiated crime, and more importantly from the point of view of the English colonisers, a significant number of women involved in serious crimes which threatened English authority. From the time of the passing of the treason act in 1534, English authorities turned their legislative attention to crimes which women perpetrated. Garthine Walker has suggested that women were persecuted rather than simply prosecuted.[31] She made this remark with reference to local witchcraft trials, but it would appear to be applicable to other areas of criminality, and the persecution mania was certainly exported to Ireland. Early modern notions of female aggression and criminal and disorderly behaviour were explained by contemporaries through biological and cultural models. Biological explanations centred on women's inherent weakness: women were imperfect creatures, more prone to temptation than men. Cultural explanations acknowledged women's active involvement in criminality and wider disorderly behaviour. Across Europe male expressions focused upon the female sex as the disorderly one.[32] These were not straightforward models, however, and were often applied together. Certain crimes were considered unnatural when committed by women. Violence committed by women within the family was treated exceptionally harshly. Murder of husbands, or 'petty treason', and infanticide were deeply abhorrent. Women in military roles were treated with deep suspicion. However, unnatural crimes were relative. In Ireland, and to a lesser extent Scotland, the warrior woman tradition was deeply rooted, and not just in mythology. Irish sources such as the fifteenth-century text Cath Fintraga are clear about the female warrior tradition in Ireland. Violence and aggression were forms of behaviour resorted to by women as well as men.[33]

In Ireland particularly women's behaviour came to be increasingly defined as disruptive, and disorderly behaviour became increasingly defined as criminal. The background to these tensions over women in England has commonly been seen as part of the growing influence of the Reformation and the accompanying ideas of familial or more specifically patriarchal control which helped to shape the ways in which society came to be organised.[34] In Ireland these influences were not prevalent, and even in the towns which came to be dominated by an English model of criminal justice it proved difficult to drum up the hatred and suspicion of women which manifested itself in many European towns in this period.

Superstitions and popular beliefs about women's potential as witches in Scotland operated in an entirely different way in Ireland.[35] In sixteenth- and seventeenth-century Scotland the witch-hunt reached its peak. Scottish clergy were trained to recognise the signs of witchcraft. Torture of witches was used even after prohibition. Witch beliefs were often related to popular culture, but for officials in Scotland this proved to be a threat to orthodoxy. Protestant judges and magistrates saw themselves as a godly magistracy.

Although this happened in Ireland, the scale was smaller. Beyond settler towns there was little legal interest in witchcraft. Popular Irish beliefs had always held women to be potential shape-shifters, seers, prophets, and capable of supernatural and transcendental powers which were not possessed by men. It was also believed that these extra and special talents of women should be respected and not obstructed. Prophecy was also relied upon in Irish culture, and many septs had their own prophet. The Fitzgeralds employed the Abbess of Shanagolden to advise and predict for them. For the English this was also a threat as prophecy was often linked to rebellion in early modern mentalities. Jansen's work on the sixteen-year-old nun Elizabeth Barton, and her execution for political prophecies against Henry VIII, shows that prophecy was considered as sedition and treason.[36] In most areas of Ireland it was priests who often supported the popular beliefs in women's supernatural powers. This appears to have infuriated incoming colonial authorities. Henry Pyerce, recorder at Westmeath in the 1680s, expressed the typical outrage and surprise of the incomer when he recorded that the Irish do not prosecute witches, but instead allow 'ignorant priests' to use excorcisms, holy water, consecrated relics and amulets which they hang around the children's necks.[37] This does reveal the mindset of the coloniser, but also that the power of the English to prevail over the customs of Irish society was limited.

The growth areas of female crime in England and lowland Scotland, including gossip, scolding, slander, sedition, drunkenness, theft, witchcraft, profanity, fornication and adultery appear to a limited extent across the whole of Ireland. In Scotland witchcraft in particular became a focus for godly authorities. Torture was sometimes used as part of the initial investigation process in order to establish a case. Torture was never allowed in Ireland during the few cases which reached the court process. Conviction and sentencing rates were low throughout Ireland. For many women appearing in both secular and religious courts with a plea of mitigation and a show of remorse, there was a small sermon on morality and a public punishment, or a fine.

The area of female criminality that attracted most attention and legislation was that of rebellion. For the English lawgivers women's activity in the various periods of rebellion, whether directly or indirectly involved, was at the heart of colonial concerns over female criminality, violence and aggression. Another significant concern was that of racial impairment through intermarriage, and early theories of degeneracy were often expressed when English or Scottish men married Irish women. The English government passed a statute in 1557 making intermarriage, or the hiring of Scottish mercenaries a capital offence.[38] This legislation was largely ignored, although it was a clear indication of the colonisers' awareness of the links between intermarriage and the supply of Scottish mercenaries as dowries.

A number of case studies illustrate the response to the corrupting influence of Irish women. Most of the surviving sources relate to elite women, or women with some status, although the 1641 depositions cite the widespread involvement of women from the lower orders in rebellion. The State Papers of Ireland contain a number of accounts of women as negotiators, go-betweens, spies, raisers of finance and instigators of rebellions. Many of these women dealt directly with major European powers. After the flight of the Earls from Ireland in 1607 many Irish settled in Spain, France and the Low Countries, establishing permanent settlements, and making significant contributions to the military, schools, colleges and universities. Many Irish women became spies, particularly those who worked for the Spanish monarchy and government. As early as 1577 the wife of the Earl of Fitzmaurice was recorded as a go-between and negotiator between Fitzmaurice and the Pope, who promised the rebels eight galleys in support against the English.[39] Lady Fitzmaurice had also written to the French King for his support. She and her husband were the most conspicuous rebels in the early 1570s. Between 1574 and 1579 she had visited France, Spain and Italy; however, her activities were closely monitored by the English authorities. In July 1577 Elizabeth I wrote to Sir Amyas Poulet that she had discovered letters between the couple relating to European aid for the rebels in Ireland.[40] This does reveal the extent of the network between the rebels and their supporters, but also the level of intelligence work which the English were forced to undertake.

One of the most famous female networks credited with playing a direct part in early sixteenth-century revolts was Agnes Campbell and her daughter Finola O'Donnell. Lady Agnes was the sister of the Earl of Argyll, and came to Ireland to marry Turlough Luineach O'Neill in 1569, after the death of her first husband, James MacDonnell, Lord of the Isles of Scotland. When Agnes arrived in Ireland, she brought with her a dowry of twelve hundred Scottish mercenary troops. So did her daughter who married the other Ulster chief, Hugh O'Donnell.[41] This in itself was a typical if frightening prospect for the colonial authorities, as they feared the Scottish mercenaries as much as they feared Irish rebels. What was perhaps more significant was that Agnes was swiftly credited with ruling and directing her chieftain husband and 'making herself strong in Ireland'.[42] Agnes' role in the Desmond rebellion of 1579 to 1583 was to make a new Scotland of Ulster.[43] It was Agnes who was commissioned to raise munitions from Scottish supporters.[44] Agnes was recorded as highly educated and intelligent, and it was she with whom the English negotiated in 1579 when she met with Sir Henry Sidney. They recorded that her husband was, by contrast, a 'rude, wild savage'.⁴⁵ It was also recorded that O'Neill 'accepts the lewd counsel of his wife'.⁴⁶ Agnes claimed that 'the Scots would be the only hope the Irish had to sustain them'.⁴⁷ Agnes visited Scotland during the summer of 1583 in order to raise financial aid. The Irish looked to O'Neill for a lead against the English. When Agnes returned to Ireland, she was questioned by English officials and is recorded as having reassured them that her visit was 'for no disloyal purpose'.⁴⁸ The Lord Justice who questioned Agnes recorded that she replied to him in Latin.⁴⁹ Scottish and Irish women were renowned for their education and linguistic abilities. Sir John Perrot, the Lord Deputy, sent specially trained forces to Ireland, but deplored the fact that he did not have better spies in Scotland and Spain.⁵⁰ This reveals that the English were unable to muster spies against the Irish, even though they undoubtedly offered a considerable payment for these services.

It was Agnes and Finola who united the O'Neills and the O'Donnells, who then banded together against the English in the north of Ireland. This was a result which the women had facilitated. Previously the O'Neills and the O'Donnells had been sworn enemies. Agnes and Finola were central to training the Scottish mercenaries in Ireland, and worked as go-betweens and negotiators. The redshanks employed by the O'Neill sept were joined by some of the Campbell clan. The unity of these two powerful groups intensified the fears of the English, although these alliances were not ultimately strong enough to repel the colonial forces. Nevertheless, these two women were at the centre of the Irish-Scottish network. They worked to keep Ulster independent from Dublin. Both women worked together, and under their own direction. Lord Malbie recorded that Agnes and Finola worked in the north with other rebels in order to control Connaught.⁵¹ Ireland saw the arrival of a large number of Scottish mercenaries in the summer of 1592. The English feared an Ulster rebellion. In 1592 a captured Catholic priest reported that the King of Spain was intending to send ships and money and to transport Scottish mercenaries to Ireland. As widespread fear increased, Lord Burghley recorded that the whole of Ulster was open to Scottish support.⁵² Agnes and Finola had plans in 1590 to overthrow the English sheriff of Donegal; however, by 1600 the rebellion was weakening against superior English numbers. After the flight of the Earls the O'Donnells left Ireland for Spain. The eventual defeat also marked the end of a period when Ireland could call upon Scottish military aid through appeal to a shared Gaelic identity. The suspicions which surrounded these women were well founded. The evidence of women who were spies include an alert in 1581 over a Spanish woman who was also described as being

Irish. She was travelling in the company of the Spanish Ambassador, and used the name Imperia Romana. What alerted Lord Burghley to her (as well as the company she kept) was her ability to speak Spanish, Irish and English. Her activities included many secret talks, and she was called 'a fit instrument for spying', but because she travelled with the ambassador she had a degree of diplomatic immunity.[53] She was recorded as having carried documents from the Spanish King, and stayed for lengthy periods at the home of the Spanish Ambassador.[54] The master of the ship she sailed on was questioned and reported that she travelled with money and many packets of letters. What made her behaviour even more suspicious was that she conveyed packets to other Spaniards. She remained with the Ambassador in a position of diplomatic immunity, reducing the English, who were already paranoid at this period about Spanish intervention, to a state where they constantly monitored her covert activities. The Ambassador later requested her safe passage, which technically had to be granted, provoking further outrage amongst Elizabeth's ministers and spymasters. There are a number of comments about the clearly perceived alliances between Ireland and Spain, but there appears to be nothing that English officials could do about a person under Ambassadorial protection.[55] Lord Burghley and Sir Francis Walsingham continued to comment upon Imperia Romana, but were ultimately unable to arrest or detain her. Female spying was already established by 1581, with women able to travel through Europe with protection.

Women's own testimonies also appear to support female agency in crime and aggression. Finola O'Donnell stated in 1588 that she would hire the Spaniards to stir up wars against the English.[56] The Earl of Tyrone's wife announced publicly, in the presence of English officials, that 'she would to God that Essex would stir up trouble in England', in order that foreign powers would leave Ireland.[57]

Women were directly involved in the military conflicts of the 1640s. Their activities included supplying ammunition and weapons, like Mary Burke who was found to be travelling in a coach full of gunpowder out of Dublin to the rebels in Westmeath.[58] Bridget Darcy was burned to death in Dublin in 1660 for admitting to murdering a number of Englishmen, and claiming to have made candles out of their fat.[59] Darcy's testimony, given when she knew that she would be executed, reveals her concentration upon English officers as legitimate political targets. This would appear to indicate a determined focus upon a specific group of colonisers, rather than a generalised attitude to all English plantation communities.

Further down the social scale there are numerous accounts of the activities of 'she soldiers', women who were part of troop activity. During one battle between the Irish and parliamentary troops at Connaught, amongst

the dead on the Irish side was a young soldier who had his hat pulled off
to reveal long tresses of hair, and upon being further searched was found
to be a woman.[60] Although O'Dowd and Whelan discuss women's role
in war, it is Higgins who has produced evidence on the weaponry which
women used, confounding the idea that women were unlikely to carry
muskets.[61] Other lower strata women involved in wider criminal activities
surrounding rebellion and civil war were the network of prostitutes and
receivers. The Dublin corporation records which cover the period from
1573 to 1634 detail women tavern keepers and prostitutes who worked
as conduits, receiving stolen goods and trading them from taverns.[62] The
numbers of indictments for trading for the rebellion increased steadily
throughout the sixteenth and seventeenth centuries, alongside an increase
in statutes attempting to prevent prostitution and suppress bawdy houses.
English soldiers were constantly warned to avoid these women as they
might be tempted to give information to them.[63] The 1641 depositions
also contain many accounts of women acting as receivers, sometimes
with huge stores of hardware and ammunition, and the most improbable
excuses for having them. However, increasingly during the seventeenth
century the intelligence service of the English government became more
ruthless in their investigation and interrogation procedures.

Gender was an important dynamic in rebellion and warfare. As far as
the English were concerned, women, and wives specifically, incited their
menfolk to rebel. Sir Francis Rush, writing to Lord Justices Loftus and
Carey in 1600, gave having an Irish wife as the cause of men's treason.[64]
Not only did wives spy, but they used their husbands. An Irish wife would
corrupt an Irishman, but for an Englishman, an Irish wife was simply
beyond any kind of control. Scottish chieftains' wives were viewed with
similar suspicion, although they were not vilified to the same extent. The
political developments from the mid-sixteenth century onwards put many
Irish outside the law. The suspicions attaching to women in the context
of ethnic conflict are particularly interesting as intermarriage was seen
as the key to degeneration. Intermarriage bred the problem of dubious
loyalty. The state papers of Ireland are replete with accounts of wives
betraying secrets to the rebels, and acting as duplicitous interpreters and
spies. An account of Captain Tom Lee's wife cites that Lee and his wife
parted because he had used his wife as a translator and go-between. She
then went over to the rebels' side after interpreting for them.[65] Andrew
Trollope wrote to Lord Burghley asking for the removal from Ireland of
all English soldiers and government officers who were married to Irish
women, on the grounds that they would be compromised and corrupted.
Conversely, English observers believed that an English wife would have a
calming effect upon an Irish husband. In 1564 Sir Thomas Cusacke told

Lord Cecil that, after years of notable rebellion, Shane O'Neill 'preserves good conformity', and this was due to his new English wife.[66] However, they were mistaken: a few months later O'Neill was rebelling and asking Queen Mary Stewart for financial assistance.

Whilst English government officials believed Irish women to be dangerous, barbarous, and, in the case of Eleanor O'Donnell, pestiferous, and all capable of turning men from reason, recorders such as Edmund Spenser, Fynes Moryson, Barnaby Rich and William Camden all concentrated on the savage aspects of Irish women. Not only were they politically influential and subversive, but their behaviour was described as licentious boldness.[67] They were sexually promiscuous, and what most scandalised Fynes Moryson was the way Irish women of all strata did not name their children's father until they were about to die.[68] This was intolerable to the English, who maintained primogeniture as an essential support for patriarchy.

The language used by these writers is hyperbolic; for instance, in 1610 William Camden stated that once Irish women 'had given themselves over to lewdness they are more lewd than lewdness itself'.[69] The language used was often sexualised. Francis Rush described one Irish wife of an Englishman suspected of treason as being 'his whore wife', and having recourse to the rebels.[70] This in itself was not unusual. The conflation of disorder and sexuality went on throughout early modern Europe. However, accusations of lewdness appear to intensify in Ireland. There was not the same degree of hostility towards Scottish women. Scottish women did not incur the same level of retribution that Irish women did. The constant use of 'whore wife', 'bitch wife', 'lewd woman' and 'amazon' in the cases of women cited in the 1641 depositions indicates that Irish women were seen as much from a sexual as a criminal angle. Their behaviour came under increasingly constant scrutiny during the seventeenth century when the colonial powers stepped up the level of violence used to impose authority. In external views of Irish women the cultural and the criminal were conflated.

It would appear that by the end of the seventeenth century English legal control in Ireland was widespread, although the Reformation was only partially successful. What is significant is the excessive hostility of colonial authorities towards Irish women, and the early development of racist policies. Gender played a crucial role in early modern Ireland. Whilst sixteenth- and seventeenth-century Englishmen feared the power of women on many levels, their fear of Irish women appears to have been excessive. Scottish and Welsh women were not feared in the same way. The retribution meted out to Irish women was not mirrored anywhere else in Scotland, England or Wales. Apart from the women examined by Jansen, who were tried for rebellion against Henry VIII, there is no comparable display of brutality against women.[71] However, early racist views were contradictory, including both prejudice and voyeuristic interest in Irish women as exotic, highly sexualised creatures. Mikalachki maintains that the English had a fear of 'savage feminity', which was a hangover from Boadicea and the ancient warrior queens who epitomised early-modern beliefs in the inevitable excess and failure of female rule.[72] Powerful women loom large in early-modern visions, and for colonisers these unruly women who challenged the patriarchal order were doubly threatening because they also challenged colonial authority.

Scottish and Irish women were clearly motivated by sept and kin interests. However, they also identified with each other on grounds of culture and politics. For the English, identifying Irish and Scottish women as potentially deviant, disorderly and threatening classified them as subversive subjects.

The question remains whether Scottish and Irish women who were violent and rebellious were acting independently as groups of women. Some appear to have done so, but not always. A significant number of women, and not just elite women, networked very effectively. Armaments and munitions, as well as information, were passed through these groups. Often this was without the knowledge of their immediate families. Sometimes women did instigate rebellion and lead the men in their sept. On rare occasions an elite Englishwomen, such as Elizabeth Cary, defied her husband, Viscount Falkland, senior governor to Elizabeth I in Ireland, in order to criticise his and his government's treatment of the Irish. Other women tried for more covert activities often worked without the need of men.

Deviancy is not a given in any situation: it is relative and dependent upon the society in which it takes place. In early-modern Ireland and Scotland women of the septs were deviant. Irish and Scottish women were violent compared to English women of the period, partly because of the prevailing colonialism, and clear opposition to it. In Scotland and Ireland there was a longer history of involvement of women in the military, and in other aggressive acts against colonisers.

Finally, what was it about Irish society that, despite the continuing efforts of these seriously criminal women, prevented the misogyny, tortures and executions which existed during this period in England, lowland Scotland and much of Europe? In the sixteenth and seventeenth centuries the English were attempting to destroy Irish culture. However, the west of Ireland and some of the rural south outside the colonised towns did not demonise or persecute women. The continued identification with the septs worked actively to prevent the subjugation of the Irish.

Despite colonisation there remained a greater cohesion within Irish and Scottish than in English communities, despite the fact that society as a whole was much less integrated. This cohesion appears to have had the effect of minimising misogyny outside the colonial towns and areas, with the result that there was less aggression between the genders in indigenous Irish communities than there was in plantation areas of Scottish and English communities. Irish women and men do not appear to have adopted English views of gender, morality and crime throughout the sixteenth and seventeenth centuries.

NOTES
1. Gowing, L. (1996), *Domestic Dangers: Women, Words and Sex in Early Modern London*, Oxford: Clarendon Press; Jansen, S. L. (1996), *Dangerous Talk and Strange Behaviour: Women and Popular Resistance to the Reforms of Henry VIII*, New York: St Martin's Press.
2. *Ibid.*
3. Sharpe, J. A. (1984), *Crime in Early Modern England, 1550–1750*, London: Longman Press. Includes a critique of early crime studies.
4. *Ibid.*
5. See Jansen and Sharpe.
6. See Chambers, A. (1979), *Granuaile, The Life and Times of Grace O'Malley, c. 1530–1603*, Dublin; Wolfhound Press; Chambers, A. (1986), *As Wicked a Woman, Eleanor Countess of Desmond, c. 1545–1638*, Dublin: Wolfhound Press.
7. For Scottish witch-hunting, see Larner, C. (1983), *Enemies of God: The Witch-Hunt in Scotland*, Oxford: Blackwell; Levack, B. P. (1980), 'The Great Scottish Witch Hunt of 1661–1662', *Journal of British Studies*, 20, pp. 90–108.
8. MacCurtain, M. and O'Dowd, M., eds. (1991), *Women in Early Modern Ireland*, Edinburgh: Edinburgh University Press; Ewan, E. and Meikle, M., eds. (1999), *Women in Scotland c. 1100–c. 1750*, East Linton: Tuckwell Press.
9. Read, C. (1969), *The Government of England under Elizabeth I*, Virginia: University of Virginia Press.
10. Graham, M. F. (1999), 'Women in the Church Courts in Reformation-Era Scotland', in Ewan and Meikle, pp. 187–198.
11. See Irwin, L. (1977), 'The Irish Presidency Courts, 1569–1672', *The Irish Jurist*, 12, pp. 106–114.
12. Manuscripts relating to disorderly women include Dublin City Library, Gilbert MS. 42; Trinity College Dublin, MSS. 817, 836 and 883; and Public Record Office, Kew, Calendar of State Papers Ireland, and Calendar of State Papers Foreign.
13. Cosgrove, A. (1985), 'Marriage in Medieval Ireland', in Cosgrove, A., ed., *Marriage in Ireland*, Dublin: College Press, pp. 1–16.
14. Nicholls, K. W. (1991), 'Irishwomen and Property in the Sixteenth Century', in MacCurtain and O'Dowd, eds. (1991), pp. 17–31.
15. *Ibid.*, p. 19.

16. Nicholls, K. W. (1970), 'Some Documents on Irish Law and Custom in the Sixteenth Century', *Analecta Hibernica*, 26, pp. 102–130.

17. See Amussen, S. D. (1985), 'Gender, family and the social order, 1560–1725', in Fletcher, A. and Stephenson, J., eds., *Order and Disorder in Early Modern England*, Cambridge: Cambridge University Press.

18. Graham, M. F., p. 190.

19. Patterson, N. (1991), 'Gaelic law and the Tudor conquest of Ireland: the social background of the sixteenth-century recensions of the pseudo-historical Prologue to the Senchas Mar', *Irish Historical Studies*, 27 (7), pp. 193–215.

20. Coutts, W. (1999), 'Wife and Widow: The Evidence of Testaments and Marriage Contracts c. 1600', in Ewan and Meikle, p. 177.

21. Patterson, N., p. 195.

22. Haderman, M. (1980), 'Irish Women and Irish Law', *The Crane Bag Book of Irish Studies*, 4 (1), pp. 55–59.

23. Stiubhart, D. U. (1999), 'Women and Gender in the Early Modern Western Gaedhealtachd', in Ewan and Meikle, pp. 233–249.

24. MacCurtain, M. (1985), 'Marriage in Tudor Ireland', in Cosgrove, A., pp. 51–66.

25. *Ibid.*, p. 51.

26. O'Dowd, M. (1999), 'Women and the Irish chancery court in the late sixteenth and early seventeenth centuries', *Irish Historical Studies*, 31 (124), pp. 470–487.

27. Dawson, J. E. A. (1987), 'Two Kingdoms or Three?: Ireland in Anglo-Scottish Relations in the Middle of the Sixteenth Century', in Mason, R., ed., *Scotland and England, 1286–1815*, Edinburgh: John Donald, pp. 113–138.

28. *Ibid.*, p. 131.

29. Haderman, M., p. 55.

30. Ellis, P. B. (1975), *Hell or Connaught! The Cromwellian Colonisation of Ireland, 1652–1660*, London: Hamish Hamilton, p. 26.

31. Walker, G. (1994), 'Women, theft and the world of stolen goods', in Kermode, J. and Walker, G., eds., *Women, Crime and the Courts in Early Modern England*, London: University College London Press, pp. 81–106.

32. See Davis, N. Z. (1987), *Society and Culture in Early Modern France*, Oxford: Blackwell, p. 124.

33. Meyer, K. (1885), ed. and trans., *Cath Finntraga, or the Battle of Ventry*, Oxford: Clarendon Press, vols. 1–4.

34. Amussen, S. D. (1985).

35. See Larner, C. (1983) and Levack, B. P. (1980).

36. See Jansen, S. L., p. 57.

37. Trinity College Dublin (T.C.D.), MS. 883/1, p. 297.

38. Ellis, S. G. (1998), *Ireland in the Age of the Tudors, 1447–1603*, Harlow: Longman, p. 247.

39. Public Record Office (P.R.O.), Calendar of State Papers (C.S.P.) Foreign, 1575–77, vol. 2, p. 102.

40. P.R.O., C.S.P. Ireland, 1574–85, p. 173.

41. P.R.O., C.S.P. Ireland, Letter from Lord Piers to the Lord Chancellor, 5th Aug., 1569, vol. 1, p. 30.

42. Lambeth Palace Library (L.P.L.), Carew MS. vol. 1, pp. 490–491.

43. L.P.L., Carew MS. vol. 2, p. 277.

44. P.R.O., C.S.P. Ireland, 1570, vol. 30, p. 428.
45. P.R.O., C.S.P. Ireland, 1579, vol. 65, p. 103.
46. P.R.O., C.S.P. Ireland, 1574–1585, p. 107.
47. P.R.O., C.S.P. Ireland, 1571, vol. 2, pp. 244–245.
48. P.R.O., C.S.P. Ireland, 1571, vol. 2, p. 451.
49. P.R.O., C.S.P. Ireland, 1571, vol. 2, p. 477.
50. P.R.O., C.S.P. Ireland, 1571, vol. 2, p. 148.
51. P.R.O., C.S.P. Ireland, 1571, vol. 2, p. 202.
52. P.R.O., C.S.P. Ireland, 1590, vol. 4, p. 453.
53. P.R.O., C.S.P. Foreign, 1581, vol. 15, p. 12.
54. Ibid.
55. P.R.O., C.S.P. Foreign, 1581, vol. 15, p. 13.
56. P.R.O., C.S.P. Ireland, vol. 3, 1588–1592, p. 63.
57. P.R.O., C.S.P. Ireland, vol. 6, 1600–1601, p. 282.
58. T.C.D., MS. 813, pp. 35–36.
59. MacNeill, M. (1990), *Maire Rua. Lady of Leamaneh*, Clare: Ballinakella Press, p. 75.
60. Dublin City Library (D.C.L.), Gilbert MS., vol. 1, p. 107.
61. O'Dowd, M. (1991), 'Women and War in Ireland in the 1640s', in MacCurtain, M. and O'Dowd, eds. (1991), pp. 91–112; Whelan, B., 'Women, Politics and Warfare in the Late Seventeenth Century', in Whelan, B. ed., *The Last of the Great Wars. Essays on the War of the Three Kings in Ireland, 1688–91*, Limerick: University of Limerick Press, pp. 139–161; Higgins, P. M. (1965), Women in the English Civil War, unpublished M. A. thesis, University of Liverpool.
62. D.C.L., Gilbert MS. 42, p. 169.
63. Dublin Records Office, Calendar of the Marquis of Ormonde, vol. 2, pp. 463–464.
64. P.R.O., C.S.P. Ireland, MS. 63, 1600, vol. 207.
65. P.R.O., C.S.P. Ireland, 1588–1592, vol. 3, p. 131.
66. P.R.O., C.S.P. Ireland, 1509–1573, p. 230.
67. Kew, G. (1998), ed., *The Irish Sections of Fynes Moryson's Unpublished Itinerary*, Dublin: Irish Manuscripts Commission, p. 37.
68. Moryson, F. (1617), *An Itinerary of the present state of Ireland*, vol. 4, London, pp. 198–199, and p. 237.
69. Camden, W. (1610), *Britain, or a Chorographical Description of England, Scotland and Ireland*, London, p. 120.
70. P.R.O., C.S.P. Ireland, 1599–1600, vol. 6, p. 398.
71. Jansen, S. L. (1996).
72. Mikalachki, J. (1998), *The Legacy of Boadicea. Gender and Nation in Early Modern England*, London: Routledge.

FURTHER READING

Cosgrove, A., ed. (1985), *Marriage in Ireland*, Dublin: College Press.
Ellis, P. B. (1975, repr. 2000), *Hell or Connaught! The Cromwellian Colonisation of Ireland, 1652–1660*, London: Hamish Hamilton.
Ewan, E. and Meikle, M., eds. (1999), *Women in Scotland, c. 1100–c. 1750*, East Linton: Tuckwell Press.

Gowing, L. (1996), *Domestic Dangers: Women, Words and Sex in Early Modern London*, Oxford: Clarendon Press.

Jansen, S. L. (1996), *Dangerous Talk and Strange Behaviour: Women and Popular Resistance to the Reforms of Henry VIII*, New York: St Martin's Press.

Larner, C. (1983), *Enemies of God: The Witch-Hunt in Scotland*, Oxford: Blackwell.

MacCurtain, M. and O'Dowd, M., eds. (1991), *Women in Early Modern Ireland*, Edinburgh: Edinburgh University Press.

Mikalachki, M. (1998), *The Legacy of Boadicea: Gender and Nation in Early Modern England*, London: Routledge.

Sharpe, J. A. (1984), *Crime in Early Modern England, 1550–1750*, London: Longmans.

Sharpe, J. A. (1996), *Instruments of Darkness: Witchcraft in England, 1550–1750*, Harmondsworth: Penguin.

Smout, T. C. (1969, repr. 1987), *A History of the Scottish People, 1560–1830*, London: Collins.

THREE

Death, Removal and Resignation: The Succession to the Office of Prioress in Late Medieval Scotland*

Kimm Perkins

The Indult of 1487 from Pope Innocent VIII gave King James III of Scotland the right to recommend his candidate to vacant offices, or benefices,[1] in cathedral churches and monasteries, providing these were worth more than two hundred gold florins. In the indult the Pope agreed to wait at least eight months to make his appointment to allow the king to supplicate for his own candidate. This right of presentation was called *sede vacante*.[2] If the pope and the king were content, 'appointments might be made smoothly and satisfactorily, but the possibilities of obstruction and friction were infinite'.[3] There was usually some motivation behind particular appointments made by the king, whether they were his illegitimate sons or the children of families that were in the king's favour.[4]

What I hope to do in this essay is to present some of the cases in the ecclesiastical records concerning the succession to the office of prioress in medieval Scottish convents. In these cases, there was litigation concerning impediments to the office of prioress, the value of the office, as well as reasons for the vacancy. Also, I would like to point out which family these prioresses may have come from and show that familial support may have 'allowed' for some individuals to obtain the office of prioress, whether they deserved it or not. The houses that I will concentrate on are the Cistercian houses of Coldstream, Eccles, Elcho, Haddington, Manuel and North Berwick.[5] All of these houses have some presence in the ecclesiastical records, some houses more than others. These records include presentations to the office of prioress for election, complications with succession, and most importantly the names of the prioresses themselves.

The materials that I will focus on are the Scottish entries listed in Vatican Archives, which Leslie Macfarlane called 'the most important repositories of ecclesiastical material in the world'.[6] The Scottish material in the Vatican Archives contains a wealth of information concerning the medieval church and society.[7] Individuals petitioned Rome to obtain a papal grace, valid in canon law, or to request a form of justice. The Register of Supplications, for example, contains the records of petitions to the Pope for 'dispensations or graces of every sort: for provisions of benefices, . . . promotions to higher dignities; for absolutions sought for defect of birth and dispensations from marriage irregularities; . . . for release from pilgrimage vows; and for much else besides'.[8] There are other registers that are equally important to the supplications – those of the series of letters and bulls of the Vatican and Lateran registers that were copies of the letter of 'papal grace' after being granted.[9] We must keep in mind that the material is not as cut and dried as it appears. In controversial cases if the supplicant was an interested party, the underlying meaning may have been hidden in the legal terminology or not written down at all.

Medieval Scottish women were usually offered few choices in their life, and although becoming a nun may not have been a woman's *first* choice, it was evident that a convent had much to offer. To start with, if a woman committed herself to the monastic life and took religious vows, it became impossible for her to marry.[10] Also, although she became 'dead to the [secular] world', and technically to her own family, she became part of a much larger extended family. Her religious vows removed her from a personal place in the social structure and kept her from *individual* legal concerns.[11] Her new 'community' encompassed the whole of Europe – she was committed to a lifestyle shared by thousands, and in her convent she enjoyed the company of her 'sisters'. And lastly, the convent was a place that allowed a woman to choose her vocation and her occupation. The structure of medieval convents reveals the opportunity these houses presented to all women. If a convent held small numbers of women, usually under twenty, almost every woman there would have held some office, executive or otherwise.

The prioress needed to fill many offices in the convent that held a great deal of responsibility.[12] There was someone in charge of the supervision of the guesthouse; someone who called the nuns to their offices and cared for the vestments of the church; and others who took care of the wardrobe, the distribution of alms, and attended to the sick. The cellaress, for example, managed the domestic servants and secured food for the convent either through purchase or from the convent's farm. Some of these offices were permanent appointments while other offices were held for a year and some for as short as a week.[13] The executive offices included the subprioress, who was required to supervise and implement the superior's commands and to act in her place when the prioress was absent on business. Another executive office was the treasurer, who was responsible for keeping account of the income collected from spiritualities and temporalities of the convent and paying expenses of the nunnery.[14]

The governance of Cistercian houses was done by the strict observation of the Rule of St Benedict. According to the Rule, the head of the house was the most important person in the monastery. While the Rule mainly applied to the administration of an abbey and the responsibilities of the abbot and monks, because female monastics belonged to the same order, the Rule was to be applied to them as well. The administrators of convents (abbesses and prioresses) had the same similar rights and privileges as abbots, and the internal life was consistent with the life and customs of the monasteries for men.[15]

The qualifications for the head of the house required the candidate to be of good name, legitimate birth, and a professed nun for five years, and at least twenty years of age, although Cistercian requirements indicated that they must be thirty years of age. If the candidate did not meet any or all of the requirements, then a special dispensation had to be granted by the pope in order that candidate be validated. Another requirement in the Rule was that [she] must have a 'merit of life and wisdom'.[16] Once installed in the office, the prioress held it until she died, resigned, or was removed.

Prioresses were powerful heads of their communities and there was no other institution, other than monasticism, where women could participate so fully in shaping their own lives.[17] The role of the prioress as head of her house, similar to that of an abbot or prior, has rarely been fully evaluated as being a significant role or occupation for women. The exclusion of these religious women reveals a serious lack of understanding of the female religious since they should have enjoyed a degree of autonomy in the operation of the management of their affairs often denied to their female counterparts in other areas of society.[18] The prioress would have enjoyed a considerable amount of freedom both in relation to her convent and to the outside world.

To the women in the convent, the prioress occupied a position that had great meaning and influence for all sisters. She had direct authority over the lives and wills of the others, for better or worse.[19] She had to have the skills necessary, not only to protect the convent's interests, but also to follow the Rule set out for her and her sisters. As head of her house she had to be 'chaste, sober and merciful' in her dealings with all those in her convent and with the outside world and to love all her sisters.[20] She also needed to seek a balance in the way she handled herself – never too excitable, worried, headstrong, exacting, jealous, or over-suspicious.[21] For most female religious, and men for that matter, this was an immense responsibility.

A prioress was not only an example to her convent but also to her contemporaries and would have enjoyed the same prestige as their local lords. She was always busy with the immediate administration of the convent and was responsible for running all its affairs: operating its estates, ruling and counselling younger nuns, and managing sizeable monastic households, which contained servants and boarders.[22] If the prioress was a member of a particular family or a member of the higher nobility, she may have been able to attract wealthy patrons to continue the maintenance of the convent.[23] Additionally, she had to make sure that she was on good terms with them and other officials, including the king and the bishop. For if there were any disagreements, especially concerning the convent's claim to lands, rents, and rights, the prioress would have to protect the interests of her convent, whatever the cost.[24]

The head of the house had to meet particular requirements before being presented as a candidate for the office. Two requirements were that a candidate must be of legitimate birth and legal age to succeed to office. According to the Supplications to Rome from Scotland and papal letters, at least four candidates for prioress asked for a special dispensation to rid themselves of defects:[25]

On 4 October 1403, Janet Wardlaw, a nun from the convent of Haddington, was dispensed from her defect of birth as the 'daughter of an unmarried nobleman and an unmarried women to be eligible to hold all kinds of dignities and offices'.[26]

25 March 1501: Elizabeth Hume, a nun from the convent of Eccles, supplicated for a dispensation for her defect of age. She was twenty years old and wished to hold the office of prioress, or any other 'office or dignity to which she might be elected'.[27]

2 October 1517: Elizabeth Hepburn, a professed nun from the convent of Haddington, supplicated to Rome for the office of prioress after the death of Beatrice Hepburn, her predecessor.[28] Elizabeth was a daughter of an Augustinian canon and an unmarried woman, and twenty-four years old. She had a dispensation for the defect of her birth from the archbishop.[29]

6 November 1526: Euphemia Leslie, a nun from the convent of Elcho, asked for a dispensation from her defect of birth and age. She was only eighteen years old and wanted to become the prioress of Elcho. Leslie was the daughter of an unmarried woman and a priest and was dispensed from her defect of birth, but further litigation ensued for the office of prioress between her and her predecessor Margaret Swinton.[30]

Litigation for the office of prioress could go on for years. In the instance of Janet Wardlaw, some three years later she was still in the process of confirming her status as legitimate and securing her office as prioress.

On 23 June 1408, the bishop of Whithorn confirmed that she was of the canonical age to become the prioress of the monastery of Haddington, after the death of the previous prioress, Alice. The convent elected her, 'notwithstanding the defect of birth, which she claimed to have been dispensed by papal authority'.³¹ She was also consecrated by ordinary authority and received the possession of the goods of the monastery.³² However, less than three weeks later, Robert, Duke of Albany, uncle of King James I, called upon the bishop of Brechin to examine the validity of her claim and to have her removed from office. Robert's petition against her argued that she was placed in office before she received papal dispensation of her defect of birth; therefore she had 'illegally' taken office.³³ From the few surviving records available, we can assume that she continued as prioress until approximately 1437.³⁴

The process of becoming the head of house usually started after the death or removal of the current prioress. The bishop of the diocese was usually notified of the death of the prioress and authorised the election of another. On 30 April 1474, Elizabeth Forman, a nun of the monastery of North Berwick, was given provision by the Pope to become the prioress after the death of Mariota Ramsay.³⁵ Another example was in 1548 when Marion Hamilton was promoted to office after the death of Janet Hunter and given the fruits of the monastery of Eccles.³⁶

Besides the death of a prioress, sometimes a bishop instigated the removal of a prioress. On 30 December 1402, Ellen Carrick, prioress of North Berwick, petitioned to Avignon that Walter Trail, bishop of St Andrews, had unjustly removed her from office, after a visitation, and had made the nuns elect another woman, Matilda Leys, in her place.³⁷ It is not clear why Carrick was taken from her office, after holding it for eight years.³⁸ Since prioresses remained in office for life, it was possible that the bishop had found that she was lacking the ability necessary to provide guidance for the nuns under her, or had misused the funds of the convent, or had engaged in immoral conduct.³⁹ Another possibility was that Leys usurped Carrick while Carrick was in office and Carrick wanted 'justice'. Ellen Carrick disputed the election of Matilda Leys and continued to plead her case at Avignon. Five years later, on 25 February 1407, the case was left undecided. Ellen claimed that the convent upon the death of her predecessor, Beatrice, had elected her and that Matilda was prioress unlawfully.⁴⁰

Another case of removal occurs at the convent of Haddington. Prior to 1440, Henry, bishop of St Andrews, deprived Agnes Maul, prioress of Haddington, of her office for her demerits.⁴¹ As a nun of Haddington she appealed to Rome against her successor, Mariota Douglas. The convent elected Mariota, who was twenty years old, and the bishop consecrated and confirmed the election. Mariota took possession of the office despite her defect of age.[42]

On 11 December 1443 litigation was still in progress against Douglas. King James II and James, bishop of St Andrews, supported Mariota and appealed to the pope to dissolve the suit against her by Maul. Maul had appealed to the pope against the election of Mariota, and after the appeal she had neglected it for several years, for whatever reason. She then decided to again pursue the cause against Mariota in the Roman Curia.[43]

On 28 January 1444, the Curia granted an investigation into the case. Douglas, now twenty-six years old, was granted the office of prioress and was blessed by the ordinary, 'on whose behalf James, king of Scotland and James, bishop of St Andrews had petitioned the Pope'. She was also dispensed of her impediment of her defect of age, and by 30 May 1444 she was rehabilitated to the office of prioress.[44]

Another cause for an election was after the resignation of the current prioress of the convent, and there are several cases in the ecclesiastical records. At the convent of North Berwick, for example, Alison Hume resigned in favour of Isabella Hume, a nun of Eccles, in 1524/5.[45] Alison herself had received the office of prioress after the death of Mariota Ramsay and the resignation of the 'clandestinely' elected Elizabeth Forman in 1473.[46] In 1544, however, Isabella Hume resigned her office in favour of Margaret Hume and Margaret was confirmed as the prioress of North Berwick.[47] There is no clear indication why the current prioresses resigned their offices. We can assume that it was for practical reasons of age or ill health, since there were no other indications.

There were two cases which highlight *continued* litigation between the predecessor and the successor in office. We can assume from the records that for some reason the succession may have been 'unlawful', and the resignation was obtained by coercion. The conflict for the headship of house could happen for different reasons: one, incompetence of the current head of house; two, family rivalries, within and outwith the house; three, favouritism; and lastly, for Scotland, the nominated head of house having been chosen by the king but not approved by the house, creating friction and discontent. Secular intrusions, like the king's, could ultimately affect the entire house. The candidate who was not well trained or a good administrator could cause tremendous financial difficulties and conflicts within the house. Two particular houses had problems with succession, and continued litigation ensued – the houses of Eccles and Elcho.

Eccles

Prior to the sixteenth century, the prioresses of Eccles came from a variety of local families. From the records we know that they came from the families of Fraser, Graham, and Cant.[48] By the beginning of the sixteenth century there was a strong tradition of a particular local family holding the office of the head of house. At Eccles, it was the Humes. The Humes were descendants of the Earls of Dunbar and March, who had held East Lothian for three hundred years until they were deprived of the earldom in 1400 and again in 1435.[49] The Dunbars were the founders and patrons of the house of Eccles, and the Humes were vassals of the Earls of March. The Humes became influential in the Eastern Borders during the rise of the Black Douglas's, and in 1400 Archibald, 4th Earl of Douglas, gave concessions to the Hume family, particularly Alexander Hume and his brother Patrick.[50] These 'promotions' by Douglas did much to change the nature of local politics in the Eastern Borders, and for the next century the many-branched Hume family dominated the region, extending as far as North Berwick.[51]

The priory of Eccles came into the possession of the Humes in the sixteenth century, only after a struggle between the Formans and Hamiltons for the office of prioress. In appointing the head of a female house, the king and the pope naturally believed that their choice was the 'legal' and rightful one. The king did not want to distance himself too much from his loyal supporters, and often he chose individuals for head of house to satisfy particular families and to keep them loyal to the crown. This continued struggle for the office of head, to receive the fruits, or monies, from the priory was not a problem that arose just in female houses; it was a widespread problem in all vacant benefices in Scotland in the late Middle Ages, a direct result of the Indult of 1487 and the royal minorities that plagued the first half of the sixteenth century.[52]

In 1501 Janet Forman, a nun from the convent of North Berwick, had removed herself from North Berwick and for some reason desired to go to Eccles.[53] She was admitted to the convent of Eccles and also granted its possessions, including its lands and rents, on 27 February 1501 by the crown.[54] According to a supplication to Rome, Janet Forman was given the office of prioress after E had vacated it before 10 March 1501.[55]

On 10 March 1501, Elizabeth Hume was in dispute with Janet Forman, current prioress, who contested the incursion of Elizabeth Hume. Because Hume had the defect of canonical age to take the office, legally she could not become prioress. Forman also contested the appointment because she was given papal acceptance and crown nomination on 9 December 1500.[56]

By 23 March 1501, the pope granted Elizabeth a special dispensation for her defect of age, to become the prioress of Eccles, in her nineteenth year.[57] Two days later in the Roman Court she was also granted a dispensation to hold the office of prioress, or any other monastic office in any other Cistercian house in the diocese of St Andrews.[58] This supplication is unusual in that it allows for Elizabeth to be provided to any vacancy of any office in any convent. Elizabeth must have felt that she might not win her case and needed a desperate back-up plan. Subsequently, two days later on 25 March, she was given the office.[59]

On 27 March 1501, Margaret Cant wanted to resign her office into the hands of the Pope. We can assume from this entry that the nuns of Eccles either elected Margaret Cant in spite of Elizabeth Hume, or she had assumed the office illegally. At the same time, Elizabeth Hume supplicated to become the prioress of Eccles. The profits of the office were listed as £80 sterling and, according to the supplication, the office was vacated by the resignation of Margaret.

We might assume by the last entry that Elizabeth Hume had become the prioress of the convent. According to a later supplication to Rome, however, another candidate for prioress, Janet Hunter, was given the office of prioress on the death of Janet Forman in 1529.[60] Elizabeth may have been 'given' the office of prioress, but for some reason Janet Forman still held it. The convent had elected Christina Macdowell, after the death of Forman, but the election was considered null and void.[61] The struggle between the two candidates began sometime after the death of Forman. Christian Macdowell (Dougal) was apparently the candidate selected by King James V, and Hunter was the Pope's candidate.[62] The archbishop, Andrew Forman, also claimed that the sub-prioress and the nuns had elected J H, who had been a professed nun for twenty years and that C M, a nun of Haddington, had intruded herself and uplifted the fruits of the priory and forced the nuns to obey her.[63] Margaret Cant did not appear to be involved in this litigation between Hunter and Macdowell.

After the death of Hunter, there were continued problems with succession at Eccles until the house was taken into commendation in 1575.[64] From 1548 to 1575 the Humes and Hamiltons disputed each other's claims to the office of prioress – each receiving crown grants. Marion Hamilton, daughter of James Hamilton of Innerwick, received the gift of the priory on 18 April 1548, after an election had taken place, and on 19 June 1548 she was given the benefice by the crown.[65] Isobel and James Hume were both given all the benefices of the priory of Eccles on 21 August 1566.[66] Isobel Hume must have expected or assumed that Marion Hamilton would vacate her office and surrender the priory sometime in 1566, but Hume was premature.[67] It has also been suggested that the incursion of the Humes, at an earlier date with Elizabeth and now Isabel, was an attempt by the Humes to take the convent.[68] Once the house was

given in commendation to James Hume, the struggle to retain the fruits
of the office, now valued at £100 sterling, ended.

Elcho

The conflict for the head of house and the damage it could do to a house
is best represented with a case from the priory of Elcho. The prioresses,
prior to 1490, were Agnes of Arroch, Elizabeth of Aberlady, Isobella,
and Margaret.[69] By c. 1493, a Margaret Swinton appears in Perthshire
as the prioress of Elcho.[70] The Swintons were a local family originating
in Berwickshire and in the fifteenth century related to the Dunbars by
marriage.[71] It is not clear why the Swintons appear in Perthshire when their
influence and patronage tended to focus on houses in East Lothian and
Berwickshire.[72] Janet Burton suggested that if the house a family *usually*
patronised was small or poorly resourced, or there was a restriction placed
on the number of women allowed in the convent, recruits or officeholders
might have been forced to go where there were places available.[73] This
may have been the case at Elcho.

On 28 July 1511 Margaret Swinton, the prioress, was asked to resign
her office and the priory into the hands of the pope or 'some other father of
God, Alexander, Archbishop of St Andrews'. The crown had given license
to Elizabeth Swinton, a professed nun of Elcho, to purchase the said priory
(sic) with permission of the archbishop. She was to raise confirmation
and provision as 'she thought expedient and the resignation of Margaret
Swinton and purchase of the priory by herself should not cause danger
or peril to either two parties'.[74]

For approximately fourteen years Elizabeth held the office of prioress,
with no contest, and we can assume, after holding the office for that length
of time, that her local bishop confirmed her. On 26 March 1526 the pope
acknowledged Elizabeth Swinton as prioress at Elcho and the value of the
office was listed at £40 sterling.[75] Sometime later in the year, however,
Swinton was in litigation with a nun, Euphemia Leslie, for the office of
prioress.[76]

On 2 May 1526 Elizabeth Swinton pleaded her case in the Roman Court
that she was the lawful prioress of Elcho. She asked that the decision and
the office be placed in the hands of the pope. However, much to her
surprise, the pope compelled her to resign the office with a pension of
40 marks Scots, £6 sterling. Euphemia Leslie was then granted the office
of prioress despite having a defect of birth.[77]

The litigation between Swinton and Leslie continued. On 6 November
1526 Swinton pursued the case further, claiming that Leslie could not
become prioress because of her defect of birth and that she was unlawfully

appointed prioress, but there is no mention how she unlawfully obtained the office.[78] It seems that although Swinton had resigned her office into the hands of the pope, she still had some claim of the office. Again on 29 March 1527 Elizabeth Swinton resigned freely as prioress of Elcho and Euphemia Leslie supplicated again for the office. By this time the records show that Leslie not only had a defect of birth, 'being the daughter of a priest and unmarried woman', but that she was also not of the canonical age to take office, being only eighteen years of age.[79]

Many months after resigning the office, twice, into the hands of Leslie, Elizabeth continued to appeal to anyone outside the Roman Court to hear her case. On 20 December 1527 letters were purchased by Dame Elizabeth Swinton, prioress of Elcho, against Dame Euphemia Leslie, alleged prioress, and these letters stated that the Earl of Atholl[80] and the Bishop of Caithness[81] came to the priory with eighty armed men and forced an entry into the monastery. After forcing their way through the priory, they took Elizabeth Swinton and confined her to a chamber. After being confined, she was compelled 'for fear of her life to constitute procurators to resign at Rome in favour of Euphemia'. Leslie's brother attended the transaction, procured bulls, and was able to persuade the court to decide in Leslie's favour. Dame Elizabeth immediately appealed to Rome, where the case was still pending. 'The Lords, for anything they have yet seen, declare Leslie's admission to the temporality to be in order as conform to the bulls.'[82]

Almost a year later, on 6 September 1528, Swinton still claimed that she was the prioress of Elcho and was presented to the office by the king.[83] She supplicated again to Rome to continue in her office, stating that Leslie's claim was still invalid. Before, the objection had arisen that Leslie had a defect of birth, being a daughter of a priest and an unmarried woman.[84] Her age then became another impediment to office, she being only eighteen and not the age of thirty required for office. Swinton, using every *legal* option available to her, found that Leslie still could not become prioress because her mother and father were related in the third degree of consanguinity, i.e. they were second cousins. The last line of her supplication reinforced her concern that she had resigned under coercion and she appealed to Rome to hear her case and to reinstate her 'against all adversaries'.[85]

Months later the litigation was still present at the Roman Court. On 14 January 1529 the priory of Elcho was assumed vacant by the resignation of Swinton and Leslie supplicated despite her defects of age and birth. The interesting note regarding this supplication was that the value of the office had gone up from £40 sterling to £60 sterling. For Leslie, the litigation had turned to her advantage on receiving the office; she not only won the case but also was given considerable financial gain.[86] However, Elizabeth Swinton still did not recognise Leslie as the prioress of Elcho, and the last dispute between the two headstrong women was on 16 July 1529, again at the Roman Court. This time the tables had turned on Elizabeth and she was styled the 'adversary' for the office of prioress against Leslie.[87] Even with the continued efforts of Swinton, Leslie did succeed in becoming the prioress of Elcho, and she appears in the records after 1532 styled as such.[88]

The claims made by Elizabeth Swinton about being 'forced' to resign her office to Leslie may or may not be completely true. There was some evidence that Swinton had been 'deprived from her office for her excesses [and] continued to molest the nunnery'. Her 'excesses' and the turmoil caused by her continued efforts in Rome created debts that the nunnery was unable to pay.[89] Litigation, over the fruits of a benefice, was to be avoided: it was costly, time-consuming, and the outcome often uncertain.[90] There was no doubt that Swinton felt she was forced to resign her office to Leslie; the registers of the Vatican attest to that, but the real circumstances concerning her resignation are yet to be uncovered. If Leslie truly used her family's influence to send an army to deprive Swinton of her office and put herself in Swinton's place, we can be sure that the convent suffered a great deal. Those in the convent who would have to consent to election and give a majority vote may have been easily 'persuaded' to nominate Leslie for fear of repercussions.[91]

There are other cases of resignation from the office of prioress, but the litigation does not appear to have been continuous, as in the above cases from Eccles and Elcho. For example, in July 1495 Joanna Hepburn, nun of Haddington, supplicated to the Pope to be granted the office of prioress and Margaret Fawside had resigned.[92] There were no other supplications to the Roman Court doubting the validity of her claim and Hepburn continued to benefit from the fruits of the office until her death in 1517.[93] Another case was from the convent of Manuel where Elizabeth Hoppringle had resigned by 1543 and Janet Livingstone was appointed to the office on approval from the crown.[94] In both of these cases, there was no reason given for the resignation of the predecessor. We can assume that they had resigned due to pressure from inside the convent or from ill health. Also, at both of these houses, there were no continued problems with succession to the office of prioress. Resignations where an incumbent took the fruits of the office, without litigation from another, proved to be less costly affairs. There were no legal actions taken and the predecessor, if not dead, could live happily in the convent with a pension near or equal to that of the amount she received for the fruits of her office.[95]

Because of the relative lack of episcopal registers in Scotland, we have to assume that most elections were presented to the bishop by one of the executive officers of the monastery, most likely the subprioress. The bishop would then give his approval for an election either by being present himself or by sending one of his officials. Once episcopal permission for the election was obtained, the election was confirmed. For the election of the prioress of Haddington in 1517, the Archbishop of St Andrews, Andrew Forman, confirmed it, and a letter was sent to the subprioress and her convent.[96]

After episcopal confirmation that an election could take place, and the confirmation by the bishop of the candidates, the nuns held an election to determine who would hold the office of prioress. There were three authorised ways to hold an election for prioress: one was by unanimous vote or divine inspiration; two, by scrutiny, or the system by which an outside group was chosen to examine each nominee and tally the votes by the convent; and lastly by compromise, meaning that if there was no clear majority, a compromise was sought.[97] Under the Rule of St Benedict, the office must be conferred upon someone who was chosen by the whole community, for fear of God.[98]

Details of female monastic elections in medieval Scotland are lacking. There was only one recorded election, and it followed the rules outlined in the election process. It was from the convent of Coldstream in 1537 and was recorded by the public notary.

On January 6 1537, Isabella Hoppringle, the prioress, died. On 13 February an election was granted to determine the future prioress of the convent. The names of the sisters in the convent in support of the candidate, Jonet Hoppringle, were written down: Isobell Rutherford, subprioress, Katherine Fleming, Jonet Brown, Mariota Rutherford, Jonet Kingorne, Elizabeth Hoppringle, Katrina Stevenson, Christina Todric, Katrina French, Jonet Shaw, and Ellen Riddall.

Jonet Hoppringle, candidate for the office of prioress, was found to be a professed nun of the convent, clearly of good merit (*virtutum meritis insignatum*), a person fit for the duties of office, and qualified in spiritual and temporal matters as needed for the guidance and rule of the convent. She was also of legitimate birth and good name. So (with *una voca et una anima*) there was a unanimous vote to choose Jonet Hoppringle as the new prioress of the convent.[99]

On February 23, 1537, the public notary, Edward Dickson, clerk of the official of St Andrews, wrote down the confirmation of the election. Present for the confirmation of the election were Robert Hoppringle, rector of Arnotston, Patrick Cockburn, rector of Pettikis, John Donaldson, Cuthbert Hinde, Andrew Curry, chaplain, William Cockburn of Schoslie,

Robert Watson of Yselye, Archibald Hoppringle, Adam Cockburn, James Hoppringle, Sir Arthur Crawford, subprior of the monastery of Newbattle, and Sir James Watson, monk from Newbattle.[100]

In nunneries exempt from diocesan control, the election ceremony would have been presided over by an abbot from a nearby Cistercian monastery for men. In this case, the abbot sent someone in his place, the subprior of Newbattle. Other representatives present at the election would be those who had a vested interest in the convent. More than likely they would be the patrons of the monastery and would also have to give approval of the candidate. In this particular election, the patrons appear to have been from the same family, or were closely linked to, the Hoppringles.

It appears that this election carried on with no contest from any other candidate, and the record seems to indicate that no other nun was presented or nominated for the office of prioress. From approximately 1434 to 1588, a prioress was elected at Coldstream with what seems to have been no clear opposition after each death of the predecessor. This could have been due to the continual succession of a powerful family, the Pringles of that Ilk.

Having strong families represented in the monasteries could create a power vacuum. If local families had influence in the secular world, the power could spread to the monastic by having a member of that family elected as head of house. This individual would be considered an important person, being a member of an influential family and also because she was the head of a house. Heads of religious houses in medieval society could command great respect and reverence and some extra admiration on account of their religion.[101] They could also wield a great deal of power, especially over local landholding and rents. These women, with their family connections and control over their monastic revenues, were powerful individuals. Having a woman of local influence and rich connections as a prioress promoted the wealth and prosperity of the convent.[102] But even though these women may have been wealthy landowners and powerful locally, they were often involved in their own litigation for the office of prioress, as well as control over their lands, rents, tithes and protection of their holdings.

With few religious options available to medieval Scottish women, the convent provided an outlet for particular talents, and opportunities for 'advancement' for many women. These important women may also have been from powerful local families. Currently, we know of 78 women who succeeded to the office of prioress from c. 1100 to 1600 – the women discussed here are only a few.[103] The case studies outlined above demonstrate that many women fought long and contested battles for the office of prioress. To fully understand the role of the prioress and her importance in medieval Scottish society, additional information in the Vatican archives will need to be collected. Only with this material will we be able to see 'the world in which medieval [women] lived, the problems they had to face, and how they dealt with them'.[104]

NOTES

* I am indebted to Norman Shead at the University of Glasgow for his work on the heads of religious houses in medieval Scotland, especially those of the female monastic houses. His information about the prioresses has been invaluable.

1. A benefice was an income from a church living, usually in return for the spiritual care of its inhabitants. See also, Cameron, Annie I., *The Apostolic Camera and Scottish Benefices, 1418–1488* (Oxford, 1934); Cameron (Dunlop), Annie I. *et al, Calendar of the Scottish Supplications to Rome, 1418–1432*, Vols. 1–3 (Scottish History Society [hereafter SHS] 1934–1970); Dunlop, Annie I. *et al, Calendar of the Scottish Supplications to Rome, 1433–1471*. Vols. 4–5 (Glasgow, 1983–1997); Donaldson, Gordon, ed., *Accounts of the Collectors of the Thirds of Benefices, 1561–1572* (SHS, 1949); Kirk, James, ed., *The Books of Assumption of the Thirds of Benefices: Scottish Ecclesiastical Records at the Reformation* (Oxford, 1995); Williamson, Eila, Scottish Benefices and Clergy during the Pontificate of Sixtus IV (1471–84): the evidence in the *Registra Supplicationum*. Unpublished PhD thesis (University of Glasgow, 1998).

2. Donaldson, Gordon 'The Rights of the Scottish Crown in Episcopal Vacancies', *Scottish Historical Review* [hereafter *SHR*], Vol. XLV, I, No. 139 (April 1966), 34; Donaldson, Gordon *et al, Scottish Historical Documents* (Edinburgh, 1970), 89–90; Macdougall, Norman, *James III* (Edinburgh, 1982), 229–30.

3. Anderson, William James, 'Rome and Scotland, 1513–1625', in *Essays on the Scottish Reformation, 1513–1625*' ed. David McRoberts (Glasgow, 1962), 465.

4. James IV promoted his illegitimate son, Andrew, as archbishop of St Andrews at the age of eleven. James V supplicated to the Pope to have his illegitimate sons promoted to the abbeys of Kelso, Melrose, Holyrood, and the priories of St Andrews and Pittenweem – while they were still infants. See Macfarlane, Leslie, 'The Primacy of the Scottish Church, 1472–1521', *Innes Review*, Vol. 20, No. 2 (Autumn, 1969), 111–129.

5. Lincluden (B), St Evoca, South Berwick, St Bothans (C), Iona, St Leonards (A), Dundee, Aberdour (F), Sciennes (D). Many of these houses have very few records, if any at all. By 1400, three of the houses had been dissolved or converted into collegiate churches. See also, Cowan, Ian B, 'Church and Society,' in *Scottish Society in the Fifteenth Century*, ed. Jennifer Brown (London, 1977), 115–122; Cowan, Ian B. and D.E. Easson, eds., *Medieval Religious Houses of Scotland*, 2nd Edition (London, 1976), 143–156. Although the mendicant orders fall into the period I am covering, their rules for succession to head of house and rules of the order were different than those of the other orders.

6. MacFarlane, Leslie, 'The Vatican Archives as a Source for Scottish Medieval Historians: An Update', in *Freedom and Authority: Scotland 1050–1650, Historical and Historiographical Essays Presented to Grant Simpson*. Ed. T. Brotherstone and D. Ditchburn (East Linton, 2000), 183; see also, Cowan, Ian B, 'The Vatican Archives: A Report on Pre-reformation Scottish material', *SHR*, Vol. 48 (1969), 227–242; Foggie, Janet, 'Archivium Sacrae Penitentiariae Apostolicae in the Vatican Archives as a source for Scottish Historians,' *Innes Review*, Vol. 47, No. 2 (Autumn, 1996), 110–126; Robertson, James, 'Scottish Legal Research in the Vatican Archives: a preliminary report', *Renaissance Studies*, Vol. 2, No. 2 (1988), 339–346; Watt, D.E.R, 'Sources for Scottish History of the Fourteenth Century in the Archives of the Vatican', *SHR*, Vol. 32, No. 114 (1953), 101–122.

7. My research into the Scottish material contained in the Vatican archives is at the preliminary stages. Over time, some of the information and ideas expressed here may change due to new developments and information that will come with continued use of the material.

8. MacFarlane, 184.

9. The Register of Supplications, and both the Vatican and Lateran registers, were all from the records of the Papal Chancery. The Scottish Vatican material is held at the University of Glasgow, Scottish History Department on microfilm [hereafter: GUS *Reg. Supp.*; *Reg. Lat.*; *Reg. Vat.*].

10. *Decretum Gratian*, CC.27.C1.C3., Question 1, C10; *Extravagantes of John XXII*, Title VI, CI: *Corpus Iuris Canonici*.

11. Labarge, Margaret Wade, *Women in Medieval Life: A Small Sound of the Trumpet* (London, 1986), 28.

12. Nichols, John, 'The Internal Organization of English Cistercian Nunneries', *Citeaux: Commentarii Cisterciense*, Vol. 30 (1979), 31–32; Power, Eileen, *Medieval English Nunneries, c.1275–1535* (Cambridge, 1922), 131–34.

13. Nichols, 31–32. The offices of the cellaress, infirmaress, and novice mistress were permanent and yearly appointments because they required special skills that not all of the nuns would have. The kitcheness, however, was a position that rotated week by week.

14. Power, 131–34; Eckenstien, Lina, *Women Under Monasticism* (New York, 1896), 368–370; Nichols, 30–32.

15. Lekai, Louis, *The White Monks: A History of the Cistercian Order* (Wisconsin, 1953), 239–41.

16. Doyle, Leonard, trans., *Rule of St Benedict* Ch. 64.

17. Johnson, Penelope, *Equal in the Monastic Profession: Religious Women in Medieval France* (Chicago, 1991), 206.

18. Nichols, 23; Lowe, K.J.P., 'Female Strategies for Success in a Male Ordered World: The Benedictine Convent of Le Murate in Florence in the Fifteenth and Sixteenth Centuries,' in *Women in the Church*, ed. Derek Baker (Oxford, 1990): 209–212; see also, Dilworth, Mark, *Scottish Monasteries in the Late Middle Ages* (Edinburgh, 1995), Introduction, *passim*; Easson, D.E., 'The Nunneries of Medieval Scotland', *Transactions of the Scottish Ecclesiological Society*, 13 Pt 2 (1940–1), 22–38; Cowan, Ian B., *Medieval Church in Scotland*, ed. James Kirk (Edinburgh, 1995); Dickson, W. Croft, *Scotland from Earliest Times to 1603* (Edinburgh, 1961), n. 133; Nicholson, Ranald, *Scotland: The Later Middle Ages* (Edinburgh, 1974), 234–5.

19. Johnson. 167.

20. *Rule*, Ch. 64.
21. *Ibid.*
22. Olivia, Marilyn, 'Aristocracy or Mediocracy? Office Holding Strategies in Late Medieval English Nunneries', in *Women in the Church*, ed. Derek Baker, 207.
23. Power, 42–3.
24. Labarge, 28–30.
25. It was possible that there were more candidates for the office of prioress that did not meet these specific requirements. More research into the archives of the Vatican will need to be done to determine if this was the case, especially those of the Apostolic Penitentiary.
26. *Calendar of Papal Registers, Papal Letters* (hereafter *CPL*), Benedict XIII, 100.
27. GUS *Reg. Supp.*, 1119, fos. 158v–59r.
28. GUS *Reg. Supp.*, 1583, fo. 255r.
29. Donaldson, Gordon and C. Macrae, eds. *St Andrews Formulare, 1516–46* (hereafter *St.A.Form.*) (Stair Society, 1942–44), 104–5, No. 94.
30. GUS *Reg. Lat.*, 1490, fos. 215r/v-216r/v.
31. See above.
32. *CPL, Benedict XIII*, 177.
33. *CPL, Benedict XIII*, 180–1.
34. Wardlaw was listed as becoming the head of house in 1408, *CPL, Benedict XIII*, 110; in 1421 there was a mention of a Jonet as the head of house, Easson, D.E. and Angus Macdonald, eds., *Charters of the Abbey of Inchcolm* (SHS, 1938), 47–49; the next prioress in the written record in Agnes Maul in 1437.
35. *CPL*, xiii, part 1, 29–30.
36. *Registrum Secreti Sigilli* (hereafter *RSS*), iii, No. 2822.
37. *CPL, Benedict XIII*, 100.
38. *Ibid.*
39. Daichman, Graciela, 'Misconduct in the Medieval Nunnery: Fact, Not Fiction', in *That Gentle Strength: Historical Perspectives on Women in Christianity*, eds. Lynda Coon, Katherine Haldane, and Elisabeth Sommer (Charlottesville, 1990), 101–103; Daichman, Graciela, *Wayward Nuns in Medieval Literature* (New York, 1986), *passim*.
40. *CPL, Benedict XIII*, 161.
41. *CPL*, ix, 326.
42. *Ibid.*
43. *Calendar of Scottish Supplications to Rome, 1443–1447* (hereafter *CSSR*), iv, 238, No. 963.
44. *CPL*, ix, 326–7; Bull of Rehabilitation from Pope Eugene IV, GUS: PRO 31/9/28, 149 fo. 258 (University of Glasgow, microfilm).
45. GUS *Reg. Supp.*, 1550, fo. 132r; *Carte Monialum de Northberwic* (hereafter *N.B. Chrs.*) (Bannatyne Club, 1847), Nos. 33–34.
46. See above. *CPL*, vol. xiii part 1, 23; Alison Hume had paid dues in the Camera in 1473. Cameron, Annie, I., ed., *Apostolic Camera and Scottish Benefices, 1418–1488*, 176.
47. *N. B. Chrs.*, No. 38; GUS *Reg. Supp.*, 2510, fos. 226v-267s; GUS *Reg. Lat.*, 1749, fos. 226v–228.
48. Ada Fraser, c. 1296, *Calendar of Documents Relating to Scotland.*, ii, 206;

Annabelle Graham, cousin of King James II and sister of James Kennedy, bishop of St Andrews, c. 1444, *CSSR*, iv, 247–8, Nos. 994, 250, & 1005; Margaret Cant, c. 1501, GUS *Reg. Supp.*, 1119, fo. 267.

49. The land of Hume was given as a dowry in c. 1215 to Ada, daughter of the 5th Earl Patrick of Dunbar. William of Hume was said to have married Mariota, Lady of Hume, widow of Patrick Edgar, and descendant of the Earls of Dunbar. The Humes were loyal subjects of the Dunbar family until it deemed it 'unfavourable' and 'risky' to be so. See Nicholson, 319; Brown, Michael. *The Black Douglases: War and Lordship in Late Medieval Scotland, 1300–1455* (East Linton, 1998), 112–3.

50. Alexander was made deputy of the priory of Coldingham and Patrick was given the lands of Wedderburn.

51. Brown, *Black Douglases*, 177–8.

52. See above. Also, Cowan, *Medieval Church*, Ch. 12.

53. Janet Forman may have been related to the Humes by marriage. Helen Rutherford's second husband was John Forman of Dawane, and her fourth husband was Patrick Hume of Broomhouse.

54. *RSS*, No. 645.

55. GUS *Reg. Supp.*, 1118, fo. 247.

56. GUS *Reg. Supp.*, 1114, fo. 54; *RSS*, i, No. 645.

57. *CPL*, xvii, pt. I, 274, No. 410.

58. GUS *Reg. Supp.*, 1119, fos. 158–159r.

59. See above.

60. Janet Forman was alive in 1517 and gave her consent, as prioress, to Sir William Myrton for the erection of the Collegiate Church of Crail. *Register of the Collegiate Church of Crail* (hereafter *Crail Register*) (Grampian Club, 1877), 4.

61. GUS *Reg. Supp.*, 1970, fo. 204r.

62. See above. Also, Meikle, Maureen, 'Victims, Viragos, and Vamps: Women of the Sixteenth-Century Anglo-Scottish Frontier', in *Government, Religion, and Society in Northern England, 1000–1700*, ed. J.C. Appleby and P. Dalton (Gloucestershire: Sutton Hoo Publishers), p. 183.

63. *St A. Form.*, 370, No. 302.

64. A commendator was the holder of the revenues of a monastic house, usually a secular lord.

65. GUS *Reg. Supp.*, 2661, fo. 2v; *RSS*, iii, Nos. 2822–3.

66. *RSS*, v, pt. 2, No. 3041.

67. Isobel Hume was the daughter of Alexander, 5th Lord Hume and Agnes Gray, Marion Hamilton was her cousin, daughter of Helen Hume who was the daughter of Mungo Hume married to Elizabeth Stewart who then married Patrick Sinclair, familiar of James IV. Isobel was very close to James Hume. She was styled his 'loved and special friend', see above, *RSS*.

68. Graham, T.W., Patronage, Provision and Reservation: Scotland and the Papacy during the Pontificate of Paul III. Unpublished Ph.D. thesis (Glasgow University, 1993), 82.

69. Agnes Arroch, c. 1282, *Cartulary of the Abbey of Lindores, 1195–1479* (SHS, 1903), 158, No. 125; Elizabeth de Aberlady, c. 1405, *St Andrews Copiale*, 77, No. 39; Isobella, c. 1445, Fraser, W., *Memorials of the Family Wemyss of Wemyss*, ii (Edinburgh, 1888), 67–69, No. 51; Margaret, c. 1470, Anderson, Joseph, *The Oliphants of Scotland* (Edinburgh, 1879), 4, No. 5.

70. Swinton, A.C., ed., *The Swintons of that Ilk and their Cadets* (Edinburgh, 1883), 35 & app., lxxv., No. 55.
71. John Swinton married Lady Marjory Dunbar, daughter of George Earl of March, c. 1424.
72. The Swintons patronised the convents of Haddington. North Berwick, and Coldstream and appear on witness lists in charters to the above houses.
73. Burton, Janet, 'Yorkshire Nunneries in the Middle Ages: Recruitment and Resources', in *Government, Religion and Society in Northern England, 1000–1700*, ed. John Appleby and Paul Dalton (Glouscestershire, 1997), 111–112.
74. *RSS*, i., No. 2273.
75. GUS *Reg. Supp.*, 1888, fos. 277r–278r. Margaret received a pension of 40 marks Scots and £6 sterling to remain a nun at Elcho.
76. GUS *Reg. Vat.*, 1281, fo. 265.
77. Elizabeth was granted the same pension amount as Margaret, see above. PRO, 31/9/32/104 (microfilm, University of Glasgow).
78. GUS *Reg. Lat.*, 1490, fos. 215r-216v.
79. GUS *Reg. Supp.*, 1922, fo. 176r-v.
80. This would be John, the 3rd Earl of Atholl, who succeeded his father in c. 1521–22. His second wife, Janet Forbes, took as her third husband, William Leslie. According to the peerage, there is no Euphemia Leslie listed as daughter of this marriage between Forbes and Leslie nor is there a Euphemia listed in the Leslie line.
81. Alexander Stewart II, son of Sir John Stewart, 1st Earl of Atholl, died c. 1541. John Stewart was the brother of James II and was married first to Margaret Douglas, heiress to Archibald, 5th Earl of Douglas and, secondly, to Eleanor Sinclair.
82. *Acts of Lords of Council in Public Affairs, 1501–1554: Selections from the Acta Dominorum Concilii*, ed. R.K. Hannay (Edinburgh, 1932), 273–4.
83. See above, *RSS*.
84. It is not clear from the 'supposed' lineage who her father, the priest, actually was. Further investigation of her case will be necessary to determine if she was actually illegitimate.
85. GUS *Reg. Supp.*, 1949, fo. 164v.
86. GUS *Reg. Supp.*, 1965, fos. 72r.v.–73r.
87. GUS *Reg. Supp.*, 1984, fos. 189r.v.-190r.
88. *Registrum Magni Sigilli Regum Scotorum*, Vol. 3, No. 2746. In 1540 she appeared in the record of the *Apostolic Penitentiary*, Vol. 25, 23x85. In 1532, a tack by her was granted to John Swinton for lands, *Swintons*, App., cxiii, No. 81.
89. Fraser, W., *Wemyss, ii*, No. 190.
90. Cowan, *Medieval Church*, 208.
91. See election process above.
92. GUS *Reg. Supp.*, 1007, fo. 207r.
93. *Crail Register*, 32, No. 47. Beatrice Hepburn was listed as the prioress who died in 1517 but it could be an error for Jonet, *Ibid.*, 37–40, No. 55; 14 November 1526, Joanna was listed as the former prioress and her successor was Elizabeth Hepburn, *Acts of the Parliaments of Scotland, 1424–1547*, Vol. 2., App. 398–399, No. 12.
94. *RSS*, iii, 46, No. 332.

95. Margaret Swinton at Elcho at her resignation to Elizabeth received a pension of £40 sterling per year that was more or less equal to that of her yearly sum as a prioress. See above, *Reg. Supp*; Johnson, 172.
96. *St A. Form.*, No. 94.
97. Johnson, 169. *Corpus Iuris Canonici: Liber Sextus* 1.6.43; Mellinger. L., 'Politics in a Convent: The Election of a Fifteenth Century Abbess', *Church History*, Vol. 63 (1994), 528–540.
98. *Rule*, CH. 64.
99. *Chartulary of the Cistercian Priory of Coldstream*, App. I, No. V, 83–85.
100. *Ibid.*
101. Power, 69.
102. Power, 43.
103. The role of the prioress in Scotland is an ongoing research project. The names of the 78 women are only what have been discovered so far – there may be more.
104. *CSSR*, i., 1418–1422 (SHS, 1934), xii.

FURTHER READING

MANUSCRIPT SOURCES
University of Glasgow, Scottish History Department
GUS   Microfilm, Vatican Registers
GUS   Microfilm, Public Record Office, London,
   Transcripts of Vatican Registers

PUBLISHED PRIMARY SOURCES AND WORKS OF REFERENCE

Abbotsford Club (1845) *Liber Officialis Santi Andree*, Edinburgh.
Acts of the Parliaments of Scotland (1814) House of Commons, London.
Anderson, J. (1879) *The Oliphants in Scotland*, Edinburgh.
Bain, J., ed. (1881-8) *Calendar of Documents Relating to Scotland*, 4 vols., Edinburgh.
Bannatyne Club (1847) *Carte Monialum de Northberwic*, Edinburgh.
Baxter, J.H. (1930) *Copiale Prioratus Santiandree*, Oxford.
Black, G.F. (1946) *The Surnames of Scotland: Their origin, meaning and history*, New York.
Bliss, H. *et al* (1893-) *Calendar of Entries in the Papal Registers relating to Great Britain and Ireland: Papal Letters*, London.
Cameron, A.I. and E.R. Lindsay, eds. (1934) *Calendar of Scottish Supplications to Rome, 1418–22, i.*, Scottish History Society, Edinburgh.
Cameron. A.I. (1934) *The Apostolic Camera and Scottish Benefices, 1418–88*, Oxford.
Cowan, Ian B. and D.E. Easson, eds. (1977) *The Medieval Religious Houses of Scotland*, London.
Donaldson, G. and C. Macrae, eds. (1942-4) *St Andrews Formulare, 1514–46*, Stair Society, Edinburgh.
Donaldson, Gordon, ed. (1949) *Accounts of the Collectors of the Thirds of Benefices, 1561–1572*, Scottish History Society, Edinburgh.
Donaldson, Gordon, ed. (1970) *Scottish Historical Documents*, Edinburgh.
Dunlop, A. I., ed. (1956) *Calendar of Scottish Supplications to Rome, 1423–28, ii*, Scottish History Society, Edinburgh.

Dunlop, A.I. and Ian B. Cowan, eds. (1970) *Calendar of Scottish Supplications to Rome, 1428–1432, iii*, Scottish History Society, Edinburgh.

Dunlop, A.I. and D. MacLauchlan, eds. (1983) *Calendar of Scottish Supplications to Rome, 1433–1447, iv*, Glasgow.

Dunlop, A.I., James Kirk, and Roland Tanner, eds., (1997) *Calendar of Scottish Supplications to Rome, 1447–1471, v*, Glasgow.

Easson, D.E. and Angus Macdonald, eds., (1938) *Charters of the Abbey of Inchcolm*, Scottish History Society, Edinburgh.

Fraser, W. (1888) *The Memorials of the Family of Wemyss of Wemyss*, Edinburgh.

Friedburg, Emil and Aemilus L. Richler, trans., eds. (1879–1881) *Corpus Iuris Canonices*, 2 vols., Leipzig.

Grampian Club (1879) *The Cartulary of the Cistercian Priory of Coldstream*, London.

Grampian Club (1877) *The Register of the Collegiate Church of Crail*, London.

Hannay, R.K., ed. (1932) *Acts of the Lords of Council in Public Affairs, 1501–1554: Selections from the Acta Dominorum Concilii*, Edinburgh.

Livingstone, M. *et al* (1908–) *Registrum Secreti Sigilli Regum Scotorum*, 8 vols., Edinburgh.

McGurk, F., ed. (1976) *Calendar of Papal Letters to Scotland of Benedict XIII of Avignon, 1399–1419*, Scottish History Society, Edinburgh.

Paul, Sir James Balfour (1904–14) *The Scots Peerage*, 9 vols., Edinburgh.

Scottish History Society (1903) *Cartulary of the Abbey of Lindores*, Edinburgh.

Swinton, A.C., ed. (1883) *The Swintons of that Ilk and their Cadets*, Edinburgh.

Thompson, J.M. *et al* (1882–1914) *Registrum Magni Sigill; Regum Scotorum*, II vols., Edinburgh.

SECONDARY SOURCES

Unpublished Theses

Graham, T.W. (1993), Patronage, Provision and Reservation; Scotland and the Papacy during the Pontificate of Paul III, unpublished PhD thesis, University of Glasgow.

Williamson, Eila (1998), Scottish Benefices and Clergy during the Pontificate of Sixtus IV (1471–84): the evidence in the *Registra Supplicationum*, unpublished PhD thesis, University of Glasgow.

Books and Articles

Anderson, Willliam James (1962), 'Rome and Scotland, 1513–1625', in McRoberts, David (ed.), *Essays on the Scottish Reformation, 1513–1625*, Glasgow: G.S.Burn, pp. 463–483.

Brown, Michael (1998), *The Black Douglases: War and Lordship in Late Medieval Scotland, 1300–1455*, East Linton: Tuckwell Press.

Burton, Janet (1997), 'Yorkshire Nunneries in the Middle Ages: Recruitment and Resources', in Appleby, John and Paul Dalton (eds.), *Government, Religion and Society in Northern England, 1000–1700*, Gloucestershire: Sutton Hoo Publishers, pp. 104–106.

Cowan, Ian B. (1977), 'Church and Society', in Brown, Jennifer (ed.), *Scottish Society in the Fifteenth Century*, London: Edward Arnold, pp. 115–122.

—— (1995), *Medieval Church in Scotland*, ed. J. Kirk, Edinburgh: Scottish Academic Press.

—— (1969), 'The Vatican Archives: A Report on Pre-reformation Scottish material', *Scottish Historical Review (SHR)*, 48, pp. 227–242.

Daichman, Graciela (1990), 'Misconduct in the Medival Nunnery: Fact, Not Fiction', in Coon, Lynda, Katherine Haldane and Elisabeth Sommer (eds.), *That Gentle Strength: Historical Perspectives on Women in Christianity*, Charlottesville: University of Virginia Press, pp. 97–117.

—— (1986), *Wayward Nuns in Medieval Literature*, New York: Syracuse University Press.

Dickinson, W. Croft (1961), *Scotland from Earliest Times to 1603*, Edinburgh: Thomas Nelson and Sons.

Dilworth, Mark (1995), *Scottish Monasteries in the Late Middle Ages*, Edinburgh: Edinburgh University Press.

Donaldson, Gordon (1966), 'The Rights of the Scottish Crown in Episcopal Vacancies', *SHR*, 45:1 (139), April, pp. 27–35.

Doyle, Leonard (1948), trans., e-c. *St Benedict's Rule for Monasteries*, Collegeville, Minnesota: Liturgical Press.

Easson, D.E. (1940–1), 'The Nunneries of Medieval Scotland', *Transactions of the Scottish Ecclesiological Society*, 13:2, pp. 22–38.

Eckenstien, Lina (1896), *Women Under Monasticism*, New York: Russell and Russell, Inc.

Foggie, Janet (1996), 'Archivium Sacrae Penitentiariae Apostolicae in the Vatican Archives as a source for Scottish historians', *Innes Review*, 47 (2), Autumn, pp.110–26.

Houston, R.A. (1989), 'Women in the Economy and Society of Scotland, 1500–1800', in Houston, R.A. (ed.), *Scottish Society, 1500–1800*, Cambridge: Cambridge University Press, pp.118–147.

Johnson, Penelope (1991), *Equal in the Monastic Profession: Religious Women in Medieval France*, Chicago: University of Chicago Press.

Kirk, James., ed. (1995), *The Books of Assumption of the Thirds of Benefices: Scottish Ecclesiastical Records at the Reformation*, Oxford: Oxford University Press.

Labarge, Margaret Wade (1986), *Women in Medieval Life: A Small Sound of the Trumpet*, London: Hamish Hamilton.

Lekai, Louis (1953), *The White Monks: A History of the Cistercian Order*, Wisconsin: Cistercian Fathers.

Lifshitz, Felice (1996), 'Is Mother Superior? Towards a History of Feminine Amtscharisma', in Parsons, John, Carmi and Bonnie Wheeler (eds.), *Medieval Mothering*, New York: Garland Publisher Inc., pp. 117–138.

Lowe, K.J.P. (1990), 'Female Strategies for Success in a Male Ordered World: The Benedictine Convent of Le Murate in Florence in the Fifteenth and Sixteenth Centuries', in Baker, Derek (ed.), *Women in the Church*, Oxford: Basil Blackwell, pp. 209–221.

Macdougall, Norman (1982), *James III*, Edinburgh: John Donald.

Macfarlane, Leslie (2000), 'The Vatican Archives as a Source for Scottish Medieval Historians: An Update', in Brotherstone, Terry and David Ditchburn (eds.), *Freedom and Authority: Scotland 1050–1650, Historical and Historiographical Essays Presented to Grant Simpson*, East Linton: Tuckwell Press, pp.183–189.

Macfarlane, Leslie (1969) 'The Primacy of the Scottish Church, 1472–1521', *Innes Review*, 20 (2), Autumn, pp. 111–129.

Marshall, Rosalind K. (1983), *Virgins and Viragos: A History of Women in Scotland*, 1080–1980, London: Collins.

Meikle, Maureen (1997), 'Victims, Viragos, and Vamps: Women of the Sixteenth-Century Anglo-Scottish Frontier', in Appleby, John and Paul Dalton (eds.), *Government, Religion, and Society in Northern England, 1000–1700*, Gloucestershire: Sutton Hoo Publishing, pp. 172–184.

Mellinger. L. (1994), 'Politics in a Convent: The Election of a Fifteenth Century Abbess', *Church History*, 63, pp. 529–540.

Nichols, John (1979), 'The Internal Organization of English Cistercian Nunneries', *Citeaux: Commentarii Cistercienses*, 30, pp.23–40.

Nicholson, Ranald (1974), *Scotland: The Later Middle Ages*, Edinburgh: Oliver and Boyd.

Noonan, John T., trans. Thompson, Augustine, O.P., ed.(1994), *Marriage Canons from The Decretum of Gratian and The Decretals, Sext, Clemetines and Extravagantes*, Oregon: Augustine Thompson.

Oliva, Marilyn (1990), 'Aristocracy or Mediocracy? Office Holding Strategies in Late Medieval English Nunneries', in Baker, Derek (ed.), *Women in the Church*, Oxford: Basil Blackwell, pp. 197–208.

Power, Eileen (1922), *Medieval English Nunneries, c. 1275–1535*, Cambridge: Cambridge University Press.

Robertson, James (1988), 'Scottish Legal Research in the Vatican Archives: a preliminary report', *Renaissance Studies*, 2 (2), pp. 339–346.

Watt, D.E.R. (1953), 'Sources for Scottish History of the Fourteenth Century in the Archives of the Vatican', *SHR*, 32 (114), pp. 101–122.

FOUR

The Bewitchment of Christian Shaw: A Reassessment of the Famous Paisley Witchcraft Case of 1697

Hugh McLachlan and Kim Swales

Introduction

Christian Shaw is called 'The Bargarran Impostor'. She was the daughter of the Laird of Bargarran and lived in Erskine, Renfrewshire. As the brains behind the Bargarran Thread Company, she can be regarded as a founder of the sewing thread industry on which the prosperity of Paisley was based. However, she is notorious rather than famous and more commonly thought of as having been a particularly deceitful and malicious child than as having been a successful businesswoman and entrepreneur. For instance, Robbins entitles the section of *The Encyclopedia of Witchcraft and Demonology* which deals with the Paisley witchcraft prosecution of 1697: 'Bargarran Impostor'. He writes that '. . . one eleven-year-old girl . . . could cause twenty-one persons to be indicted, and seven of them burned at the stake'.[1]

Those who denigrate Christian Shaw as the 'Bargarran Impostor' have not, as one might have thought, based their case upon a consideration of the record of the trial of the alleged witches in question. Indeed, the first person (to the best of our knowledge) who expressed the 'impostor theory' in print – Hugo Arnot in 1785 – explicitly states that no record of the trial exists.[2] Christian Shaw's reputation as a spectacularly evil child – which was not the one she had during her own lifetime – is based upon an interpretation which later generations, following Arnot, have put upon a book entitled *A True Narrative of the Sufferings and Relief of a Young Girle; Strangely molested by Evil spirits and their instruments in the West*.[3] It was published in Edinburgh in 1698, very shortly after her alleged imposture and after, it should be noted, the trial of those who were accused of having bewitched several people including her.

We shall re-assess the claim that Christian Shaw was 'The Impostor of Bargarran' by giving a more careful interpretation of the *Narrative* than is provided by Arnot and other commentators. The allegation that Christian Shaw was a deceitful fraudster is not only unfair but it presents, we shall suggest, an implausible and inaccurate historical interpretation of the relevant actions and occurrences in an around Paisley in the mid-1690s.

As a background to the re-assessment, we shall present a statement of our methodological position and a brief introduction to ancient Scottish witchcraft belief and prosecution.

Postmodernism, the Enlightenment and Diversity of Thought

We aim to offer not merely a different interpretation of Christian Shaw's alleged bewitchment but a better one than the more usual ones. Lest it be thought that there are well founded objections to such an attempt, some comments on so-called 'postmodernism' are in order.

Some postmodernists claim or, more characteristically, imply that now-adays there is great diversity of beliefs and that in the past there was uniformity. Even if this claim were true, it is not at all apparent what – if anything – would follow from it. Diversity of beliefs about some issue or other does not imply that there are no true or false beliefs about it nor that rational discussion of the issue is not possible. Once, there was much disagreement about what shape the earth is. It does not follow that then the earth was of indeterminate shape: then, as now, some statements about the earth's shape are true and some are false; some are rationally defensible, others are not. Now, unlike then, it is easier to distinguish between true and false theories about the earth's shape but the truth and falsity of the particular theories is unaltered. However, this postmodernist claim is, we would suggest, false. At the very least, it has not been established. There would seem to have been as much- or more-diversity of thought in the past as there is now.

Postmodernists associate what they call 'modernity' particularly with what they consider was the mental attitude of the Enlightenment. They think that this attitude was one of unbounded admiration of and enthusi-asm for reason and science and that it carried the conviction that science would lead to the wise control of nature and society. Perhaps some people had that attitude then just as some people have it now. However, there cer-tainly were people living at the time of the Enlightenment who did *not* have it. Consider, for instance, David Hume, who was one of the key figures and arguably *the* key philosopher of the Enlightenment. His views were about as nearly the opposite of what the postmodernists call 'modernism' as it is possible to get.[4] Hume thought that reason is and ought to be 'the slave of the passions'. He thought too that 'ought' statements could not be derived from 'is' statements and that this, somehow, showed that they are not rationally founded.[5] His famous scepticism – which might well remind one of postmodernism relativism: the beliefs which we entertain about a reality beyond our perceptual experiences are without a rational basis according to Hume – is well summed up in his claim '. . . that all our reasonings concerning causes and effects are deriv'd from nothing but custom; and that belief is more properly an act of sensitive, rather than the cogitative part of our natures'.[6]

In so far as one can measure diversity of beliefs, we would say that, even in relation to witchcraft, the example of which might be thought supportive of the postmodernist case, there was as much and probably even more diversity of beliefs regarding witchcraft in the past – in, for instance, Paisley, Scotland, in the 1690s – than there is now. For instance, then (as now) many people were atheists and disbelieved completely in even the possibility of witchcraft. Then, some people believed that the devil, in the form of a man – the devil, for the purpose, occupied the body of a recently deceased person: hence the devil was cold when witches had sexual intercourse with the female ones and hence, so James VI and I argued, the devil did not make witches pregnant – appeared to people some of whom, by renouncing Christ and their Christian baptism to him, became witches. Who, if anyone, believes these particular things in, for instance, Paisley, Scotland, nowadays?[7]

Paradoxical though it might initially seem, the Paisley witchcraft trials of the 1690s came about precisely because of the diversity of beliefs which existed pertaining to witchcraft. The *Narrative* would not have been written had belief in witchcraft been universal in Paisley and its surroundings in the 1690s, or so we suggest.

Language Games and Cultural Relativism

Postmodernists are uncomfortable with – and like to hint that there are good reasons for being uncomfortable with – the notions of truth and falsity. They seem to think that someone or other – Wittgenstein, perhaps – has shown that truth and falsity and rationality pertain solely to the moves of language-users within particular language games and that different language games are incommensurate. They are tempted to think that the truth and rationality of 'narratives' and 'discourses' are internal to the particular discourses concerned.

It is our view that there is an important distinction between meaning and truth. The rules of language games determine the meaning but not the truth of linguistic expressions. It is true but trivial to say that the *meaning* of a word or expression is relative to the linguistic context in which it is used. It is not trivial but it is not *true* to say that the truth of an expression is relative in the same way to that context. For instance, the term 'The Loch Ness Monster' has whatever meaning it has solely in relation to the linguistic rules of whoever might use it. However, *given what the term happens to mean*, the proposition 'No Loch Ness monsters exist' will be true or false depending on what does exist and does occur in Loch Ness quite independently of the linguistic rules and practices of any language users. Note too that the linguistic context which gives meaning to the expression 'I believe in the existence of The Loch Ness Monster' also gives meaning, equally readily, to the expression 'I do *not* believe in the existence of The Loch Ness Monster'.[8]

Not all 'narratives' are equally true. There are various reasons for this. For instance, users of language can make mistakes and mistakes of different sorts. As Wittgenstein insists, conventional rules are central to language and to the meaning of language. It makes sense to talk about following rules only if it is possible to fail to follow rules correctly. If everything were to count as adherence to a rule, then there would be no rule to adhere to. For instance, one can say something other than what one intends to say through a misunderstanding of what a particular linguistic rule is. Furthermore, even when one understands and is able correctly to use a particular word, one can misapply it. Misclassification is a persistent possibility with the use of language.[9]

If some one or thing is called by someone else an 'X', then the person or thing might but might not be an X. You might call someone a 'procrastinator' and be mistaken. You might have made a mistake about what the word means. You might have made a mistake about what are the person's time management skills. If Christian Shaw is called, say, an 'impostor' or a 'bewitched person', then she might be but might not be an impostor or a bewitched person.

Another reason why not all 'narratives' are equally true is that not all narratives are equally truthful. For instance, someone might say to another: 'I will never kiss anyone else but you'. This statement might be true: shortly after stating it, the person might, *en route* to a tryst with his mistress, die of an unexpected heart attack. Truth and truthfulness are related but different things.

Witchcraft in Scotland in the Sixteenth and Seventeenth Centuries

The meaning of language derives from its use and social context. Hence – and for other reasons as well – a general sketch of witchcraft belief and prosecution in seventeenth-century Scotland will be a useful background to our consideration of the Paisley case.[10]

Witchcraft in Scotland was thought of in essentially theological terms. It was considered as a sort of inverse of Christianity. It was believed that the devil appeared to prospective witches in the form of a man. People

were thought to become actual witches by the voluntary act of entering
into a pact with him and renouncing Christ and their Christian baptism
to him. They became the servants of the devil and enemies of God rather
than followers of Christ. To become a witch was a wilful act. Exercises
of witchcraft – and this could be the use of diabolical power to help as
well as to harm people (*beneficium* as well as *maleficium*) – were also
thought of as wilful and, of course, sinful acts. Witches were believed to
hold meetings with other witches at which the devil presided.[11]

There were are least three aspects to the crime of witchcraft in the
sixteenth and seventeenth centuries (not all of which featured in every
case). There was the alleged spiritual offence of being in league with
the devil. There was the alleged physical harm done by accused witches
(*maleficium*). There was the offence of purporting to have supernatural
powers. The Act of the Parliament of Scotland (1563) by which witchcraft
became a crime laid great emphasis on the third aspect: the Act could be
interpreted as an early form of 'consumer protection legislation'.

The devil loomed larger in witchcraft cases in Scotland and Europe than
in England. It seems to have been the case that generally, in Scotland and
in Europe, there was a tendency to focus attention upon the spiritual and
theological aspect of witchcraft, whilst in England there was much more
concern with the *maleficia* which were performed.[12]

In Scotland, female suspected witches were typically accused of having
sex with the devil. For instance, Manie Halieburton who was burnt as a
witch in 1649 confessed that when she was at home:

> . . . in come the devil and lay with her (she being yet in bed) and had
> carnal copulation with her, his nature being cold. He desired her to
> renounce Christ and her baptism and become his servant which she
> did . . .[13]

Male suspected witches in Scotland were not accused of having sex with
the devil although in other respects – the allegation of a pact with the devil,
meetings with other witches and the performing of *maleficia* – the pattern
was the same.

Of the 1,891 Scottish cases collated by Larner, Lee and McLachlan
where individuals were known to have been tried as witches or merely to
have had preliminary proceedings taken against them in pre-trial processes,
the sex of the accused is known in 1,733 of them.[14] Of these, 86% involved
females and 14% involved males.[15] There was clearly a sexual bias of
some sort involved in the social interactions whereby it came about that
the vast majority of those who were brought before the courts as accused
witches were female. Thereafter, within the legal process, the existence
of a sexual bias is not manifest. The Scottish courts did not seem to treat

accused females more harshly than accused males.[16] We have written elsewhere that:

> . . . the data presented suggest that the treatment of male and female Scottish witchcraft suspects is very similar. The chi-square value is relatively low, suggesting only a random difference between the male and female samples. Moreover, although a greater proportion of those women who were accused of witchcraft were executed (55.8% against 52.3% of men) a greater proportion were acquitted (21.7% against 19.8%).[17]

Prior to the bulk of the actual witchcraft hunts and trials, James VI and I had speculated that the ratio of female to male witches was 20:1. His explanation for the assumed preponderance of female witches was as follows:

> The reason is easie, for as that sexe is frailer than men is, so it is easier to be intrapped in these grosse snares of the devil, as was over will proved to be true, by the Serpent's deceiving of Eva at the beginning, which makes him the homlier with that sexe sensine.[18]

The evidence used in Scottish courts against accused witches took three forms; physical signs; confessions; evidence of witnesses.

There was the putative evidence of the witch's mark, which the devil was supposed to have placed upon his servants. Suspects would be stripped and their bodily hair removed. Pins would be inserted into their bodies in order to find a part which did not bleed and was insensible to pain.

There was the evidence of confessions. Given that the use of torture was legal in witchcraft cases and commonly employed, confessions were readily forthcoming and were of a standardised form. Accused witches would confess to having attended meetings with the devil and other named witches. The named witches would confess to having attended meeting with the devil and the same other named witches: there was no 'domino effect' whereby entire communities might have been in danger of being wiped out by witch hunts.

There was the evidence of events as described by witnesses. This was typically of a circumstantial nature. Typically, too, the events described would not in themselves be of a fantastic nature: that the events were evidence of witchcraft would involve a fantastic interpretation of common-place (or, at least, readily believable) occurrences. For instance, consider the case of Helen Symen who was accused of witchcraft in Aberdeen in 1671. In the documents which detailed the case against her, it was put to her that she had:

> . . . conceived a cruel malice against Alexander Blackhall for taking

of your house . . . you out of hatred and revenge menaced and
threatened that he should not long enjoy it . . . And shortly thereafter
you came to him wishing him welcome home and laid your hand
and touched him on the shoulder and immediately by your devlish
sorcery and witchcraft the power and strength of his shoulder was
taken away and he fell sick and shortly thereafter deceased. And
being dead, his shoulder which you by your sorcery touched was
found blue and bruised and corrupted in a very noisome manner.[19]

In another case, Jean Drummond from Kilbarchan was said to have
fallen out with Jean Houston, spouse to John Young in Glenlyein, and
cursed her and threatened that the devil would make her as great as the
Kirk of Kilbarchan and clasped her hand and spat in her face. Within a
quarter of a year, Jean Houston contracted a strange sickness and swelled
prodigiously until she died. It is said that all the neighbours blamed Jean
Drummond for having bewitched her.[20]

Not all Scottish witchcraft cases were the same but a common pattern
was as follows. X and Y would have a quarrel. X would mutter some
vague or specific threats concerning Y or Y's dependents or property.
Later – sometimes many years later – a misfortune would befall Y or Y's
dependents and the threat would be remembered and adduced as evidence
that the misfortune was caused by witchcraft on the part of X. Notice
that although, in this model, children were sometimes victims, they were
not the accusers: rather, parents would accuse people of having bewitched
their children.

Most of the officially authorised Scottish witchcraft accusations and
prosecutions took place before 1697. Only a trickle continued thereafter,
and only a trickle had occurred in the decades – not merely the years –
immediately prior to the case. Larner, Lee and McLachlan write:

> The great majority of prosecutions and executions for witchcraft
> took place between 1590 and 1680. Before 1590, when James VI
> personally conducted a large scale sorcery trial, and after 1680, cases
> were rare and isolated, apart from the Paisley outbreak of 1697.[21]

It seems reasonable, then, to say that most people in and around Paisley
in the 1690s would not have been familiar with official witchcraft prosecutions and trials.

In Scotland in the later part of the seventeenth century, the only courts
competent to deal with witchcraft cases were the High Court and those
authorised by specific commissions from the Privy Council. In the records
of the Privy Council, one has to go back as far as 1677 for even the mention
of a witch Annabell Stewart – in or remotely near Paisley.[22] In the same

year there was a commission for the trial of five accused witches across the Clyde in Dumbarton.[23] Bessie Neveing was tried for witchcraft in the (High) Circuit Court in Renfrew in 1658 – almost forty years before the Bargarran incidents.[24] We can find no High Court case which is prior and closer in both space and time to the Bargarran incidents – they occurred almost forty years later – than that.

As will be shown, the incidents and alleged incidents which centred around Christian Shaw were, in some respects, less isolated than they might seem: there were other and subsequent incidents and alleged incidents – previously unknown (or very little known) and not written about – involving other people in and near Paisley. The concentrated historical focus on Christian Shaw gives a distorted impression of her significance in the overall pattern of acts and occurrences.

The Narrative of the Sufferings . . .

The *Narrative* (Anon., 1698) – i.e. *A True Narrative of the Sufferings and Relief of a Young Girle; Strangely molested by Evil spirits and their instruments in the West* – is somewhat like an extensive diary in form. The detailed chronological account of the alleged suffering and bewitchment of Christian Shaw (and of only her) gives an impression of detached objectivity.[25]

In it, she is said to have accused particular people of tormenting her. They, it is implied, bit her – and their bite marks and the effects of their nipping of her could be seen on the girl's body – tore her flesh and forced various things – for instance, straw, pins, egg shells, orange pills, hair, bones and another substance that we shall specify shortly – into her mouth. Later, the child removed the stuff from her mouth in the presence of witnesses. Christian's tormentors, it should be noted, were said in the *Narrative* to be visible to Christian while they were tormenting her but to be invisible to Christian's parents and to the other people who were said to be there at the time.

It is narrated that she fell into 'sore fits', in some of which she seemed to be dead. In others, she seemed deaf or blind and could not speak. She had 'swooning fits' and would laugh and giggle when the Scriptures were read out to her. Sometimes, she would go as stiff as a board and her head would bend backwards towards her heels. In some of her fits, her belly swelled like a pregnant woman's and her eyes sank so deeply into her skull that the onlookers thought that she would never more be able to see.

The devil would appear to the child and people would observe the girl holding lengthy theological discussions with him. Christian is said to have reported that the devil, who was unseen by the other people who were present, had hairy arms and hairs like the bristles of a pig on his face. He was said too to have been naked when Christian declared:

> God Almighty keep me from thy meetings. I will rather die than go to them. I will never, through the grace of God, renounce my baptism; for I certainly will go to hell if I do . . . And although I should never recover, I am resolved never to renounce my baptism. It is God that hath kept me all this time from being a witch, and I trust He will yet by His grace, not because of any thing in me, but of His own mercy . . .[26]

She tried to throw herself into a fire during one of her fits and, the *Narrative* says, it took four strong men to restrain her. It says too that she was seen to fly around the room without her feet touching the ground.

Christian was said to have fallen into a fit one evening in the presence of the Rev. Patrick Simpson, Lady Northbar and others. When she recovered, Mr Simpson expounded on Psalm 110 whereupon Christian fell into another fit and her mouth bled. The spectators discovered that one of her teeth had been pulled out but, despite a search, it could not be found.

On another occasion, it is said that she dropped her glove on the ground and one of her invisible tormentors picked it up and gave it back to her.

A Highlander, who was said by Christian to be one of her tormentors, was brought before Christian and a blanket was placed over her head. Various people then, in turn, touched the child and nothing happened. However, whenever the Highlander touched her, she went into a fit.

Christian is said to have predicted events which turned out as she predicted they would and to have revealed the occurrence of events of which she could not have had knowledge in any obvious natural way. For instance, she said that, at a particular time, her tormentors were then holding a meeting in Bargarran Orchard at which the devil was present. What she said was later discovered to have been true. Sometimes, too, when her tormentors were arrested, they immediately ceased to torment her even although, it is noted, she could have had no natural way of knowing that they had been arrested.

Between her fits, she is said to have been normal and well. Local ministers prayed with her and held services in her house. Her parents and other concerned people did all they could, it is said, to explain these events but they were unable to do so. They took her to a famous medical authority, Dr Brisbane, in Glasgow. Here, the child spat out a coal cinder which was as big as a chestnut and – warmer than body temperature – was almost too hot to handle. After conducting a thorough examination of the child and the case, so the *Narrative* infers, Dr Brisbane announced that her affliction was preternatural and so too did Henry Marshall, an apothecary in Glasgow.

On 21 August, 1696, when the strange afflictions and behaviour of Christian Shaw were reported to have commenced shortly after she had quarrelled with Katherine Campbell, a highland servant of the family who was subsequently and, perhaps, consequently executed as a witch, the child was only ten years old. On 28 March, 1697, Christian Shaw was said to be, 'by God's great mercy toward her', perfectly recovered.

In the period between these dates, the *Narrative* gives an account of a battle between good and evil. Christian Shaw is presented as a child who was bewitched. She is presented as a child whom God, for a season, allowed the devil to torment. She is presented too as someone who resisted with valour the temptation to become a witch.

The Bargarran Impostor?

The traditional and common interpretation of the reported events is that Christian Shaw was a trickster. For instance, the anonymous author of the introduction to the 1877 edition of the *History of the Witches of Renfrewshire* writes that Christian '. . . was only 11 years of age, but manifested an amount of cunning and artifice extraordinary at her years'.[27]

Sharpe takes the same view. He says:

> To sum up a long story in a few words, the young girl, who seems
> to have been ancient in wickedness, having had a quarrel with one of
> the maid-servants, pretended to be bewitched by her, and forthwith
> began, according to the common practice in such cases, to vomit
> all manner of trash; to be blind and deaf on occasion; to fall into
> convulsions, and to talk a world of nonsense, which the hearers
> received as the quintessence of afflicted piety.[28]

'Vediovis' – this is the *nom de plume* of a writer for *The Scots Law Times* – repeats the claim that no record of the trial is available and says of Christian Shaw:

> Her acting abilities, e.g. pretending to hear and speak to invisible
> beings soon impressed and terrified people in her locality and she
> found this a convenient and efficient way of getting people to do
> exactly what she wanted them to do at her whim, the dream of every
> capricious little 11 year old girl . . . It is thought that this cunning
> little girl who caused these tragic deaths had accomplices who were
> never identified. There is no doubt that she was a gifted little actress
> who was able to convince intelligent adults whose brains were
> perhaps tainted by superstition, prejudice and ignorance.[29]

All this echoes the thoughts and words of Arnot who writes: 'She seems to have displayed an artifice above her years . . . and to have been aided by accomplices, which dullness of apprehension or violence of prejudice forbade the bystanders to discover'.[30] There might also, he considers, have been an element of hysteria behind the girl's behaviour.

Notice that even if Arnot's interpretation were true, it would be most unfair to focus on Christian Shaw as the central villain of the piece. A child would not have adult *accomplices* in the sort of situation which Arnot envisages; she would, rather, be the *stooge of adult manipulators*. However, although Arnot's interpretation might have a superficial plausibility and it might seem to give a reasonable account of *some* of the events described in the *Narrative*, it has only that and gives only that. It will not bear a close and systematic study of the *Narrative*. Similarly, Sharpe does not accurately sum up a long story in a few words. He gives, rather, a superficial reading of parts of the story.

If the child was an impostor, *why* did she do what she did? It is all very well to say that she did it, for instance, out of spite and/or to attract attention to herself, but some of the things which were reported to have happened must have been, if they did happen as reported, extremely unpleasant. Less unpleasant actions could have attracted as much attention and vented as much spite. For instance, among the things which Christian is said to have removed from her mouth was dung.

One might, of course, want to explain such incidents in terms of hysteria rather than of fraud. However, if one does this, it is difficult to avoid making the unlikely claim that the child was *simultaneously* a rational, methodical, amazingly skilful conjurer and a passionate hysteric. One explanation tends to cancel out rather than reinforce the other.

If she was an impostor, then *how* was she, a young girl ten or eleven years old, able to perform such tricks? How did she learn them? Who taught her? It is possible that one or other particularly good professional conjuror could perform the sorts of tricks which might deceive an inquiring and sceptical audience and a learned authority such as Dr Brisbane into thinking that supernatural actions were taking place before their very eyes. It is implausible to say that Christian Shaw (even with the aid of accomplices) could have performed them. For instance – and other examples could be cited – could you drop a glove onto the ground and then make it jump back into your hand as if an invisible tormentor had replaced it there? Could you fly through the air without touching the ground and/or give the impression that you were doing so?

Four strong men, it is said, were required to stop Christian Shaw from ending up in the fire. How could the child, through trickery, give the impression that such amazing physical force was required to subdue her?

How could the child, with a blanket over her head, have recognised the Highlander? According to McDonald, Thom and Thom, 'There is no mystery in this as his smell, clothes and manner would differentiate him from local people'.[31] Perhaps he did have a distinctive odour which the child might have detected. However, it seems reasonable to assume that if the child could smell the Highlander, then so too could the adult onlookers. Similarly, if we would be wary of this as a possible and obvious means of deception, so too would have been the adult onlookers.

Mental Illness?

Recently, Christian Shaw has been argued to have been suffering from some sort of mental illness. For instance, Adam writes: 'If Christian's bewitchment happened now, it would be diagnosed at once as a case for psychotherapy. She was suffering from hysteria . . .'.[32] Similarly, three psychiatrists, McDonald, Thom and Thom, have recently expressed the view that: 'While the story is bizarre, modern psychiatry could certainly explain Christian Shaw's condition'.[33] They say it is likely that she was suffering from 'dissociative disorder/conversion disorder'; 'trance and possession disorder'; 'pica of infancy and childhood'; 'localisation-related (focal) (partial) idiopathic epilepsy and epileptic syndromes with seizures of localised onset, and 'acute and transient psychotic disorder'.

Some aspects of the case, for instance the levitation, cannot be explained, according to Adam, in terms of mental illness, and rather than putting them down to Christian's trickery, she says that they were paranormal. She writes: 'Much of the reporting in the *Narrative*, once considered exaggerated and credulous can now be seen as factual and accurate'.[34] McDonald, Thom and Thom say that 'the most likely explanation' of the reported levitation is that the child was sleepwalking in a dim light and those who were watching over her and reported her behaviour were tired.

Now, it is possible that *some* of the events described in the *Narrative* could be accounted for in terms of Christian Shaw's mental health. However – as in the case of the theory of the child as an impostor – not all of the events could be. Furthermore, various events can be explained by neither the theory that she was mentally ill nor that she was an impostor.

Reconsider some of the incidents which we have noted. Suggested mental illness on the part of Christian Shaw would not explain, say, how she was able to fool adult spectators into believing that a glove dropped from her hand was replaced there by an invisible tormentor nor how she was able to seem to fly around the room without touching the ground. Mental illness too would not have given her the ability to predict occurrences nor could mental illness have enabled her to know, when she was covered with a blanket, whether the Highlander or some other person was touching her.

It is said in the *Narrative* that Christian Shaw knew the precise moment when Mary Morrison, one of her tormentors, was apprehended and that she knew because an invisible being had told her. How could mental illness account for this knowledge if she had it? How could trickery on the part of Christian account for it? Similarly, Christian is said to have told her mother that her tormentors were having a feast in Bargarran Orchard and, later, James and Thomas Linday and Elizabeth Anderson, three of her tormentors, are said to have confirmed that they actually did have a feast there at the time the child had – remarkably! – indicated to her mother. How is this to be explained?

In a reported theological conversation with the previously mentioned servant Katherine Campbell, who was said to have been visible in this incident only to Christian Shaw, the child is reported to have said:

> 'Thou sittest there with a stick in thy hand to put in my mouth, but through God's strength thou shalt not get leave; thou are permitted to torment me, but I trust in God thou shalt never get my life though it is my life thou designest . . . Come near me Katie, and I'll let thee see where a godly man was given up to Satan to be tormented but God kept his life in His own hand . . .'.[35]

The child then, it is narrated, read from the relevant passages in Job and then said to her:

> 'Now, Katie, what thinkest thou of that? Thou seest for all the power the Devil got over Job, he gained no ground on him: and I hope he shall gain as little on me. Thy master the Devil deceives thee; he is a bad master whom thou servest, and thou shalt find it to thy smart, except thou repent before thou die. There is no repentance to be had after death. I'll let thee see, Katie, there is no repentance in hell'. And turning over the book, citing Luke, Chap. xvi, near the latter end thereof, and reading the same over, said . . .[36]

The *Narrative* claims:

> Thus she continued for more than two hours space, reasoning at this rate, and exhorting her to repent, quoting many places of Scripture through the Revelation and the Evangelists.[37]

The passage in Luke, Chapter 16, which the girl is said to have referred to is particularly relevant to the point which the girl is said to have been making. It contains the story of the rich man and Lazarus and of the torment the rich man suffered in hell.

In another similar reported conversation with her tormentors, Christian is said to have argued as follows:

'It is God that gives us every good gift. We have nothing of our own. I submit to His will, though I never be better, for God can make all my trouble turn to my advantage, according to His Word, Romands [sic] viii 28' – which place she then read, and thus continued reasoning for the space of an hour.[38]

Again, when we consult the Bible, we find that this text is particularly appropriate. It is: 'And we know that all things work together to them that love God, to them who are called according to *His* purpose'.

It does not seem plausible that an eleven-year-old child – whether or not an impostor and whether or not suffering from a mental illness – could possess sufficient knowledge of the Scriptures to realise the pertinence of these passages to the highly sophisticated theological points which she was said to be making. It is plausible that other adults – for instance, local ministers – could have had the required level of scriptural knowledge, linguistic sophistication and theological acumen to devise monologues like these.

The mental illness theory is no more plausible than the impostor theory. It might be even less plausible.

The Bewitchment of Christian Shaw: a Re-assessment

Arnot talks of gullible people being deceived by Christian Shaw. We suggest that, perhaps, the gullible people are those like Arnot, Adam and 'Vediovis' who believe too readily that what is written in the *Narrative* is an authentic account of what people who were observing Christian Shaw heard and saw or, at least, believed they heard and saw.

Some of the events described in the *Narrative* are, we would suggest, fantasies: they did not occur or, at least, did not happen quite as they are described. They do not require an explanation. What requires to be explained, rather, is why it was said that the events occurred. In so far as there were hoaxes and impostures going on, they were carried out by those who said that Christian Shaw did the things which she was said to have done.

The author or authors of the *Narrative* says or say, with reference to Christian's alleged conversations with the devil, that, although the child had a knowledge of the Scriptures which was quite remarkable for her age, 'Yet we doubt not in so strong a combat, the Lord did, by his good

Spirit, graciously afford her more than ordinary measure of assistance'.[39]
Is there here a guilty apprehension of having 'over-egged the pudding'?
Did he or they realise that this was a particularly weak part of the story
because he or they knew that it was a part he or they had been particularly
inventive in relating?

Who Wrote the Narrative?

What credence should be given to the *Narrative*? Is it trustworthy? Among
the considerations that make it difficult to answer these questions is the
fact that the *Narrative* is anonymous. Who wrote it? According to Sharpe,
'The particulars of this comic tragedy were collected by John MacGilchrist,
town-clerk of Glasgow, and embodied in a pamphlet [i.e. the *Narrative*]
written by Mr Francis Grant, advocate, afterwards a knight, and lord of
session, with the style of Lord Cullen'.[40] (Sharpe, 1884, pp. 169–170)
Francis Grant was the judge in the witchcraft trial of 1697 in Paisley. It
is interesting and perhaps relevant to note that John MacGilchrist, who
was a solicitor in Glasgow, was Christian Shaw's mother's brother. The
grounds of Sharpe's claim are not made clear by him.

We have a different – or at least a complementary – theory. Prior to
anything which Grant and MacGilchrist might (or might not) have done
with the material, we suggest that the *Narrative* was written, or compiled,
collated and/or edited by the Rev. Andrew Turner, minister at Erskine, and
the Rev. James Brisbane, minister at Kilmacolm. The latter was, according
to Adam, 'a young relative of Dr Brisbane'.[41] As we shall show below, the
Rev. Mr Brisbane concerned himself with witchcraft cases, gave evidence
in them and believed that his own child had been killed by witchcraft.

In the *Record of the Presbytery of Paisley* for 13 December, 1696, it
says:

> This day Mr Turner represented to the Presbytery a deplorable case
> of Christine Shaw daughter to the laird of Bargarran, in the paroch
> of Erskine, who since the beginning of September last, hath been
> under a very sore and unnatural distemper . . . The Presbytery being
> deeply sensible of the sad circumstances of that Damsel and family,
> does appoint the exercise of fasting and prayer to be continued as it
> is already set up by Mr Turner in that family every Tuesday, leaving
> him to call to his assistance whom he pleases from time to time. And
> further, appoints Mr Turner and Mr Brisbane to repair to Bargarran,
> Friday next, there to take up a particular narrative of her whole
> trouble, of its rise and progress . . .[42]

About four months later – and in the meantime, the Presbytery had sought a commission from the Privy Council in Edinburgh to try Christian's suspected tormentors as witches – there is mention of the revising and copying of 'the narrative of Christine Shaw's trouble'. According to the minutes of a meeting of the Presbytery of Paisley held on 14 April, 1697:

> The meeting of this day considering that the revising of the narrative of Christine Shaw's trouble was recommended unto them by the Synod, therefore they appoint Mr Turner to cause transcribe four copies, and to send one to Principal Dunlop and Mr Ja. Brown, another to Mr Ballantyne, another to Mr Wylie, and another to Mr Wilson, allowing them to advise with any of the brethren of their respective presbyteries in the revising thereof, appointing them ere they leave to meet and appoint time and place of their next meeting that they may compare their animadversions, and put the whole relation in a suitable dress . . .43

The minutes of a meeting of the Presbytery of Paisley held on 10 May, 1697 say:

> This day it was reported that those appointed to revise the narrative had obeyed, and their thoughts and animadversions thereupon being this day produced and compared; the whole thereof was committed to Mr Sympson, Mr Turner, and Mr Blackwell, to draw up the whole relation in mundo. It having been formerly recommended to Mr Jo. Wilson by this meeting to draw up a preface to the narrative which was this day produced, read, and approven, and left in Mr Turner's hands . . .44

It is of interest to note that there is a preface to the *Narrative*, in which the existence of God, the devil and witchcraft is affirmed; atheism and disbelief in witchcraft are deplored. It is indicated that the subsequent *Narrative* will furnish proof of the existence of witchcraft and, by implication, of the existence of God. To refute atheism, which is suggested in the preface to have been all too common, could have been a cardinal motive for the writing of the *Narrative*.

The *Narrative*, the preface says, will serve to glorify God's name. It says too that:

> . . . the abundant and efficacious grace of God is conspicuous in enabling a young girl to resist to the utmost the best laid assaults of the evil one, as it is certain that he shews the greatest malice in countries where he is hated and hateth most, and the nearer his reign be to an end.45

Perhaps there were anticipations of the Second Coming as 1700 drew ever nearer.

We suggest that the narrative referred to in these minutes of the Presbytery of Paisley is the *Narrative* and that – probably with the aid of other local ministers – the Rev. Mr Turner and the Rev. Mr Brisbane were instrumental in the writing and/or compilation of it. It would not be surprising if Grant and/or MacGilchrist obtained a copy of it nor if one or other of them edited or amended it in some way. The question of who presented it for publication is not the same question as who wrote it?

Erskine and Salem

There is an important feature of the Bargarran witchcraft case which tends to be overlooked and which we would like to highlight, and that is the fact that it is very unusual – perhaps even unique – in the Scottish experience. However, within a wider geographical and historical context, the case is not so unusual and can be seem to conform to a pattern involving the elements of, first of all, fantastic ailments and also fantastic behaviour of children; invisible tormentors; assiduous clergymen; prestigious, independent experts; and, secondly, a pamphlet written about the children, tormentors, clergymen and experts, purporting to prove the occurrence of supernatural events and the existence of supernatural phenomena.

The case of the Warboys Witches in England in the 1590s is a good early example of this.[46] Of particular relevance too is the case of the Lowestoft Witches, who were tried at Bury St. Edmunds in 1662. This is discussed most notably and thoroughly by Geis and Bunn.[47] Sir Thomas Browne, the celebrated author of *Religio Medici*, was the scientist appealed to in the trial of two old women, Amy Denny and Rose Cullender, who were hanged for bewitching the daughters of Samuel Pacy, a rich merchant in Lowestoft. It is interesting to note that the pamphlet narrating the case is anonymous and that Geis and Bunn are, perhaps, rather naive in accepting it at face value as a sincere, honest and true account of the trial of the two old women.[48]

The Bargarran case bears striking resemblances to the famous Salem witchcraft outbreak in New England in 1692.[49] Geiss and Bunn show conclusively links between the Lowestoft case and the Salem case: both prefigure the Bargarran case.

The earliest known account of the Salem case was written by the Rev. Deodat Lawson and published in Boston in 1692 and reprinted in London in 1693. It is entitled *A Brief and True Narrative of some Remarkable Passages Relating to Sundry Persons Afflicted by Witchcraft, at Salem*

Village which happened from the Nineteenth of March, to the Fifth of April, 1692.[50] Mr. Lawson had previously been a minister at Salem. He believed that his wife and daughter, who died there three years previously, had been killed by witchcraft.

In a sermon which Mr. Lawson delivered in London in 1696, he said that he published his account of the case in order to '. . . satisfy such as are not resolved to the Contrary, that there may be (and are) such Operations of the Powers of Darkness on the bodies and Minds of Mankind, by Divine Permission'.[51] There is, as we have seen, a preface to the Bargarran *Narrative* which too is similar in tone to Mr. Lawson's sermon.

On the face of things, the Salem outbreak might seem to differ from the Bargarran one in involving several victims, not merely a single individual. According to Lawson, there were ten alleged victims in Salem. They were all female.[52] However, we shall consider shortly a previously unknown manuscript which we have discovered: it shows the Bargarran case to be part of a broader picture of Renfrewshire witchcraft accusation, which is even more like the Salem experience than the Bargarran case in isolation might seem to be.

Both in style and content, as well as in rationale, the Salem *Narrative* and the later Bargarran one are remarkably similar. For instance, it says in Mr. Lawson's *Narrative*:

> Abigail Williams, (about 12 years of age) had a grievous fit; she
> was at first hurried with Violence to and fro in the room (though
> Mrs Ingerson endeavoured to hold her) sometimes making as if
> she would fly . . . she said there was Goodw. N. and said, 'Do
> you not see her? Why, there she stands!' . . . After that, she ran
> to the Fire, and began to throw Fire Brands, about the house;
> and run against the Back, as if she would run up the chimney,
> and, as they said, she had attempted to go into the Fire in
> other Fits.[53]

It is said that on Monday, 21st March, the magistrates of Salem and many spectators gathered in the Meeting-House to examine Martha Corey – 'Goodwife. C' – as a suspected witch. Several of the afflicted were present and they '. . . did vehemently accuse her in the Assembly of afflicting them, by Biting, Pinching, Strangling, etc. And that they did in their Fit see her likeness coming to them . . .'.[54] Bite marks were seen on their arms and wrists. It was said that after Martha Corey was arrested, she did not appear to them or afflict them any longer.

Lawson reports that he was present with Thomas Putmans and his wife when the latter had a 'sore fit' and during it had a discussion with Rebecca Nurse, who was visible only to Mrs Putnams. According to Lawson, the latter

> ... seemed to dispute with the Apparition about a particular Text of Scripture ... said she, 'I am sure you cannot stand before that Text! ... It is the third Chapter of the Revelations.' ... I began to read, and before I had read through the first verse, she opened her eyes, and was well; this fit continued near half an hour. Her husband and the spectators told me, she had often been so relieved by reading Texts that she named, something pertinent to her Case as Isa. 40.1, Isa. 49.1, Isa. 50.1 and several others.[55]

On the 26th of March, it is said that Elizabeth Parris – the daughter of a local minister and the first to appear to be afflicted – had sore fits and reported that a Black Man appeared to her. Lawson notes that, on 31st March, a public fast was held for those afflicted. Public fasts were also held in Renfrewshire for Christian Shaw.

Lawson says that he particularly wants to stress to the reader the following points:

> That their Motions in their Fits are Preternatural, both as to the manner, which is so strange as a well person could not screw their Body into; and as to the violence also it is preternatural, being much beyond the Ordinary force of the same person when they are in their right mind. The eyes of some of them in their fits are exceedingly fast closed and if you ask a question they can give no answer, and I do believe they cannot hear at that time yet do they plainly converse with the Appearances, as if they did discourse with real persons.[56]

The author or authors of the *Narrative* was or were, we suggest, familiar with Lawson's Salem narrative and/or with some other such book which closely resembled it.

Conclusion

Perhaps we have not *proved* that Christian Shaw was not an impostor, a trickster who deluded gullible but sincere adults (and nor, for that matter, have we proved that she was not bewitched!). Nevertheless, we have shown that the impostor theory is not at all plausible. At the very least, we have demonstrated that the proponents of that theory have failed to prove its truth. Our rejection of the impostor theory is not based on explaining the fantastic occurrences described in the *Narrative* in terms of Christian Shaw's alleged mental ill-health. Not all such narrated occurrences can be so explained any more than they can all be explained in terms of trickery and deceit: perhaps none of them can be so correctly explained.

Not all the narrated fantastic occurrences actually occurred. That is the essence of our case. Our view is that some of the events described in the *Narrative* occurred exactly as described; some occurred but not quite as described; some are total fabrications. Into which of these three categories each and any particular occurrence should be placed is one of the intriguing and teasing questions which renders the Bargarran witchcraft outbreak and the *Narrative* of perennial historical interest.

It is possible (at least logically possible) that the *Narrative* was a total hoax and that all the events and incidents described therein are fabrications. It might, say, have been written solely with the intention of making money. That, however, is not our view. We think that Lawson's narrative about Salem or a very similar text served as a model for the *Narrative*. It might be possible that Christian Shaw had read this book while her parents and the other adults involved were unaware of it. It seems more likely that one or more of the adults in or around Bargarran had read it. We would speculate further that the Rev. Mr Brisbane and/or the Rev. Mr Turner had read it or at least had been made very familiar with its contents. It was an adult's knowledge of this or a related text rather than the imagination of the pre-teenaged Christian Shaw which framed and flavoured the tales of the fantastic happenings in Bargarran, Renfrewshire and the production of the *Narrative*.

The *Narrative*, we suggest, is not completely true. Whether or not it was completely *truthful* – whether the errors of fact were deliberate or not – remains an open question. If there were liars, it remains an open question who they were. Notice that Mr Turner and Mr Brisbane (or one or other of them) might well have had a clerical rather than a creative role in the production of the book. We are not trying to free Christian Shaw from unfair blame at the expense of unfairly blaming some one else. In our view, the dead, no less than the living, have a moral right not to be slandered, which is to say that the living have a moral duty not wantonly to slander them.

We would speculate that the *Narrative* was written with the intention of glorifying God and of proving to atheists that God exists. Paradoxically, the *Narrative* was written not because everyone in Scotland in the 1690s believed in witchcraft but because the author or authors was or were aware that not everyone shared his or their views on the matter. However, it does not follow from this that it was written as a deliberate hoax. Perhaps the author or authors of the *Narrative* believed that Christian Shaw was bewitched. He or they might have had the *intention* of writing a true account of her condition and experiences. With the writing and rewriting of the documentation, consciously or unconsciously, various parts of the story might well have been revised, polished up and exaggerated. That *some* strange things happened to or concerning Christian Shaw – whether they were paranormal, the result of mental illness, merely mysteriously coincidental or whatever – seems to us to be likely.

Various considerations tell against the theory that the *Narrative* was a complete, deliberate fabrication. They also serve to place the reported events concerning Christian in a broader context. For instance, at the back of the *Narrative*, there is a list of witnesses although it is not indicated which particular incidents the particular people are the cited witnesses to. Included are the following: Lord Blantyre; Mr Francis Montgomery of Giffen; Sir John Maxwell of Pollock; Sir John Houstoun of that ilk; the Laird of Blackhall younger; the Laird of Glanderstone; the Laird of Craigends; Porterfield of Fulwood; John Alexander of Blackhouse; the Laird of Orbistone; Gavin Cochrane of Craigmure; Dr Matthew Brisbane; and the following ministers: the Rev. James Hutchison; the Rev. Patrick Simpson; the Rev. James Stirling; the Rev. Thomas Blackwell; the Rev. Robert Taylor; the Rev. Neil Gillies; the Rev. James Brown; and the Rev. John Gray.

The list of witnesses includes, as the last two people named: the Rev. Andrew Turner and the Rev. James Brisbane. Are they named last, as a matter of etiquette, because these two men are the authors of the book (or, at least, the compilers of the list)? Contrary to what Arnott and 'Vediovis' say, the record of the Paisley witchcraft trial of 1697 *does exist*.[57] While Christian Shaw and her alleged exploits are the central and exclusive focus of the *Narrative*, they do not loom as large in the official legal case against the accused witches. What evidence if any that Christian Shaw gave was not given under oath and was not recorded (or if it was, has not survived). However, over thirty other people were witnesses against the accused witches at their trial. Evidence too was given relating to witches' marks and to confessions. Dr Brisbane and Mr. Marshall gave evidence concerning Christian Shaw's condition.

Notice too the obvious points that Christian Shaw did not apply for a commission for the trial of the accused witches, nor did she arrest them and nor was she a member of the jury which convicted them. Robbins's claim that Christian Shaw *caused* '. . . twenty-one persons to be indicted, and seven of them burned at the stake' is, on any interpretation of the events, nonsensical.[58] Her involvement was, at the very most, like that of a speck amidst a dollop.

It says in a recent edition of the official magazine of the Renfrewshire Council – the history of Christian Shaw remains a live issue! – that 'As a result of the testimony of this young girl, six people were strangled and burnt at Gallow Green in Paisley'.[59] This is a travesty and an example of how the repetition of errors produces conventional 'wisdom' and accepted 'truths'.

It is notable that whereas being very young would seem on any reasonable interpretation to be a mitigating feature when someone is accused of having done something particularly evil, people often react absurdly as if the opposite were true and as if, the younger and less mature one is, the more culpable one is when one transgresses. The sins – or some sorts of sins – of children (and of girls even more than of boys?) are to some people more horrific than the same sins performed by adults. They – the sins, that is – seem to be more memorable too. For instance, the common misconception is that the victims/accusers in Salem were *invariably* children. However, of the ten afflicted females whom Mr Lawson identifies, only three of them were pre-teenaged girls; four were said to be married and, of the remainder, two were seventeen.

We have come across a document which indicates that in and around Renfrewshire in the 1690s, various people other than Christian Shaw – including (but not only) other children – were involved in the sorts of bizarre behaviour which she was said to have indulged in.[60] The document is dated Glasgow May 1699. Twenty-five people were charged with witchcraft and obliged to compear before their Lordships within the Tolbooth of Glasgow on 19th May, 1700. The case was deserted. This can be taken in support of the view that not everyone was convinced of the existence of witchcraft but, of course, it is possible that some people – many perhaps – believed that witches existed but were sceptical about the ability of the courts to detect them and to punish only them.[61] Note that although seven people were executed as witches in the Paisley trial of 1697, over twenty people had been charged with witchcraft.

What is one to say about the nature of the torment of the alleged victims of witchcraft mentioned in this document? Were the alleged victims impostors? Were they mentally ill? If the stories about their torment are lies, whose lies are they? At least some of the reported incidents are not readily explicable in terms either of trickery or mental illness on the part of the alleged victims. For instance, Margaret Laird – who was a child – named Janet Laing as one of her tormentors and fell into a fit when Janet's name was mentioned to her. When Janet looked into a room where Margaret Laird was, the child fell into a fit even although it is said that the child could have had no way of knowing that Janet had looked into the room. A similar thing happened when Janet was covered by a blanket.

Annabell Reid was charged with witchcraft and named by Margaret Laird as one of her tormentors. Annabell touched Margaret's hand and Margaret fell into a fit and her hand swelled and turned blackish. The

Rev. Mr James Brisbane challenged Annabell and claimed that she had laid a charm on Margaret's hand. Annabell said: 'The Lord Jesus Christ take it off for I cannot' and immediately, Margaret's hand returned to its normal colour, the swelling ceased and Margaret's pain went away.[62] If this was a trick, it was quite a trick.

Issobel Houstone was another of Margaret Laird's alleged tormentors. In the document, one reads:

> . . . when the s[ai]d Margaret Laird was in her fitts she saw the said Issobell Houstone in the roume and spoke to her and challenged her for tormenting her but the said Issobell Houstone was invisible to any other person in the roume as also the said Issobell Houstone tormented a chyld of Mr James Brisbane Minister at Kilmacomes by a pictur of wax until the chyld dyed . . .[63]

Margaret Alexander asked for alms from Margaret Cumming, spouse of James Arthur in Paisley. Margaret refused and went away muttering and then gave Margaret's son, William Arthur, a strange look for nearly a quarter of an hour. Within a fortnight, he fell into a great distemper. His tongue disappeared down his throat and his belly would swell up. He would become as stiff as a table. His head would turn to the side. He was often bent back on his bed like a bow. Three or four men could not hold him. For about a month or so he could not speak but he had been aware that he was tormented with pins and needles and awls by Margaret Alexander and others. Eventually, Margaret Alexander was given a dollar and she asked Christ to heal the child and the child was healed.

Jean Ross and Janet Stewart had a quarrel in Paisley in the month of March, April or May in 1697 and Jean Ross went away murmuring something or other. That very same night, Janet's child had extraordinary pains, stiffness and convulsions. These fits lasted from about twelve o'clock at night until five in the morning. After the fits, the child was black and blue as if he had been buffeted and pinched. Between the fits, the child was fine. This lasted for about twelve days. It is said of his condition that '. . . physitians and o[the]r skilled persons could assigne no cause for it . . .'. Then, the child died.[64] This was not a trick on the part of the child, nor does it sound like a mental illness.

It is said in the document that in 1688 (i.e. years before Christian Shaw's alleged affliction and before the Salem outbreak) Jean Ross, who seems to have been a schoolteacher, had a quarrel with Alexander Mure over his daughter who, it appears, attended Jean's school. It is said that within a week

> . . . the chyld was troubled with a strange and extraordinary sickness

as one distempered and out of her witts for she did climb up the walls with her feet and dashed herslefe to the bed so that he [i.e. Alexander Mure] could hardly hold her with all his strength and tymes she would have gone out of his hands as souple as a willow wand and the chyld continued under this distemper for three days and then she dyed and two or three nights before the chyld fell sick the hous was infested by a multitude of cats . . .[65]

What should one make of the following? Elspet Wood, a widow from Overgourock was charged with witchcraft and, among other things, it was said against her that she spoke to the Rev Mr James Brisbane immediately after he came out of the kirk at Kilmacolm and she repeated part of the first prayer of the morning and discussed with him the sermon which he had delivered in the afternoon. Yet, she or the shape of her had been seen sitting for the whole of that same day in a church in another town.

With the debunking of the Bargarran impostor theory, a puzzling historical mystery still remains: the plot, one might even say, thickens. Why was the *Narrative* written? Is our explanation, or partial explanation, a correct one? Why were the witchcraft allegations made? In relation to them, what that was out of the ordinary – if anything – happened to or was done by Christian Shaw? What a marvellous film the mystery might make.

NOTES

1. Robbins, R. H. (1959), *The Encyclopedia of Witchcraft and Demonology*, New York: The Hamlyn Publishing Group, p. 59.
2. Arnot, Hugo (1785), *A Collection of Celebrated Criminal Trials in Scotland, 1536–1784*, Edinburgh.
3. Anon. (1698), *A True Narrative of the Sufferings and Relief of a Young Girle; Strangely molested by Evil spirits and their instruments in the West: With a preface and postscript containing Reflections on what is most Material or Curious either in the history or trial of the Seven Witches who were Condemn'd to be Execute in the country*, Edinburgh: Watson.
4. See McLachlan, Hugh V. and Swales, J. K. (1998), 'The Methodology Rather Than the Rhetoric of Economics: McCloskey on Popper and Hume', *Journal of Interdisciplinary Economics*, Vol. 9, No. 2, 125–143.
5. See McLachlan, Hugh V. (1979), 'The Is/Ought Question: A Needless Controversy', *Journal of the British Society for Phenomenology*, Vol. 10, No. 2, 134–137.
6. Hume, David (1969), *A Treatise Concerning Human Nature*, Harmondsworth: Penguin Books, p. 234.
7. See McLachlan, Hugh V. and Swales, J. K. (1980), 'Witchcraft and Anti-Feminism', *Scottish Journal of Sociology*, vol. 4, no. 2, pp. 141–166; McLachlan, Hugh V. and Swales, J. K. (1982), 'Tibbetts's Theory of Rationality and Scottish Witchcraft', *Philosophy of the Social Sciences*, Vol. 12, No. 1,

pp. 75–79; McLachlan, Hugh V. and Swales, J. K. (1983), 'Rationality and the Belief in Witches: A Rejoinder to Tibbetts', *Philosophy of the Social Sciences*, Vol. 13, No. 4, pp. 475–477; and McLachlan, Hugh V. and Swales, J. K. (1984), 'Review of Witch-Hunting, Magic and the New Philosophy by Brian Easlea', *Philosophy of the Social Sciences*, Vol. 14, No. 4, pp. 577–580.

8. See McLachlan, Hugh V. (1979), 'The Is/Ought Question: A Needless Controversy', *Journal of the British Society for Phenomenology*, Vol. 10, No. 2, pp. 134–137 and McLachlan, Hugh V. and Scott, Michael (1985), 'Rationality and Relativism: A Defence of Strong Absolutism', *The British Journal of Sociology*, Vol. 36, No. 6, pp. 604–610.

9. See McLachlan, Hugh V. (1981), 'Wittgenstein, Family Resemblances and the Theory of Classification', *International Journal of Sociology and Social Policy*, Vol. 1, No. 1, pp. 1–16 and McLachlan, Hugh V. (1981), 'Is "Power" an Evaluative Concept?', *British Journal of Sociology*, Vol. 32, No. 3, pp. 392–410.

10. See Black, George, F. (1938), *A Calendar of Cases of Witchcraft in Scotland 1510–1727*, New York: New York Public Library; Larner, Christina (1981), *Enemies of God: The Witch-Hunt in Scotland*, London: Chatto and Windus; and Larner, C. J., Lee, C. H., and McLachlan, H. V. (1977), *A Source-Book of Scottish Witchcraft*, Glasgow: University of Glasgow.

11. See McLachlan, Hugh V. and Swales, J. K. (1979), 'Stereotypes and Scottish Witchcraft', *Contemporary Review*, Vol. 234, No. 1357, February, pp. 88–94 and McLachlan, Hugh V. and Swales, J. K. (1992), 'Scottish Witchcraft: Myth or Reality?', *Contemporary Review*, vol. 260, no. 1513, February, pp. 79–84.

12. See, for instance, Macfarlane, Alan (1970), *Witchcraft in Tudor and Stuart England*, London: Routledge and Kegan Paul, pp. 3–20 and Le Roy Ladurie, Emmanuel (1987), *Jasmin's Witch*, Harmondsworth: Penguin Books, pp. 5–29.

13. *Register of the Privy Council*, 2nd series, Vol. 8, p. 194.

14. See Larner, C. J., Lee, C. H., and McLachlan, H. V. (1977), *A Source-Book of Scottish Witchcraft*, Glasgow: University of Glasgow. This is the most comprehensive general account of witchcraft prosecutions in Scotland. At present, there is an attempt to supersede it with an online database of Scottish witchcraft cases and/or witches. This project is the 'Survey of Scottish Witchcraft, 1563–1736'. It is funded by the E.S.R.C. and based at the Scottish History Department of Edinburgh University. The project is jointly directed by Dr Julian Goodare of the Department of Scottish History and Dr Louise Yeoman, Curator of Manuscripts at the National Library of Scotland. Dr Joyce Miller and Ms Lauren Martin are Research Fellows on the project. Unlike the *Source-Book of Scottish Witchcraft*, this database will be computer-searchable as well as being more comprehensive. The interactive website for the survey is, minus the full-stop which ends this sentence: www.arts.ed.ac.uk/witches.

15. The figure of 1,891 represents the number of cases and not the number of individual witches since the same individual could be accused of witchcraft on more than one occasion and tried for witchcraft more than once.

16. See McLachlan, Hugh V. and Swales, J. K. (1978), 'Lord Hale, Witches and Rape: A Comment', *British Journal of Law and Society*, Vol. 5, No. 2, pp. 251–261; McLachlan, Hugh V. and Swales, J. K. (1979b), 'Witchcraft and the Status of Women: A Comment', *British Journal of Sociology*, Vol. 30,

No. 3, pp. 349–358; McLachlan, Hugh V. and Swales, J. K. (1980), 'Witchcraft and Anti-Feminism', *Scottish Journal of Sociology*, vol. 4, no. 2, pp. 141–166; and McLachlan, Hugh V. and Swales, J. K. (1994), 'Sexual Bias and the Law: The Case of Pre-Industrial Scotland', *International Journal of Sociology and Social Policy*, Vol. 14, No. 9, pp. 20–39.

17. McLachlan, Hugh V. and Swales, J. K. (1980). 'Witchcraft and Anti-Feminism', *Scottish Journal of Sociology*, vol. 4, no. 2, p. 145.

18. James VI and I (1597), *Daemonologie, in the Form of a Dialogue*, Edinburgh: Robert Walde-Grave, pp. 43–44.

19. National Archives of Scotland (NAS) manuscript JC26/38 (Aberdeen Roll, 1671).

20. NAS manuscript JC26/81/D9.

21. Larner, C. J., Lee, C. H., and McLachlan, H. V. (1977), *A Source-Book of Scottish Witchcraft*, Glasgow: University of Glasgow, pp. iv–v.

22. See *Register of the Privy Council*, 3rd Series, Vol. 5, p. 148.

23. See Larner, C. J., Lee, C. H., and McLachlan, H. V. (1977), *A Source-Book of Scottish Witchcraft*, Glasgow: University of Glasgow, pp. 145–146.

24. See Larner, C. J., Lee, C. H., and McLachlan, H. V. (1977), *A Source-Book of Scottish Witchcraft*, Glasgow: University of Glasgow, p. 55.

25. It was reprinted, along with other relevant material, in *A History of the Witches of Renfrewshire who were Burned on the Gallowgreen of Paisley*, published in Paisley in 1809 by the Editor of the *Paisley Repository* and again in 1877 by Alexander Gardner, with an introduction embodying extracts from the Records of the Presbytery of Paisley. Apart from the introduction, the pagination is identical in both editions. The editorship in both instances is anonymous.

26. Anon., editor (1877), *A History of the Witches of Renfrewshire who were Burned on the Gallowgreen of Paisley*, Paisley: Alexander Gardner, p. 123.

27. Anon., editor (1877), *A History of the Witches of Renfrewshire who were Burned on the Gallowgreen of Paisley*, Paisley: Alexander Gardner, p. xxv.

28. Sharpe, C. K. (1884), *A Historical Account of the Belief in Witchcraft in Scotland*, London and Glasgow, p. 172.

29. 'Vediovis' (1982), 'The Abuse of Justice by Means of Sorcery', *The Scots Law Times*, December 3, p. 319.

30. Arnot, Hugo (1785), *A Collection of Celebrated Criminal Trials in Scotland, 1536–1784*, Edinburgh, p. 202.

31. McDonald, S. W., Thom, A. and Thom, A. (1996), 'The Bargarran Witchcraft Trial: A Psychiatric Reassessment', *Scottish Medical Journal*, vol. 41, p. 156.

32. Adam, Isabel (1978), *Witch Hunt: The Great Scottish Witchcraft Trials of 1697*, London: Macmillan, p. 222.

33. McDonald, S. W., Thom, A. and Thom, A. (1996), 'The Bargarran Witchcraft Trial: A Psychiatric Reassessment', *Scottish Medical Journal*, vol. 41, p. 157.

34. Adam, Isabel (1978), *Witch Hunt: The Great Scottish Witchcraft Trials of 1697*, London: Macmillan, p. 224.

35. Anon., editor (1877), *A History of the Witches of Renfrewshire who were Burned on the Gallowgreen of Paisley*, Paisley: Alexander Gardner, p. 76.

36. Anon., editor (1877), *A History of the Witches of Renfrewshire who were Burned on the Gallowgreen of Paisley*, Paisley: Alexander Gardner, p. 77.

37. Anon., editor (1877), *A History of the Witches of Renfrewshire who were Burned on the Gallowgreen of Paisley*, Paisley: Alexander Gardner, p. 79.

38. Anon., editor (1877), *A History of the Witches of Renfrewshire who were Burned on the Gallowgreen of Paisley*, Paisley: Alexander Gardner, p. 84.

39. Anon., editor (1877), *A History of the Witches of Renfrewshire who were Burned on the Gallowgreen of Paisley*, Paisley: Alexander Gardner, pp. 79–80.

40. Sharpe, C. K. (1884), *A Historical Account of the Belief in Witchcraft in Scotland*, London and Glasgow, pp. 169–170.

41. Adam, Isabel (1978), *Witch Hunt: The Great Scottish Witchcraft Trials of 1697*, London: Macmillan, p. 42.

42. Anon., editor (1877), *A History of the Witches of Renfrewshire who were Burned on the Gallowgreen of Paisley*, Paisley: Alexander Gardner, pp. xxvii–xxviii.

43. Anon., editor (1877), *A History of the Witches of Renfrewshire who were Burned on the Gallowgreen of Paisley*, Paisley: Alexander Gardner, pp. xxxii–xxxiii.

44. Anon., editor (1877), *A History of the Witches of Renfrewshire who were Burned on the Gallowgreen of Paisley*, Paisley: Alexander Gardner, p. xxxiv.

45. Anon., editor (1877), *A History of the Witches of Renfrewshire who were Burned on the Gallowgreen of Paisley*, Paisley: Alexander Gardner, p. 64.

46. See, for instance, Robbins, R. H. (1959), *The Encyclopedia of Witchcraft and Demonology*, New York: The Hamlyn Publishing Group, pp. 527–530.

47. Geis, Gilbert and Bunn, Ivan (1997), *A Trial of Witches: A Seventeenth-Century Witchcraft Prosecution*, London: Routledge.

48. Notice that Geis and Bunn are, in our view, hypercritical of Lord Hale, the trial judge in the case. See McLachlan, Hugh V. and Swales, J. K. (1978), 'Lord Hale, Witches and Rape: A Comment', *British Journal of Law and Society*, Vol. 5, No. 2, pp. 251–261.

49. See, for instance, Boyer, Paul and Nissenbaum, Stephen (1974), *Salem Possessed: The Social Origins of Witchcraft*, Cambridge: Cambridge University Press; Rosenthal, Bernard (1993), *Salem Story: Reading the Witch Trials of 1692*, Cambridge: Cambridge University Press; and Hill, Francis (1995), *A Delusion of Satan: The Full Story of the Salem Witch Trials*, New York: Doubleday.

50. It was reprinted in Burr, G. L., editor (1914), *Narratives of the Witchcraft Cases*, New York and we shall refer to this edition.

51. Burr, G. L., editor (1914), *Narratives of the Witchcraft Cases*, New York, pp. 149–150.

52. Burr, G. L., editor (1914), *Narratives of the Witchcraft Cases*, New York, pp. 154–155.

53. Burr, G. L., editor (1914), *Narratives of the Witchcraft Cases*, New York, pp. 153–154.

54. Burr, G. L., editor (1914), *Narratives of the Witchcraft Cases*, New York, p. 155.

55. Burr, G. L., editor (1914), *Narratives of the Witchcraft Cases*, New York, pp. 157–158.

56. Burr, G. L., editor (1914), *Narratives of the Witchcraft Cases*, New York, p. 162.

57. See the NAS manuscript JC 10/6, pp. 1–81.

58. Robbins, R. H. (1959), *The Encyclopedia of Witchcraft and Demonology*, New York: The Hamlyn Publishing Group, p. 39.

59. *Renfrewshire*, Issue Fifteen, Autumn 2001, p. 8.
60. The NAS manuscript JC/26/81/D9.
61. See Russell, Steven (2001), 'Witchcraft, Genealogy, Foucault', *The British Journal of Sociology*, Vol. 32, No. 1, pp. 121–137.
62. The NAS manuscript JC/26/81/D9.
63. The NAS manuscript JC/26/81/D9.
64. The NAS manuscript JC/26/81/D9.
65. The NAS manuscript JC/26/81/D9.

FURTHER READING

Adam, Isabel (1978), *Witch Hunt: The Great Scottish Witchcraft Trials of 1697*, London: Macmillan.

Anon. (1698), *A True Narrative of the Sufferings and Relief of a Young Girle; Strangely molested by Evil spirits and their instruments in the West: With a preface and postscript containing Reflections on what is most Material or Curious either in the history or trial of the Seven Witches who were Condemn'd to be Execute in the country*, Edinburgh: Watson.

Anon., editor (1877), *A History of the Witches of Renfrewshire*, Paisley: Alexander Gardner.

Arnot, Hugo (1785), *A Collection of Celebrated Criminal Trials in Scotland, 1536–1784*, Edinburgh.

Black, George F. (1938), *A Calendar of Cases of Witchcraft in Scotland 1510–1727*, New York: New York Public Library.

Boyer, Paul and Nissenbaum, Stephen (1974), *Salem Possessed: The Social Origins of Witchcraft*, Cambridge: Cambridge University Press.

Burr, George, editor (1914), *Narratives of the Witchcraft Cases*, New York.

Geis, Gilbert and Bunn, Ivan, (1997), *A Trial of Witches: A Seventeenth-Century Witchcraft Prosecution*, London: Routledge and Kegan Paul.

Hill, Francis (1995), *A Delusion of Satan: The Full Story of the Salem Witch Trials*, New York: Doubleday.

James VI and I (1597), *Daemonologie, in the Form of a Dialogue*, Edinburgh: Robert Walde-Grave.

Larner, Christina (1981), *Enemies of God: The Witch-Hunt in Scotland*, London: Chatto and Windus.

Larner, C. J., Lee, C. H., and McLachlan, H. V. (1977), *A Source-Book of Scottish Witchcraft*, Glasgow: University of Glasgow.

Lawson, Deodat (1693), *A Brief and True Narrative of some Remarkable Passages Relating to Sundry Persons Afflicted by Witchcraft, at Salem Village which happened from the Nineteenth of March, to the Fifth of April, 1692*, London.

Le Roy Ladurie, Emmanuel (1987), *Jasmin's Witch*, Harmondsworth: Penguin Books.

Lyotard, J.-F. (1988), *The Differend: Phrases in Dispute*, Manchester: Manchester University Press.

Lyotard, J.-F. (1989), *The Lyotard Reader*, Benjamin, A. (ed.), Oxford: Blackwell.

Macfarlane, Alan (1970), *Witchcraft in Tudor and Stuart England*, London: Routledge and Kegan Paul.

McDonald, S.W., Thom, A. and Thom, A. (1996), 'The Bargarran Witchcraft Trial: A Psychiatric Reassessment', *Scottish Medical Journal*, vol. 41, pp. 152–158.

McLachlan, Hugh V. (1976), 'Functionalism, Causation and Explanation', *Philosophy of the Social Sciences* vol. 6, No. 3, pp. 235–240.

McLachlan, Hugh V. (1979), 'The Is/Ought Question: A Needless Controversy', *Journal of the British Society for Phenomenology*, Vol. 10, No. 2, pp. 134–137.

McLachlan, Hugh V. (1981a), 'Wittgenstein, Family Resemblances and the Theory of Classification', *International Journal of Sociology and Social Policy*, Vol. 1, No. 1. pp. 1–16.

McLachlan, Hugh V. (1981b), 'Is "Power" an Evaluative Concept?', *British Journal of Sociology*, Vol. 32, No. 3, pp. 392–410.

McLachlan, Hugh V. (1982), 'Buchanan, Locke and Wittgenstein on Classification', *Journal of Information Science*, Vol. 3, No. 4, pp. 191–200.

McLachlan, Hugh V. and Scott, Michael (1985), 'Rationality and Relativism: A Defence of Strong Absolutism', *The British Journal of Sociology*, Vol. 36, No. 6, pp. 604–610.

McLachlan, Hugh V. and Swales, J. K. (1978), 'Lord Hale, Witches and Rape: A Comment', *British Journal of Law and Society*, Vol. 5, No. 2, pp. 251–261.

McLachlan, Hugh V. and Swales, J. K. (1979a), 'Stereotypes and Scottish Witchcraft', *Contemporary Review*, Vol. 234, No. 1357, February, pp. 88–94.

McLachlan, Hugh V. and Swales, J. K. (1979b), 'Witchcraft and the Status of Women: A Comment', *British Journal of Sociology*, Vol. 30, No. 3, pp. 349–358.

McLachlan, Hugh V. and Swales, J. K. (1980), 'Witchcraft and Anti-Feminism', *Scottish Journal of Sociology*, vol. 4, no. 2, pp. 141–166.

McLachlan, Hugh V. and Swales, J. K. (1982), 'Tibbetts's Theory of Rationality and Scottish Witchcraft', *Philosophy of the Social Sciences*, Vol. 12, No. 1, pp. 75–79.

McLachlan, Hugh V. and Swales, J. K. (1983), 'Rationality and the Belief in Witches: A Rejoinder to Tibbetts', *Philosophy of the Social Sciences*, Vol. 13, No. 4, pp. 475–477.

McLachlan, Hugh V. and Swales, J. K. (1984), 'Review of Witch-Hunting, Magic and the New Philosophy by Brian Easlea', *Philosophy of the Social Sciences*, Vol. 14, No. 4, pp. 577–580.

McLachlan, Hugh V. and Swales, J. K. (1990), 'Friedman's Methodology: A Comment on Bolland', in *Milton Friedman: Critical Assessments*, J.C. Wood and R. N. Woods, editors, London: Routledge and Kegan Paul, Vol. 3, pp. 438–457.

McLachlan, Hugh V. and Swales, J. K. (1992), 'Scottish Witchcraft: Myth or Reality?', *Contemporary Review*, vol. 260, no. 1513, February, pp. 79–84.

McLachlan, Hugh V. and Swales, J. K. (1994), 'Sexual Bias and the Law: The Case of Pre-Industrial Scotland', *International Journal of Sociology and Social Policy*, Vol. 14, No. 9, pp. 20–39.

McLachlan, Hugh V. and Swales, J. K. (1998a), 'The Methodology Rather Than the Rhetoric of Economics: McCloskey on Popper and Hume', *Journal of Interdisciplinary Economics*, Vol. 9, No. 2, pp. 125–143.

McLachlan, Hugh V. and Swales, J. K., 1998b, 'Sraffa, Wittgenstein and the Nature of Economic Theory', *Journal of Interdisciplinary Economics*, Vol. 9, No. 4, pp. 253–271.

Robbins, R. H. (1959), *The Encyclopedia of Witchcraft and Demonology*, New York: The Hamlyn Publishing Group.

Rosenthal, Bernard (1993), *Salem Story: Reading the Witch Trials of 1692*, Cambridge: Cambridge University Press.

Russell, Steven (2001), 'Witchcraft, Genealogy, Foucault', *The British Journal of Sociology*, Vol. 32, No. 1, pp. 121–137.

Sharpe, C. K. (1884) *A Historical Account of the Belief in Witchcraft in Scotland*, London and Glasgow.

Thompson, S. and Hoggett, P. (1996), 'Universalism, Selectivism and Particularism: Towards a Postmodern Social Policy', *Critical Social Policy*, 46, Vol. 16.

'Vediovis' (1982), 'The Abuse of Justice by Means of Sorcery', *The Scots Law Times*, December 3, pp. 317–320.

FIVE

The Fair Sex Turns Ugly: Female Involvement in the Jacobite Rising of 1745

Maggie Craig

In July 1745, on a day of driving wind and rain, a young man of twenty-four was rowed ashore from a French trading brig to the small island of Eriskay in the Outer Hebrides. As he jumped from the rowing boat onto the white sands, he stepped also into history, myth and the collective consciousness of Scotland.

Destined with astonishing rapidity to become the Bonnie Prince Charlie of romantic song and legend, he had landed in this remote corner of the British Isles with high hopes that the Highland clans would remember their traditional loyalty to the Stuarts and rally to the Jacobite Cause.

Scotland's royal house, the traditional *Stewart* spelling of its name allegedly changed by Mary Queen of Scots to make it more pronounceable by French speakers, had made both love and war with its English counterparts for centuries. The resulting family relationships led to the Scottish King James VI becoming also James I of England when he succeeded the childless Queen Elizabeth I in 1603 at the birth of the modern United Kingdom.

His grandson, James VII and II, was both a devout Roman Catholic in an overwhelmingly Protestant country and not noticeably enthusiastic about reigning as a constitutional monarch. Deposed at the Glorious Revolution of 1688 in favour of William of Orange, his Protestant son-in-law, he went into exile.

Like many of Scotland's kings, James VII and II's son was yet another James. This regrettable lack of originality gave the supporters of the House of Stuart their designation of Jacobites, *Jacobus* being the Latin for *James*. The James raised in exile broke the pattern, naming his elder son Charles and his younger one Henry. The former was Prince Charles Edward Stuart to his friends and the Young Pretender to his enemies. The *Scots Magazine* was just one of several contemporary publications which avoided offending any of its readers by the use of a tactful abbreviation: Charles was referred to as 'The Pr.'

The '45 was the last attempt to restore the House of Stuart to the throne of the United Kingdom, and women played a highly significant role in it.

Indeed, the charge that Charles was 'under petticoat patronage' was one often levelled at him throughout the months which followed his landfall on Eriskay, the time subsequently referred to as the Year of the Prince.

Before and during the military campaign which followed the Raising of the Standard at Glenfinnan in August 1745, women recruited men to the Cause, gathered together horses, money and supplies and acted as spies, gatherers and transmitters of information. Their role in keeping the home fires burning – with everything which that entails – and providing morale-boosting hospitality and succour to weary fighting men was also absolutely crucial. It's a contribution often denigrated and often ignored.

After the campaign and the bloody aftermath of the final defeat at the Battle of Culloden on 16 April 1746, women nursed and hid the wounded and helped prisoners to escape. Huge risks were run. The blood-letting which began on the battlefield and continued throughout the summer and autumn of 1746 all too often spiralled off from duty into sport. Government officers such as the notorious Captain Caroline Frederick Scott gave their men tacit, and sometimes overt, permission to indulge. Stories of rape are legion.

Most of those stories are contained within the pages of *The Lyon in Mourning*, a compilation of eye-witness accounts and other statements gathered together by the Jacobite Bishop Forbes. Some modern historians continue to dismiss these stories as coming from a biased source. It's a somewhat ludicrous point of view.

Rape was, some would say still is, a crime in which the victim bore almost as much shame as the attacker. It was hard for a woman to admit to having been assaulted in this way. These stories were not easy to tell, and just why would so many women have lied about something whose stigma they would have had to live with for the rest of their lives, unless it was to bear witness to a real event?

It's a regrettable but unavoidable fact that we can only know something about those women who participated in the '45 if they appear in the written record and that those about whom we know most are inevitably those belonging to the middle and upper classes. These were the women whose activities were reported. These were the women who wrote letters and petitions.

Some working-class women did manage the latter. Christian Hakeney travelled from Forfar to London in an attempt to get her husband released from custody. Claiming that he had been forced to join the Jacobite army, she bore written statements from her local minister and sheriff to back up her case. What her own political opinions, if any, were we cannot know.

Nor can we know what the women who followed Prince Charles's army on the abortive invasion of England thought. Some were undoubtedly prostitutes, who are of course also entitled to political opinions, but as listed in the records, the vast majority were the wives and sometimes daughters of Jacobite soldiers. Many of these women were left behind when the retreat from Derby threatened to turn into a rout. They and their children subsequently languished in gaols in York, Lancaster and Chester. A trawl through the collections of the Public Record Office in London turns up many lists and many names.

As an example, 'Rebel and treasonable persons' confined in Lancaster Castle on 24th April 1746 included:

> Flora McQuin; Margaret Dike; John Roy's son; Daniel McIntosh and
> his two children; William McKowin and his wife; Ann McKenzie;
> Mary McKenzie alias McIntire, John McKenzie; Ann McIntosh;
> Mary McDonald; Jennet Pate; Jennet McKerrow; Margery Camell;
> Duncan Hore senior and junior; Jane Herrin; Jane Cumming and
> two children; Flora Cameron and child; Effey Camron; Ann Camron;
> Margaret McDonald; Mary Shaw; Margaret Shaw; . . .

There are more female names on that list, as there are on numerous other lists tucked away in the Public Record Office. Whilst some of these women were subsequently released, others were transported along with hundreds of male Jacobite prisoners to the sugar and tobacco plantations of the New World to work as indentured servants.

Reliant as we are on a somewhat self-selected group of women, they were drawn from that most traditional of Jacobite constituencies: the Episcopalian and Roman Catholic gentry and minor aristocracy. Their geographical distribution was also traditional. Most of them belonged to families with deep roots and/or estates of varying sizes in rural Scotland: Perthshire, the Highlands, the Borders and the North East, the last in particular being a hotbed of both Episcopalianism and Jacobitism.

The role played by this part of Scotland in the Jacobite story is often forgotten. The history of the '45 having largely been written by the losers rather than the winners, this is perhaps due to the brightness of the light shone on all aspects of Highland involvement with the affair casting other areas into the shadows. Brother and sister historians Alistair and Henrietta Tayler maintained that as much as 20% of Prince Charles's fighting force originated in north-east Scotland.[1]

Jean or Jenny Cameron lived on the other side of the country, at Glendessary in the West Highlands. For her time she was a highly unconventional woman, having divorced a violent husband and come home to live quietly with her brother and his family. She led around three hundred men to the Raising of the Standard at Glenfinnan, another highly unconventional, not to mention highly rebellious, act. Those men helped form the nucleus of the army which followed the Prince through initial military success and the abortive invasion of England until the defeat at Culloden.

A similar Amazon, or so she was described at the time, was Lady Anne Mackintosh. Her story is the stuff of legend, so much so that it's often hard to disentangle the truth from the myth. Twenty-two years old when hostilities broke out, she set herself the task of persuading the men of Clan Chattan to come out in support of the Prince. Her husband Aeneas (also known as Angus) was a captain in the Black Watch, a regiment within the British army. He had raised his own company himself. The 22nd Mackintosh of Mackintosh was conveniently absent when his wife rode out from their home at Moy Hall south of Inverness to try to recruit others among his tenantry to the opposite side.

Anne Mackintosh is said to have been dressed in a tartan riding habit, with a pair of pistols at her waist and the traditional blue bonnet of the fighting Scotsman on her head. An agreement to come out for the Prince was reputedly rewarded with a kiss. One doesn't have to be a complete cynic to suspect that there might well have been as much coercion as cajoling. Lady Anne assembled a regiment three hundred strong, her recruiting efforts earning her the sobriquet of 'Colonel Anne'.

Lady Mackintosh's Regiment was commanded by her cousin, Alexander McGillivray of Dunmaglass. As letters to the Jacobite Duke of Atholl show, the Mackintosh had considered throwing in his lot with the Jacobites, but apparently took cold feet at the last moment.[2] It has been suggested that he and his wife had made a pact that each should declare allegiance to one of the combatants, hedging their bets as many families did at the time. Given the consequences of failure, one can hardly blame them.

How Charles Edward Stuart would behave if he won was an unknown quantity. (He was later to show himself magnanimous in victory.) There was already a precedent as to how the British state would react to this threat to its security, ideology and stability. Anyone over the age of 40 could remember the failed Jacobite Rising of 1715. Reprisals were likely to take the form of executions, house-burnings and the seizing of property. High treason and taking part in an 'unnatural rebellion' were potentially punishable by a spectacularly gruesome form of putting someone to death: hanging, drawing and quartering.

Jacobite women were credited with having a great influence over their menfolk. After the defeat several pleas for clemency were based on the premise that the man in question had been persuaded to support the

Cause because, like William Dunbar, he had 'had the misfortune to marry a Jacobite wife'. Lord Kilmarnock, for example, beheaded on Tower Hill in August 1746 along with Lords Balmerino and Lovat, was persuaded to nail his colours to Prince Charles' mast by his wife and his mother-in-law.

Given those dreadful possible consequences of defeat, this influence is even more remarkable. The discouragement exerted by the thought of those consequences was powerful. Lord Nithsdale was the son of a famous Jacobite father, one who had famously escaped execution after the '15 by being rescued from the Tower of London by his indomitable wife.

Persuaded by his own wife to come to Holyroodhouse to be presented to Prince Charles, and the holder of firm Jacobite views himself, the younger Lord Nithsdale went home after just one night, allegedly after nightmares involving axes and scaffolds.

In this connection, it's interesting to speculate where Jean Cameron's brother was at the time of the Raising of the Standard at Glenfinnan. He isn't mentioned in any of the accounts. Was he deceased, or merely also conveniently absent? Perhaps a pact had been entered into here too, on the basis that a woman was running less of a risk than a man. Overwhelmingly, men were the owners of lands and property. That property might be less likely to fall forfeit to the crown if a man could blame his wife, mother or sister for having raised the family and clan in armed rebellion.

Whilst that argument might be plausible, it's less easy to be certain that the state would not have been prepared to hang a lady. This was an age when mere women were routinely hanged for criminal offences. Gender itself was not an inhibitor.

The '45 was followed by treason trials in Carlisle, London and York. Eighty-six Jacobites were hanged, sixty of them officers. The latter were regarded as more guilty than the foot soldiers. Having had less of a choice about joining up themselves, there were plenty of people from humbler backgrounds prepared to make sworn statements that the officers had forced them out.

Several ladies, as opposed to women, were arrested both during and after the '45. Around twenty of them were held prisoner for varying lengths of time, some in Inverness, some in Edinburgh and some in London. None were actually prosecuted, although it was recommended in certain cases. Once the immediate danger had passed, attitudes softened. While the danger was still raw and real, many Hanoverian men were infuriated by the role certain well-born ladies had played in the proceedings and the gallant attitudes some other Hanoverian men adopted towards them.

Arrested at her home at Moy Hall in the terrifying days which followed the defeat at Culloden, Anne Mackintosh was held captive in Inverness for about six weeks. Several redcoat officers visited her there. One of them wrote home about it. 'I drank tea yesterday with Lady Mackintosh. She is really a very pretty woman, pity she is a rebel.'

The government commander known by the nickname of Hangman Hawley became infuriated when his officers began to speak of the honour due to Colonel Anne. He reportedly thumped the Duke of Cumberland's table and roared out his protest. 'Damn the woman, I'll honour her with mahogany gallows and a silken cord!' Hawley obviously saw quite clearly how dangerous women like Anne Mackintosh were.

Of all the Jacobite ladies, as opposed to mere women, she is the one who most risked the gallows. That she escaped was probably due to a combination of chivalry, her own aristocratic connections and the government's understandable desire not to make a martyr out of her.

Whether she and her husband had made some sort of pact or not, her actions throughout the '45 show her to have been a committed Jacobite. Two months before Culloden, during the notorious Rout of Moy, she played a pivotal role in the ruse which saved the Prince from being captured by a large government force. She was entertaining him and his entourage at the time.

Her own husband was captured by the Jacobites shortly afterwards. Cynics on both sides considered that he had not perhaps made much of an effort to save himself, believing perhaps that the Prince's star was in the ascendant. Charles ordered the Mackintosh to be released into his wife's custody. She is said to have received him with a laconic 'Your servant, Captain'. His reply was equally as brief: 'Your servant, colonel'. Afterwards they lived together in apparent peace and amity until Aeneas died in 1770.

Perhaps the Mackintosh's caution might have had something to do with his age. Twenty years older than his wife, he was a man in early middle age. Just as when one looks into the '45 it quickly becomes apparent how many of the participants on both sides were related to each other, it's also remarkable how often those who committed themselves to the Jacobite Cause came from opposite ends of the age spectrum.

As two examples among many, Gordon of Glenbucket was in his 70s and his comrade-in-arms Lord Pitsligo was in his late 60s and a chronic asthmatic to boot. Lord and Lady Ogilvy were at the other end of the scale, both just twenty years old when they married in early 1745. Were the young impetuous and idealistic and had the old, fed up with having tolerated a regime they considered illegitimate for too many years, rediscovered their own idealism and boldness? As the generation most involved with building up a family and its fortunes, perhaps it was the middle-aged who had the most to lose and who were therefore correspondingly much more cautious.

Born Margaret Johnston of Westerhall in Dumfriesshire, young Lady
Ogilvy accompanied her equally youthful husband on his recruiting drives
in Angus, reportedly standing at the mercat cross in Coupar Angus with a
drawn sword in her hand. She was at her husband's side throughout the
campaign, often travelling in a coach with Margaret Murray of Broughton,
wife of Prince Charles' secretary.

Margaret Murray's commitment to the Cause was robust to say the least.
She took an active part in securing money and weapons for the Jacobite
army and was accused of both verbal and physical abuse of those who
declined to co-operate. The acerbic Patrick Crichton of Woodhouselee
described her as 'gone into the spirit of the gang'.

Another committed Jacobite of mature years was Lady Nairne, the
matriarch of a large extended family. Seventy-six in 1745 and not in
the best of health, she nevertheless played as active a role as she could,
rousing herself from her sickbed to send a 40-strong detachment of her
own retainers to reinforce her son-in-law's garrison in Perth when she got
news that it was being attacked by a pro-Hanoverian mob.

Lady Nairne had a huge influence over her relations, and the '45 was
the second uprising in which she made her presence felt. The Earl of Mar,
leader of the '15, said that he wished all his men had her spirit. Two of
her sons, four sons-in-law, six grandsons and two nephews fought in the
Rising of 1745. The women of the family were not left out.

One of Lady Nairne's daughters was Lady Strathallan, arrested and held
prisoner in Edinburgh Castle for six months on a charge of 'putting out
illuminations on the Pretender's birthday in a most remarkable manner'.
Given the message an activity like that sent out to others, such offences
were taken very seriously at the time. The authorities also knew that
in Lady Strathallan's case it was backed up by a real commitment to
the Jacobite Cause and that her husband was out serving with the
Prince's army.

Lady Strathallan's sister was Charlotte Robertson, Lady Lude. So
caught up in the thrill of it all when she entertained the Prince that
one observer remarked that 'she looked like a person whose head had
gone wrong', she showed a harsher side when it came to providing
men for the Jacobite army. She had no compunction about exercising
her clout over her tenants, forcing many of them to go out for the
Prince by dint of threats to burn down their cottages or set their crops
alight.

One of the many ironies of the Jacobite story is that a later member of
the same family had a great deal to do with the construction of sentimental
and romantic Jacobitism. Carolina Oliphant, another Lady Nairne and
great-granddaughter of the matriarch of the '45, penned many songs still

sung enthusiastically today. Her oeuvre contains some fabulous works. It also includes some extremely maudlin ones. *Will ye no' come back again* springs immediately to mind.

Her *Hundred Pipers* is a rousing anthem, but it bends the truth more than somewhat. Purporting to deal with the crossing of the Esk by the Jacobite army, Lady Nairne's version has the gallant Highlanders marching victoriously into England, bagpipes skirling and flags flying. In reality, the crossing of the Esk was one of the final acts of the failed march on London.

The Duke of Cumberland called the elder of these two Lady Nairnes 'this troublesome old woman' and the Privy Council recommended that she and her daughters be prosecuted. They escaped that fate, as all of the ladies ultimately did. The contrast with the harsh treatment meted out to those working-class women who had been the camp followers of the Jacobite army is striking.

The difference in treatment of the genders is fascinating when viewed from the perspective of social class. Both working-class and middle- and upper-class male Jacobites were treated with a considerable amount of brutality, but it was the officer class who were deemed more guilty and for whom the ultimate penalty of death was largely demanded.

However, when confronted by middle- and upper-class women, Hanoverian officers and officials often displayed considerable chivalry. Working-class women, on the other hand, were a problem to be disposed of as quickly and as efficiently as possible.

The younger Lady Nairne's *Charlie is my Darling* might serve as an excellent theme tune for another, less influential and less constant, female section of Jacobite support. Many gently-born young women, a considerable number from Whig or at least politically ambivalent families, had their heads turned by the personal charisma of the Prince and the heady excitement of his army's occupation of Edinburgh in the autumn of 1745. The Jacobite emblem was the white rose of Scotland, stylised into a cockade fashioned from white ribbon. The young ladies of Edinburgh had a whale of a time stitching these onto the tartan dresses which their seamstresses had run up for them.

Despite the arguments which rage now about tartan, wearing it then sent out an unmistakeable political message. In the treason trials held after Culloden it helped damn a man if witnesses had seen him during the campaign wearing a white cockade or Highland clothes: a plaid or tartan coat or waistcoat. For the Edinburgh ladies such clothes proved to be considerably less dangerous. All the same, wearing these Jacobite symbols clearly did give them a pleasurable *frisson* at the extent of their own boldness.

Writing to her sister, one young woman described Prince Charles at his most charming:

> O lass such a fine show as I saw on Wednesday last. I went to the camp at Duddingston and saw the Prince review his men. He was sitting in his tent when I first came to the field. The ladies made a circle round the tent and after we had gazed our fill at him he came out of the tent with a grace and majesty that is unexpressible. He saluted all the circle with an air of grandeur and affability capable of charming the most obstinate Whig.[3]

Interestingly, whilst acknowledging the power of the Stuart charm, Magdalen Pringle seemed capable of resisting it herself. She went on to sadly observe that falling under the spell of that charm could prove dangerous to the individual involved.

The young ladies of Edinburgh clearly took some pleasure in feeling that in their support for the Bonnie Prince they were doing something outwith the normally acceptable parameters of female behaviour. For real Jacobite women, however, those whose commitment went back much further than the arrival in Scotland of a handsome prince, what they were doing was in no way deviant. Jacobitism was their orthodoxy.

Their political faith was just that, a faith every bit as strong and deep-rooted as their Episcopalian or Roman Catholic religion. The two tenets of their belief were intertwined, impossible to unravel and separate one from the other. Indeed, in the years running up to the '45, when rumour was rife of the imminent arrival of the young Stuart prince, Charles was whispered about almost as though he were the Saviour himself, come to right all wrongs. Sometimes he was also the longed-for lover, again the one who would cure all ills and enable those who basked in the sunshine of his favour to live happily ever after.

For Jacobites, the Hanoverian monarchy was completely illegitimate: *de facto* rather than *de jure*. King George II was 'German Geordie', 'The Elector of Hanover' or 'The Usurper'. When Lord Pitsligo set off on the campaign trail he removed his hat, lifted his face to heaven and declared, 'Lord, thou knowest that our Cause is just'.

This sometimes dangerously unquestioning allegiance continued long after the Cause itself was dead and buried. Isabella Lumsden, famous at the time of the '45 for refusing to accept her lover's hand in marriage unless he first went out for the Prince, was still arguing terminology years later, lambasting anyone who dared refer to 'the Pretender' in her presence. '*Pretender? Prince*, and be damned to ye!'

A contemporary Jacobite toast sums up this absolute belief in the rightness of their Cause rather well:

> God bless the King! God bless the Faith's Defender!
> God bless – no harm in blessing – the Pretender!
> Who that Pretender is, and who that King –
> God bless us all – is quite another Thing!

It might also be hard to argue that much of what the Jacobite women actually did was too far outwith their normal sphere of activity. Organising supplies and catering for a company of soldiers was simply an extension of the skills involved in running a large home, collecting and disseminating information a formalisation of something which went on anyway.

Their menfolk relied heavily on their back-up and few seem to have had much of a problem about leaving their wives, mothers and sisters in charge of things at home. It should be remembered that eighteenth-century women had much more freedom than their Victorian great-granddaughters. Visitors to Scotland in the earlier period often commented on how willing the women of the country were to express their own opinions, even if they differed from those of a husband or father.

It's interesting also to note that the idea of obedience between men and women was a two-way street. Writing to his lover Margaret McDonnell, Duncan McGillis signed off as 'your most obedient love'.

Scotswomen also of course retained their own names after marriage. A collection of letters from Jacobite soldiers now held in the Public Record Office makes this obvious. John McLennan, for example, addressed his letter to 'Mary Grant, spouse of John McLennan'. Adopting the husband's name was an English fashion which took a long time to catch on in Scotland.

It may seem a small point and any children of a marriage did always take their father's name, but it does seem to indicate a belief that a woman should retain her own identity when she entered into marriage. Even today, for legal purposes married Scotswomen bear both maiden and married names and long-standing friends still tend to refer to other married friends by their maiden names.

It might also be possible to argue that the Jacobites took a more enlightened view towards the equality of the sexes than the Hanoverians did, although a pamphlet entitled *An Epistle from a British Lady to her Countrywomen* does throw an interesting and somewhat contradictory sidelight on that last statement. Published in 1745 and evoking the spirit of heroic women of history such as Joan of Arc, the *Epistle* is a call to arms.

The author states that in this current crisis it is the duty of British women to be bold and cheerful as they send their men off to resist this Catholic invasion which threatens to deprive us all, especially women, of our hard-won freedoms:

> In short, in this Time of public Calamity . . . a Woman of Sense and Honour cannot fit quietly down unconcerned at the Event, in which she hath an equal, nay I think a superior Interest even to the Men themselves. To give up herself at this Time to Diversion and idle Amusement, must argue a weak and a childish Mind, and must make those Men of Sense who have hitherto been our Advocates, hereafter ashamed to vindicate our Cause, and be silent when Fools and Coxcombs lay their usual Claim to Ascendency over us in Understanding.

Jacobite soldiers certainly behaved much better towards women than did their Hanoverian counterparts. Compare and contrast the lack of stories of rape which accompany the Jacobite march into England and the opposite for the government occupation of the Highlands after Culloden.

Many thoughtful contemporary commentators, both male and female, did express real and honest distaste for 'women forcing poor men to their doom'. Isabella Lumsden, as we saw, famously refused to accept the equally famously apolitical Robert Strange's proposal of marriage until he agreed to go out for the Prince.

It's important, however, not to judge these women by modern standards and sensibilities. They may not always be easy to like, but they were participating in their own times just as men were, taking what action they thought necessary to achieve their political aims.

Well aware of the importance of the activities and influence of Jacobite women, the propaganda used as a weapon against them showed few vestiges of gentlemanly chivalry. It was designed to demonstrate how much these women had deviated from acceptable female behaviour, thus putting themselves quite beyond the pale and unworthy of the respect of decent men and women.

For a start, some tried to maintain that any woman who got involved in such things was not truly feminine. The *Scots Magazine* of May 1746 carried a letter from a redcoat officer detailing the arrest of Anne Mackintosh and describing her as 'a woman of a masculine spirit'. This rather conflicted with the view expressed, among others, by James Ray of Whitehaven, a volunteer in the Hanoverian army. He sounded genuinely confused when he reflected, 'It is remarkable. Many of the prettiest ladies in Scotland are Jacobites'.

Those who had done a lot more than wear tartan dresses and white ribbons were in danger of something a lot worse than being patronised.

Predictably enough, an attack on the morals of women was one of the favourite approaches, especially for individuals like Jean Cameron who really had stepped outwith the feminine sphere by leading soldiers to Glenfinnan. For her, the gutter press of the day dipped its quills in vitriol. Since they didn't know very much about her, they simply made most of it up.

When reports came in of her presence at the Raising of the Standard, two and two were immediately added together to make five. James Ray jumped to a conclusion which seemed obvious to him and thousands of others in his *Acts of the Rebels, Written by an Egyptian.* His unpleasant concoction is written in the style of the Bible:

> And it came to pass, that when JANE the Daughter of one of the Camerons heard that CHARLES was come, she adorn'd herself with clean Linen, and gay attire, with Frankincence and Perfumes was her Garments sprinkled nay nothing was left undone to make her person seem lovely before him. 2 And JANE carryed gifts unto CHARLES, and when she had got into his Appartment, she said unto him, Oh! Prince I have yet greater riches in store for thee which Eye hath not seen. 3 Now from that time, CHARLES began to see with the Eyes of the Flesh.4

There's a great deal more in the same vein. After availing himself of what Jenny Cameron is offering, the couple sleep together. When they awake, Charles once more takes 'the Sin offering'.

The author of *The Life of Miss Jenny Cameron, The Reputed Mistress of the Deputy Pretender* took a similar view. The pamphlet purports to tell Jean Cameron's life story. Promiscuous beyond belief, this Jenny apparently spent much of her young womanhood traipsing about Edinburgh visiting brothels. Dressed in men's clothes, she and the maid who accompanied her on these jaunts 'carried the frolic as far as their sex would permit them'.

The footman who also went with the two 'she-cavaliers' later got Jenny pregnant. After she had had the abortion, she was packed off to a convent in France where she got pregnant again, this time by a Franciscan monk . . . and so on. According to the pamphleteer, Jenny compounded her sins by later bedding her own brother, causing her sister-in-law to die of shock when she found the pair *in flagrante delicto.*

The pamphleteer did however excuse Mrs Cameron from the slur of being the Prince's lover: '. . . her age, which is within a year or two of 50, must secure her from the scandal of being his mistress'.

There is clearly a fair amount of titillation in all of this, but there's a lot more than that going on in these works of fantasy. A pamphlet entitled *The*

Female Rebels is an interesting case in point. It begins with the traditional ridicule and belittling of female opinion common to such propaganda:

> It is remarkable of the Fair Sex, that whatever Opinions they embrace, they assert them with greater Constancy and Violence, than the Generality of Mankind: They seldom observe any medium in their Passions, or set any reasonable Bounds to those Actions which result from them. As they adopt Principles without Reasoning, so they are actuated by them, to all the mad Lengths which their Whim, Caprice or Revenge can dictate to them: They have, generally speaking, weak Heads and warm Hearts; and therefore we see that this Part of the Species are the first Prosylites to the most absurd Doctrines, and in all Changes of State or Religion, the Ladies are sure to lead the Van.

Nothing daunted by hopelessly confusing Margaret Murray of Broughton with the Duchess of Perth and making the latter the Duke's wife rather than his mother, *The Female Rebels* goes on to give its readers the usual salacious details. However, it also accuses this spurious Duchess of Perth of using foul language and of being more cruel and brutal than the Jacobite officers with whom she was allegedly travelling.

Lady Margaret Ogilvy is accused of similar cruelties and generally coarse behaviour. When the Jacobites were besieging the Hanoverian garrison at Fort William, the two ladies apparently suggested the use of prisoners as human cannonballs. Such a hellish and inhumane suggestion horrified even the most savage of the Jacobite men.

It is laughable, but there is a fascinating sub-text. Women – unlike men, of course – are passionate creatures. When they espouse a cause, they do so heart and soul. They go to extremes. Allow them to step outside the domestic arena and there's no knowing where it will all end.

The idea of 'the fair sex' as one of the chief civilising forces in a potentially brutish life runs though much eighteenth-century writing. Men are savages, impelled by their natures to roughness and brutality. Women provide the softening which makes civilisation possible and a peaceable and pleasant society attainable. If women are now going to abdicate that responsibility in favour of participation in politics and other traditionally male preserves, in the parlance of the time 'unsexing' themselves, isn't it possible that the whole fabric of society might crumble?

The propaganda employed during the '45, when the danger was real and immediate, was vicious. Once that danger had begun to recede, a much more powerful weapon was brought to bear against the real threat which the Jacobites had posed to the status quo: sentimentalisation.

When London was trembling before the prospect of an onslaught by the Highland savages, the London stage had been busy whipping up anti-Jacobite and anti-Scottish fervour. Almost as soon as the hostilities ceased, the same theatres began presenting pantomimes with simple Highland lassies swooning over handsome Hielan' laddies, now transformed into *noble* savages. These plays were the forerunners of today's shortbread tin depictions of a bloody and calamitous conflict sanitised by sentimentality.

The cult of Flora MacDonald so associated with that sentimentality started very early. She was arrested in September 1746. A scrappy piece of paper now in the Public Record Office details the charge: 'Miss Flora McDonald of Milton made Prisoner for having carryed off the Pretender's Son as her Servant in Women's Apparell.'

During her captivity she was polite and co-operative, offering her captors none of the defiance which other Jacobite women showed. By the time she arrived in London after a sojourn in Edinburgh, she found herself to be something of a celebrity. Anybody who was anybody wanted to visit her.

Flora's bravery in helping a fellow human being in the direst of straits cannot be gainsaid. Crossing the Minch in a small rowing boat on a stormy night was not an activity for the faint-hearted. However, it is not part of the myth that Flora herself took considerable persuading before she agreed to carry out the role allotted to her and that the organiser of the whole thing, including the disguising of the Prince as the Irish washerwoman Betty Burke, was Lady Clanranald, a woman whose name and pivotal part in the proceedings are all but forgotten.

Flora herself was no Jacobite. Nor is the issue ever raised that without apparently any duress being applied she named names, landing other people in serious trouble. There were those on Skye who found it hard to forgive her for that.

Yet there she is, gazing out of the portrait painted by Allan Ramsay with Jacobite white roses at her breast and in her hair, tartan draped elegantly about her shoulders. That she should have become the icon of Jacobite womanhood is deeply ironic.

The cult of Flora MacDonald plumbed its sentimental depths during the upsurge of writing on the Jacobite period which spanned the end of the nineteenth and the beginning of the twentieth centuries. Later in life she and her husband Allan MacDonald joined the torrent of emigration draining out of the Highlands and Islands and settled in North Carolina. Dealing with the awkward matter of Allan's support for the British king against the American revolutionaries, one writer of the early twentieth century wrote that 'They were of the blood that is loyal to kings'. That's a quite breathtaking masterpiece of spin.

The cult has continued almost unabated to the present day. Open most histories of the '45, academic and popular, and you can more or less guarantee to find the participation of women reduced to just one. Another famous depiction, very attractive on a tin of shortbread, shows a comely yet modest dark-haired girl looking doe-eyed at the Bonnie Prince as he bends over to kiss her hand.

However she is shown, Flora is always silent. That may be what gives the myth its enduring strength. Or perhaps it hinges on just one piece of reported speech. While she was in London, the Hanoverian Prince of Wales asked her sternly why she had helped his father's enemy. Why, she replied, because the man was in trouble, enchanting the Prince of Wales by further explaining 'that she would have done the same thing for him had she found him in distress'.

In short, she had helped Charles Edward Stuart because her womanly heart had been touched, not because she was committed to his Cause. Flora played the traditional female role. Perhaps that was why nobody threatened her with mahogany gallows and a silken cord.

Many women gave succour to the wounded and helped conceal men on the run from the redcoats out of the same compassionate impulses which Flora claimed, a response not of course confined to only one side or only one gender. Given the close-knit relationships of Scotland, where then as now one only has to be five minutes in a room full of apparent strangers before discovering all the connections between those present, it was entirely predictable that many people were prepared to help relatives and friends whose political convictions had put them on the wrong side of the law, whilst at the same time disapproving of those political convictions.

One woman with many relatives on both sides was Anne Leith, a young widow from Aberdeenshire. Stranded in Inverness in the autumn of 1745, she took lodgings and put her eldest son Sandy in school there. Travel continuing to be dangerous, she was still in the Highland capital in April 1746. As soon as news reached the town of the defeat at Culloden, she gathered together what medical supplies she could find and went out to the battlefield with two other women whom we know only as Mrs Stonor and her maid Eppy.

All three of them were running the very real risk of rape and assault. Those men on the battlefield who were not yet dead were horribly injured and mutilated. It must have been absolutely terrifying.

In the days which followed, when every lockable space in Inverness was crammed full of Jacobite prisoners, Anne Leith visited as many of them as she could. She spent most of her small income on bread for them, carried messages backwards and forwards between them and their friends and families and continued to offer what medical assistance she could. She described what it was like succinctly but vividly: 'nothing then but scenes of horror every moment'.

She badgered everyone she knew on the winning side, demanding better treatment by the victors for the vanquished. She tried also to insist that the latter be treated as prisoners of war who, even then, had at least some right to a basic level of humane treatment. Her friends and relatives in high places begged her to stop what she was doing. She was in danger of getting them all into trouble by identifying herself so closely with the losing side. She despised that attitude, declaring those who held it to be 'chicken-hearted' and carried on regardless, nothing daunted by being arrested four times whilst she was doing so.

Among others, she was closely questioned by Captain Stratford Eyre. He had quickly made himself hated by the Jacobite prisoners. He seemed to actively enjoy seeing them subjected to cruel treatment. Anne Leith told him less than nothing. Suspecting that they were looking for a way to punish her, she stated that her deceased husband had been a serving naval officer. This would have entitled her to a pension which could have been withdrawn. The story was untrue but it gave her a great deal of satisfaction to send them fruitlessly searching through the lists.

Anne Leith remained a committed Jacobite throughout the rest of her life. In going out to Culloden mere hours after the end of a horrendously bloody battle, she showed great bravery. Over a period of weeks she brought practical help and emotional succour to Jacobite prisoners. She refused to be frightened out of trying to secure better treatment for them.

It's interesting, then, to ask why there is no statue to her in front of Inverness Castle, as there is to Flora MacDonald. In fact, like almost all of the women who played an active part in the events of 1745–46, Anne Leith has been totally forgotten.

As has been demonstrated, contemporary commentators reported enthusiastically on the large numbers of women involved in the '45. Subsequent chroniclers of the period have contrived to render all but one of them invisible. That the limelight has stayed fixedly on Flora MacDonald has effectively obscured the other women, many of whom might have a much better claim to being Jacobite heroines.

It would be easy to blame the Victorian historians for this. It was they who began the selection process, sifting out of some of the more assertive Jacobite women in favour of concentration on the womanly, compliant and largely silent Flora MacDonald. That they did so says a lot about their attitudes to what they considered the proper female role within their own society.

It's harder to understand why modern historians continue to peddle the construct that only one woman played a significant role in the Jacobite Rising of 1745. Academic historians are just as guilty as popular ones in this regard. Is this deliberate suppression, laziness, or lack of interest?

Whichever it is, it's profoundly dishonest. We all, perforce, see history through our own filters: nationality, cultural background, gender, education, prejudices. Our first duty to the past is surely to push all of those as far back as we can and endeavour to seek the truth: not the truth we hope to find, but the one which is actually there.

Many have tried to write the women of the '45 out of history. They have not succeeded.

NOTES
1. See *Jacobites of Aberdeenshire and Banffshire in the Forty-Five* (1928), Tayler, A. & H. (eds.), Aberdeen: New Spalding Club.
2. Reproduced in *Jacobite Correspondence of the Atholl Family* (1840), Edinburgh: Abbotsford Club.
3. As quoted in *A Jacobite Miscellany* (1948), Tayler, H. (ed): Roxburghe Club.
4. As quoted in *Damn' Rebel Bitches: The Women of the '45*, see below.

FURTHER READING
Anon. (1745), *An Epistle From A British Lady To Her Countrywomen*, London: M. Cooper.
Anon. (1747), *The Female Rebels*, Dublin: G. Faulkner.
Black, Jeremy (1990), *Culloden and the '45*, Stroud: Alan Sutton Publishing Ltd.
Craig, Maggie (1997), *Damn' Rebel Bitches: The Women of the '45*, Edinburgh: Mainstream Publishing.
Douglas, Hugh (1994), *Flora MacDonald: The Most Loyal Rebel*, London: Mandarin.
Forbes, Rev. Robert (1895), *The Lyon in Mourning*, Edinburgh: Scottish History Society.
Livingston, Aikman & Stuart Hart (1985), *Muster Roll of Prince Charles Edward Stuart's Army 1745–46*, Aberdeen: Aberdeen University Press.
Macdonald, F. (1987), *'Colonel Anne' – Lady Anne Mackintosh*, Edinburgh: Edinburgh University Press.
McLynn, Frank (1998), *The Jacobite Army in England 1745*, Edinburgh: John Donald Publishers Ltd.
Prebble, John (1961), *Culloden*, London: Penguin.
Ray, James (1759), *Compleat History of the Rebellion*, London: Robert Brown.
Seton & Arnot (1928), *The Prisoners of the '45*, Edinburgh: Scottish History Society.
Public Record Office, London, *State Papers Domestic George II, Treasury Solicitors Papers (TSII), The 1745 Rebellion Papers (TS20), Court of King's Bench Papers (Baga de Secretis), Patent Rolls.*
Woodhouselee Manuscript (1907), Edinburgh: W. & R. Chambers.

SIX

Abandoned and Beastly?: The Queen Caroline Affair in Scotland

Catriona M.M. Macdonald

From Abbotsford in the summer of 1820, Sir Walter Scott reflected on Queen Caroline's return from the Continent:

> The Queen is making an awful bustle, and though by all accounts her conduct has been most abandoned and beastly, she has got the whole mob for her partisans, who call her injured innocence, and what not. She has courage enough to dare the worst, and a most decided desire to be revenged of *him*, which, by the way, can scarce be wondered at. If she has as many followers of high as of low degree (in proportion) and funds to equip them, I should not be surprised to see her fat bottom in a pair of buckskins, and at the head of an army – God mend all. The things said of her are beyond all profligacy. No body of any fashion visits her. I think myself monstrously well clear of London and its intrigues, when I look round my green fields.[1]

Not everyone shared Scott's opinion, and the Scottish Borders, like the rest of Scotland, were not to prove immune to the controversy surrounding the Queen. The *Caledonian Mercury* admitted at the time that events surrounding the Queen 'engross . . . the attention of the public to the exclusion of every other topic'.[2] And Henry Cockburn would later reflect that the affair 'threw Edinburgh . . . into great agitation', and 'the whole nation into a ferment'.[3]

Virtue and Propriety

In June 1820, having spent the previous seven years of her life in exile on the Continent, exciting rumours of adulterous relations with an Italian servant, Caroline of Brunswick – the wife of the Prince Regent – returned to England.[4] The occasion of her return was the death of George III, and the prospect of her re-emergence in courtly circles posed a challenge both to the interests which had developed around the Prince since her departure and the Tory administration which had been recently elected. In light of such circumstances, and given her status as the mother of the late heir to the throne – the 'saintly' Princess Charlotte – Caroline proved a valuable, if unlikely, heroine for political reformers.[5] Her attempts to assert her 'rights' as the British queen would become test cases of political freedom and expressions of popular morality.

Stepping off her launch at Dover on 5 June 1820, Caroline arrived in a country experiencing a period of significant change, as industrialisation and dramatic population growth irresistibly re-made British society. Significantly, as Dorothy Thompson notes:

> many of the changes that occurred involved the moving of authority
> from the private sphere of household and family to the public one
> of local or national government . . . Institutions came under scrutiny
> and were subject to criticism, established custom and tradition lost
> much of its power and in many areas became subject to rational
> critiques and to movements for reform.[6]

In the controversy surrounding Caroline as royal wife and mother, and in the drama which accompanied the Bill of Pains and Penalties instigated by the Prince Regent against his erring wife, the worlds of private and public collided in spectacular fashion. Questions of personal morality became constitutional dilemmas; the partners in a marriage became the personifications of conflicting political 'causes'; and the cultural icons of the monarchy became motifs in popular doggerel. The institutions of marriage and the state, through the operation of the law, 'publicised' the private sphere of personal relations and brought to the fore the inherent conflicts in popular perceptions of vice and virtue.[7]

Over the years, the Queen Caroline affair has attracted historiographical controversy. Anna Clark has suggested that the affair 'enabled radicals to develop a populist political language that could mobilise a mass movement . . . decisively transformed radical notions of manhood, and . . . established a place in politics for women's issues as well as for women activists'.[8] Yet W.H. Fraser – looking at the Scottish context – has commented on the 'irrelevancy of the Queen Caroline affair' in the north.[9] More recently, however, Christopher Whatley has emphasised that evidence of the 'affair' has attracted 'remarkably little notice' among Scottish historians.[10]

At root, an analysis of Scottish events suggests that the Queen Caroline affair is most usefully 'read' as an occasion of cultural self-appraisal – a point at which the constructed and contested nature of concepts of vice and virtue/normality and deviancy were made starkly apparent, and brought to the fore important questions of power and authority. As commentators observed at the time, Caroline's guilt or innocence was largely irrelevant, and apologists rarely explained their support of the Queen in terms of her virtue.[11] Rather, the dichotomies of guilt and innocence, and vice and virtue, rarely coincided. The essence of the affair is more likely to be found in the manner in which interest groups narrativised events. Groups did not merely observe and recount events, their story-telling *created* the affair. This was as much a literary phenomenon as it was a series of material events.

Self-interest guided the narrative perspectives of competing groups who found the Queen's story remarkably malleable. What is more, it was an issue which delivered passionate public sentiment in a compelling manner to causes, such as constitutionalism and reform, which had till then seemed somewhat pale imitations of radical interests.

Close examination of the manner in which reforming interests shaped the Caroline narrative and harnessed public sentiment is instructive. After all, in Scotland, Caroline's 'cause' attracted far greater support than the fabled Radical War of April 1820 and encompassed a far wider geographical area than the depressed industrial west-central belt which had been the principal locale for the spring protests. Petitions in support of the Queen from north of the Border were numerous, and on the conclusion of the debates at Westminster, illuminations celebrating the Queen's victory were recorded in over eighty areas by the contemporary press.[12] Indeed, in Pittenweem locals rang the bell so hard in honour of the queen's triumph that it 'perished in the cause, being tumbled from its belfry'; in the Castle Douglas area 'almost every hill was surmounted by a blazing bonfire'; and in Hawick the horses of the Earl of Minto's carriage were replaced by revellers who dragged him in triumph.[13]

Two overlapping sets of values proved the most contested terrain of the affair – morality and legal authority. For Caroline to prove reforming heroine, rather than royal libertine, each of these areas of influence had to be won by popular acclaim. For the reformers, the challenge was to exploit the spaces on the margins of conventional morality and re-affirm Adam Smith's observation that 'there is . . . a considerable difference between virtue and mere propriety . . . there may frequently be a considerable degree of virtue in those actions which fall short of the most perfect propriety'.[14]

Morality

> Most gracious Queen, we thee implore
> To go away and sin no more;
> But lest this effort be too great
> To go away at any rate.[15]

Michel Foucault suggested in *The Use of Pleasure* that morality implied 'a set of values and rules of action that are recommended to individuals through the intermediary of various prescriptive agencies such as the family, educational institutions, churches and so forth'.[16] Yet he also admitted that rules and values were also 'transmitted in a diffuse manner so that, far from constituting a systematic ensemble, they form a complex interplay of elements that counterbalance each other out on certain points, thus providing for compromises and loop-holes'.[17] The Caroline affair in Scotland illustrates a number of important 'loop-holes' in the Scottish moral code which were exploited by reformers.

A cursory glance at the writings of Scottish moralists would suggest that Caroline's actions, in the context of the times, would have been considered deviant.[18] After all, as many commentators have suggested, popular belief at the time held that 'the full force of sexual desire [was] seldom known to a virtuous woman'.[19] The ideal woman depicted in the writings of eighteenth-century authors such as James and David Fordyce and John Gregory was marked by her 'sensibility', 'complacency' and tenderness within a domestic environment.[20] By contrast, the evidence of Caroline's indiscretions suggested a woman at odds with the moral ideal. At her 'trial' former employees recorded the close friendship of Caroline and her equerry Bartolemo Pergami, and shared lurid details of indiscreet embraces and intimate sleeping arrangements.[21]

Surprisingly, such behaviour *could* be both accommodated on the fringes of the code suggested by moralist authors and upheld by the Scottish reformers. The idealised vision of femininity offered by moralist authors was rooted in a complementary relationship between the partners in a marriage.[22] And in this relationship, men were responsible for sustaining a domestic environment in which the powers of female sentiment could flourish. The Caroline case provided a ready lesson in what would happen if the male role was neglected, as much as an instructive warning against female 'liberation'. George's neglect condemned Caroline to the temptations of the public realm, and deprived her of the nurture of home, household and husband.

Such values were evident in the reporting of the press at the time, in the rhetoric of reformers and in the addresses of Caroline and her supporters. As the Queen's 'trial' proceeded, and Caroline sought accommodation in the homes of supporters, the otherwise less-than-sympathetic *Glasgow Herald* noted:

> If a man will not allow his wife to live in the house with him, he must surely provide her with another. A married woman is not to lie in the streets, and if her own husband is not bound to give her lodging, we should be glad to know who is.[23]

The *Scotsman* – sympathetic to the Queen's cause – lamented that during a period of economic crisis, Parliament was being caught up in the 'criminations and recriminations of *husband and wife*'.[24] Yet it seized the opportunity to highlight George's culpability in both the moral and legal sense:

> Expelled from the roof and society of her husband, in the first year
> of her married life, while confessedly an innocent woman, and forced
> to remain in that state of cruel separation, her Majesty, even if she
> shall have subsequently erred, is to be pitied as much as blamed; and,
> in no other case, would any errors of a wife, committed under such
> circumstances of estrangement, entitle the husband to a legal remedy.
> The pain and disgrace would be held, in a court of law, to have been
> of his own seeking. He would be considered as having provoked and
> deserved his fate.[25]

According to the *Scotsman*, George's conduct was 'unfeeling and unmanly', 'dangerous and unconstitutional', leaving Caroline 'an unprotected and friendless female' – 'a persecuted woman' in the eyes of the public.[26] Not surprisingly, Caroline exploited such moral outrage. In her address to the Highland Society of London, she called on Highland sentiment, and styled herself as a 'fond mother, roaming like an exile in a distant land'.[27]

More prosaically, Carolinite sympathisers questioned whether the Queen was really more wicked than the 'moral majority'. Again, the *Scotsman* pointed to the affair as an exemplar of a more common state of affairs by highlighting that Caroline's 'faults, failings and foibles' were shared 'in common with the rest of her species'.[28] In this regard, fictional incident is instructive. In John Galt's *The Ayrshire Legatees*, Rev. Pringle writes from the vantage point of contemporary London to Mr Micklewham, the schoolmaster of Garnock, of the Queen's plight:

> Anent the queen's case and condition, I say nothing; for be she
> guilty or be she innocent, we all know that she was born in sin, and
> brought forth in iniquity – prone to evil, as the sparks fly upwards –
> and desperately wicked, like you and me, or any other poor Christian
> sinner, which is reason enough to make us think of her in the
> remembering prayer.[29]

Popular morality and its appeal to 'everyman' sentiments was a powerful force. On the Queen's return to England, Henry Brougham recorded: 'It is impossible to describe the universal and strong, even violent, feelings of the people'.[30] Galt also recorded the Queen's 'common touch' later in Pringle's letter: 'She seems to be a plump and jocose little woman: gleg, blithe and throwgaun for her years, and on an easy footing with the lower orders – coming to the window when they call for her, and becking to them'.[31]

It would be hard to overstate the fellow-feeling which Caroline's case encouraged in the population and the unprecedented interest in constitutional matters which it solicited. The moral dimension of the affair facilitated the mobilisation of popular support behind the cause of reform on a scale which petitions and parliamentary debates had failed to encourage. Cockburn reflected in later years that the sentiments of a large portion of the nation 'fixed on the Government a more intense feeling of hostility than is usually produced by ordinary party differences. It was almost a personal hostility'.[32] As Bagehot would reflect half a century later, 'A family on the throne is an interesting idea ... It brings down the bride of sovereignty to the level of petty life'.[33]

Authority

> ... both the religious and legislative establishment of the country has collected rust and dirt; but to destroy the best constitution in the world, when it only requires cleaning, would argue folly, not wisdom; ignorance not skill; vice, not virtue.
>
> *A Letter Addressed to the Honest Reformers of Scotland*
> (Glasgow, 1819)

The rhetoric of legitimacy and authority was central to the reformers' appropriation of Caroline's cause, and provided the means by which moral outrage – both public and private – attained political expression. George's failure as a husband was easily re-worked to suggest his unreliability as monarch. Caroline's response to a petition from Sunderland is instructive in its reliance on this device:

> General tyranny usually begins with individual oppression. If the highest subject in the realm can be deprived of her rank and title – can be divorced, dethroned, and debased, by an act of arbitrary power, in the form of a Bill of Pains and Penalties, the Constitutional liberty of the Kingdom will be shaken to its very base. The rights of the nation will be only a scattered wreck; and this once free people, like the meanest of slaves must submit to the lash of insolent domination.[34]

Against such a threat the Constitution promised to be freedom's sole defence, and reformers eagerly highlighted the unconstitutional nature of the King's actions. The rhetoric of constitutionalism offered a shared language to both reformers and radicals and facilitated the smooth transition of public outrage into political discontent. Few could argue against constitutional principle, and in the circumstances there was little capital to be made in squabbling over the specificities of the reform agenda.

Significantly, the constitutional dynamic inverted the conventions of morality and re-cast the 'victim' in the royal drama. Throughout, Caroline's constitutional status rather than her marital status proved the most effective line of defence. By calling on constitutional principles, Caroline appeared 'more sinned against than sinning', as the weight of parliamentary power was mustered against her in support of royal self-interest.

It is not surprising, then, that the lasting legacy of the Caroline affair was the re-affirmation of the value of constitutional government. Following the King's defeat in the Lords, the *Scotsman* reflected:

> The spirit of the country is raised – and every man who sets
> any value on the Constitution acquired by the Revolution of
> 1688, or who feels any regard for his own and the welfare of his
> family, is now exerting himself to rescue his Sovereign from the
> councils of men who have acted equally as traitors to him and the
> Constitution.[35]

In December 1820 two 'monster meetings' held in Edinburgh and Glasgow marked a renewed interest in political reform. In Edinburgh, the famous Pantheon meeting attracted a sizeable audience and generated a petition of over 16,000 signatures demanding the dismissal of the King's advisors, while in Glasgow, a two-thousand strong audience listened to a 'temperate' defence of constitutional reform.[36] Looking back, Cockburn noted: 'Old Edinburgh was no more. A new day dawned on the official seat of Scotch intolerance . . . and all Scotland felt the result'.[37]

North of the Border, the Caroline affair encouraged unlikely bed-fellows, and unusual alliances in support of reform. Notably, the ire of the Scottish churches was raised early in the drama when an order from the King was issued demanding that Caroline's name would not be used in church prayers.[38] It seemed that ecclesiastical freedoms guaranteed in the Union settlement were under attack. 'A Presbyterian' wrote at the time:

> . . . no power in the empire, and no power upon earth has a legal
> title to prescribe forms of prayer for the use of our clergy. This
> has been immemorially a distinguishing feature of our ecclesiastical
> constitution.[39]

Galt's protagonist, Rev. Pringle, took great satisfaction in the prayers for the queen delivered in his church, noting that

> [It] is a thing to be upholden with a fearless spirit, even with the
> spirit of martyrdom, that we may not bow down in Scotland to

the prelatic Baal of an order in Council, whereof the Archbishop of
Canterbury, that is cousin-german to the pope of Rome, is art and
part. Verily, the sending forth of that order to the General Assembly
was treachery to the solemn oath of the new king, whereby he took
the vows upon him, to conform to the articles of the Union, to
maintain the Church of Scotland as by law established, so that for
the Archbishop of Canterbury to meddle therein was a shooting out
of the horns of aggressive domination.[40]

Again, the King's actions against his wife seemed to fly in the face of
constitutional principles and conventions.

Scottish national sentiment was also roused by Caroline's cause. Scots
were to the fore among her principal supporters, including Henry Brougham,
Caroline's Attorney General in the Lords; Lady Anne Hamilton, her loyal
Lady-in-Waiting; Lord Archibald Hamilton, the reforming Lanarkshire
MP; the Radical Joseph Hume MP (Aberdeen Burghs); and Lord Erskine.
In numerous addresses, the iconography and history of Scotland were
mustered to style the Queen the latest in a long line of victims of royal
aggression.[41] In response to the petitioners of St Andrews, Caroline
'wrote':

> Minds cast in Scotia's mould, as the Sons and Daughters of Scotia
> undoubtedly are, must ever be as favourable to the victims and
> martyrs of power as they are indignant at, and hostile to, the assassin
> blows, aimed at the semblance, or rather mockery of Justice, through
> me, at the rights and liberty of every British subject.[42]

In the political environment of the time, the King's conjugal failures were
easily re-cast as failures of legitimate authority, and constitutional rhetoric
styled Caroline's indiscretions as the consequence of poor domestic and
public 'government'. The reformers' narrative was therefore a defensive
one in which constitutional conventions became the benchmark of good
government.

The Caroline case clearly illustrates the significance of political circumstance and self-interest in the development of effective moral codes. Vice
and virtue are seldom given in an act or personified in an historical actor,
and rarely easy to predict in high-profile cases. The narrativisation of
events, however, has been shown to be a powerful tool in determining
popular perceptions of moral, legal and political rectitude. But did the
reforming interest in 1820 reform itself? Did it really re-evaluate female
virtue or were its aims rather more limited?

The Edinburgh address in support of Caroline was considered in jeopardy when it was rumoured that the Superintendent of Police had given orders to his sergeants to use 'every exertion in their power' to get the address signed by as many abandoned females as possible.[43] The *Edinburgh Weekly Journal* questioned the authenticity of an address to Caroline from the 'ladies of Edinburgh', concluding that 'these *soi-disant Ladies* of Edinburgh belong to a very low, if not the lowest class understood by that term'.[44] The pantheon meeting in Edinburgh was celebrated as a 'brilliant' and 'superior' gathering of the 'intelligent and well-dressed', and the petition which emerged from it was signed by men over the age of 21 years – female signatures were forbidden.[45]

Clearly, while there is evidence of an awareness of the complexity of female virtue in the case of the King's consort, the male-dominated reform agenda of the middling classes was not seriously re-addressed to accommodate broader perceptions of women's public role. Caroline had for a time certainly acted as 'an embodiment of abstract constitutional issues', but the insights regarding gender gleaned in this period largely failed to have a lasting impact.[46] As Anna Clark has commented: 'the iconography of the Caroline affair never challenged the fundamental principles of sexual difference'.[47]

By July 1821, indeed, the reformers had distanced themselves from their former heroine, and – at best – considered her attempts to attend the King's Coronation as 'imprudent'.[48] In a letter to the editor of the *Edinburgh Weekly Journal*, Sir Walter Scott suggested that her 'cause' was now 'a fire of straw which was now burnt to the very embers', and warned that 'those who try to blow it into life again, will only blacken their hands and noses, like mischievous children dabbling among the ashes of a bonfire'.[49] During the coronation festivities in Edinburgh, only one window boasted an effigy of the Queen crowned.

For the reformers, Caroline's womanhood, motherhood and marital status mattered only insofar as they enlivened the case for constitutional reform, by offering moral reproach as well as legal admonishment to her oppressors. The populism inherent in the affair was also eventually surrendered, as reformers became aware that the mob could not be controlled as easily as their rhetoric.[50] Morality had proved a potent weapon in the hands of men impatient for reform, and had proved malleable enough to sustain competing interests. Yet, its diffuse nature – even when bolstered by the rhetoric of the constitution – offered unstable foundations for the future.

Caroline also lived long enough to witness changed political circumstances, and to destroy the persona created for her by reformers in more sympathetic times. The political environment of 1820 had determined that Caroline's apparently disreputable conduct would be conveniently attributed by reformers to bad government. A year later – the cause of reform invigorated – the constitutional status of this uncrowned Queen no longer animated the reforming interest.

The Queen's Jaunt

When it was suggested in August 1821 that the Queen intended to visit Scotland, the *Edinburgh Weekly Journal* – unsympathetic to her cause at the best of times – noted: 'It appears to us, that she is every day rendering herself more and more unpopular'.[51] It went on to predict that 'though *canaille* enough may follow at her heels and pursue her with their rank huzzas, the respectable Whig society of Scotland will keep as much aloof from her and hers, as the whole body of the Tories'.[52] Regarding the Scottish capital – site of her earlier support – it suggested: 'There is not a city in the empire where her Majesty is less likely to obtain than in this, the distinction which she so anxiously courts'.[53]

The paper's predictions were never to be tested: within weeks Caroline was dead. Yet what if she had pre-empted George IV's famous jaunt in the north?

Sir Walter Scott, the architect of George's triumphant entry into Scotland in August 1822, and early opponent of the Queen's cause, agreed with various personal correspondents that the outcome of the Caroline affair had been the re-kindling of 'the passion for royalty'.[54] He suggested that the lasting legacy of interest in the Queen – referred to as the 'Bedlam Bitch' in a letter of 1821 – had worked against the reformers' cause: 'Unknown to these singularly absurd devotees, there was homage to the crown necessarily comprehended in homage to the queen, and never was the fascination of royalty more spread abroad, and more powerful in its operation'.[55]

The popular response to George's Scottish visit seems to reaffirm this impression. To one poet it appeared that 'Auld Reekie's turn'd a daft woman', and to the Rev. George Crabbe, the capital in August 1822 was 'A City clothed as a Bride . . . , and her King as her Bridegroom appears'.[56] Scott's Highland extravaganza certainly caught the public's imagination, and for a time pageantry eclipsed political wrangling.[57] One commentator suggested of the people of Edinburgh that.

> though party spirit had previously raged among them to a deplorable height, they suspended their animosities as if resolved, by mutual consent, there should be no alloy to the general happiness. Both parties seemed animated by one common feeling; and thus furnished a satisfactory and gratifying proof, had proof been wanting, that

difference of political opinion by no means necessarily occasions even a shade of difference in attachment to a constitutional monarch.[58]

A few months earlier, during the King's Birthday celebrations, an effigy of Caroline in Paisley bore the words, 'Am I to be forgotten?'

NOTES

1. Sir Walter Scott to Thomas Scott (son), 23 July 1820, in H.J.C. Grierson (ed.) (1934), *The Letters of Sir Walter Scott, Vol. VI*, London, 235.
2. *Caledonian Mercury*, 10 June 1820.
3. H. Cockburn (1909 ed., orig. 1856), *Memorials of his Time*, Edinburgh, 352.
4. For further biographical information, see E. Parry (1930), *Queen Caroline*, London; E.A. Smith (1993), *A Queen on Trial: The Affair of Queen Caroline*, Dover; T. Holme (1979), *Caroline: A Biography of Caroline of Brunswick*, London; F. Fraser (1996), *The Unruly Queen: The Life of Queen Caroline*, Basingstoke.
5. Marilyn Morris notes that on the birth of Charlotte, Caroline became a 'tragic heroine', as newspapers publicised her husband's affair with Lady Jersey. See Morris (1998), *The British Monarchy and the French Revolution*, New Haven, 167.
6. D. Thompson (1987), 'Women, Work and politics in Nineteenth-century England: the problem of authority', in J. Rendall (ed.), *Equal or Different: Women's politics, 1800–1914*, Oxford, 57–81.
7. For a discussion of the role of the law in personal relations, see M. Foucault (1986), *The Care of the Self: Volume 3, The History of Sexuality*, trans. R. Hurley, London.
8. A. Clark (1995), *The Struggle for the Breeches: Gender and the making of the British working class*, London, 164. See also (1990), 'Queen Caroline and the Sexual Politics of Popular Culture in London, 1820', *Representations* (31), 47–68.
9. W. H. Fraser (1988), *Conflict and Class*, Edinburgh, 113.
10. C.A. Whatley (2000), *Scottish Society 1707–1830: Beyond Jacobitism towards Industrialisation*, Manchester, 326–7.
11. As Henry Cockburn noted:
    That her Majesty was really innocent was the belief of many: that there was at least no legal evidence of her guilt was the belief of a majority of the nation: that even though she had been guilty, and her guilt had been legally established, its exposure was so dangerous that . . . no republicans wishing to bring monarchy into disrepute, could have done worse, was the opinion of almost all judicious loyalists.
    Cockburn, *Memorials*, 352.
12. Newspapers considered when arriving at this total: *Caledonian Mercury, Edinburgh Weekly Journal, Glasgow Courier, Glasgow Herald, Scotsman*.
13. *Scotsman*, 25 November 1820.
14. Adam Smith (1822 ed., orig. 1759), *The Theory of Moral Sentiments*, Edinburgh, 27.
15. This popular 'squib' dating from 1820 is recorded in Lady Charlotte Bury (1908), *Diary of a Lady in Waiting*, London, 273. Lady Charlotte was a

younger daughter of John, 5ᵗʰ Duke of Argyll, and was in the service of the
Queen intermittently between 1810 and 1815.

16. M. Foucault (1986), *The Use of Pleasure, Vol. 2 The History of Sexuality*,
    trans. R. Hurley, Middlesex, 25.
17. *Ibid.*, 25.
18. For a full analysis of the views of the Scottish moralists, see J. Dwyer (1987),
    *Virtuous Discourse: Sensibility and Community in Late-Eighteenth Century
    Scotland*, Edinburgh.
19. See R. Tannahill (1981), *Sex in History*, London, 336; also R. Eisler (1995),
    Sacred Pleasure: Sex, Myth and the Politics of the Body, New York.
20. Dwyer, *Virtuous Discourse*, 6, 189, 191.
21. Fraser, *Unruly Queen, passim*.
22. As Dwyer makes clear. 'In order to maximise social virtue generally, the two
    sexes needed to complement one another', *Virtuous Discourse*, p. 126.
23. *Glasgow Herald*, 24 November 1820.
24. *Scotsman*, 1 July 1820.
25. *Scotsman*, 26 August 1820.
26. *Scotsman*, 28 October 1820, 18 November 1820, 25 November 1820.
27. *Glasgow Herald*, 22 December 1820.
28. *Scotsman*, 28 October 1820.
29. J. Galt (1978 ed., orig. 1820), *The Ayrshire Legatees*, Edinburgh, 106.
30. H. Brougham (1871), *The Life and Times of Henry Lord Brougham, Vol.
    2*, Edinburgh, 366.
31. Galt, *Ayrshire Legatees*, 107–8.
32. Cockburn, *Memorials*, 353.
33. W. Bagehot (1993 ed., orig. 1867), *The English Constitution*, London, 87.
34. *Glasgow Herald*, 7 August 1820.
35. *Scotsman*, 23 December 1820.
36. *Scotsman*, 30 December 1820.
37. Cockburn, *Memorials*, 355.
38. See Cockburn, *Memorials* 350. Also, A Presbyterian, *Vindication of the
    Ministers of the Church of Scotland who have prayed for the Queen by
    name not withstanding the Order in Council on that Subject*, Edinburgh, 1.
39. Presbyterian, *Vindication*, 6.
40. Galt, *Ayrshire Legatees*, 106.
41. See C.M.M. Macdonald (2002), '"Their laurels wither'd, and their name
    forgot": Women and the Scottish Radical Tradition', in R.J. Finlay and E.J.
    Cowan (eds.), *Scottish History: The Power of the Past*, Edinburgh.
42. *Glasgow Courier*, 14 September 1820.
43. *Scotsman*, 25 November 1820.
44. Extract from the *Edinburgh Weekly Journal* appearing in the *Glasgow Herald*,
    29 September 1820.
45. *Scotsman*, 23 December 1820.
46. Clark, *Struggle for the Breeches*, 165.
47. *Ibid.*, 173.
48. *Scotsman*, 21 July 1821.
49. Sir Walter Scott to the Editor of the *Edinburgh Weekly Journal*, 20 July 1821.
    As quoted in J.G. Lockhart (1902), *The Life of Sir Walter Scott, Vol. VI*,
    Edinburgh, 317.
50. In a letter to James Ballantyne, the Edinburgh printer, Sir Walter Scott noted

in July 1820: 'the fanaticism of the feeling remains entirely with the mob and is used by the others like any other means which the popular heads afford them of annoying the government'. In Grierson (ed.), *The Letters of Sir Walter Scott, Vol. VI*, London, 238.

51. *Edinburgh Weekly Journal*, 1 August 1821.
52. *Edinburgh Weekly Journal*, 1 August 1821.
53. *Edinburgh Weekly Journal*, 1 August 1821.
54. Various (1822), *Letters to Sir Walter Scott, Bart. On the Moral and Political Character and Effects of the Visit to Scotland in August 1822 of His Majesty King George IV*, Edinburgh, 128.
55. Letter referred to: Sir Walter Scott to James Ballantyne, 21 July 1821, in Grierson (ed.), *The Letters of Sir Walter Scott, Vol. VI; Ibid.*, 128–9.
56. Anon. (1822), *The King's Muster* in *A Narrative of the Visit of George IV to Scotland in August 1822*, Edinburgh, 117; G. Crabbe, *Lines, ibid.*, 113.
57. See Lockhart, *The Life of Sir Walter Scott, Vol. VII*, 48–63.
58. Anon. (1822), *A Historical Account of His Majesty's Visit to Scotland*, Edinburgh, 118.

FURTHER READING

Lady Charlotte Bury (1908), *Diary of a Lady in Waiting*, London.
A. Clark (1995), *The Struggle for the Breeches: Gender and the making of the British working class*, London.
H. Cockburn (1909 ed., orig. 1856), *Memorials of his Time*, Edinburgh.
J. Dwyer (1987), *Virtuous Discourse: Sensibility and Community in Late-Eighteenth Century Scotland*, Edinburgh.
F. Fraser (1996), *The Unruly Queen: The Life of Queen Caroline*, Basingstoke.
W. H. Fraser (1988), *Conflict and Class*, Edinburgh.
J. Galt (1978 ed., orig. 1820), *The Ayrshire Legatees*, Edinburgh.
T. Holme (1979), *Caroline: A Biography of Caroline of Brunswick*, London.
M. Morris (1998), *The British Monarchy and the French Revolution*, New Haven.
E. Parry (1930), *Queen Caroline*, London.
E.A. Smith (1993), *A Queen on Trial: The Affair of Queen Caroline*, Dover.
C.A. Whatley (2000), *Scottish Society 1707–1830: Beyond Jacobitism towards Industrialisation*, Manchester.

PART TWO

Twisted Vice: Women, Crime and Punishment

SEVEN

Crime or Culture? Women and Daily Life in Late-Medieval Scotland

Elizabeth Ewan

On 9 September 1513 the Scottish army under James IV suffered a terrible defeat at the Battle of Flodden. The following day news of the disaster began to reach Edinburgh. The town council, unsure if the rumours were true, ordered the inhabitants to ready themselves for possible English attack. Furthermore, they ordered 'all women, and especially vagabonds, that they pass to their labours and be not seen upon the street clamouring and crying, and that the other good women pass to the kirk and pray'.[1]

The town fathers wanted potentially disorderly women off the streets, safe and out of sight in the private world of the household, around which they believed women's lives should revolve. Only 'good women' were allowed onto the streets, and this only so that they could pass to the house of God to pray for the souls of their husbands. But the streets of Scottish towns were as much female space as male space. Attempts to restrict women to a secluded household world led to contradictions which could result in women's daily lives and activities bringing them into conflict with the law.

Ironically, officials' attempts to keep women off the streets, or at least to keep firm control over their activities there, actually increased women's public visibility by ensuring that they frequently appeared in the burgh court, the heart of the community's public life. From the fifteenth century onwards, burgh court records survive in some numbers for Scottish towns, casting light on women's lives. The burgh court was at the very centre of urban government.[2] Here municipal officers were elected, statutes governing townspeople's lives were decided and declared, and those who broke the laws were punished.

Because women were barred from political office, they did not participate in the making of the statutes, although this did not protect them from prosecution when they broke them. The authorities were concerned with maintaining a world of good order and regulation, of social and gendered hierarchy. The problem was that the work of caring for a household meant that women often had to ignore both regulations and hierarchy. The resulting statutes meant that certain of women's common activities became defined as 'crimes'. The women who committed such crimes would not have regarded them in this light as it was these activities which shaped women's culture, the world of their everyday lives. I will examine three areas in which this clash of crime and culture took place – providing the necessities of life, caring for the physical and material health of the household, and attempting to live outside acceptable household structures. I also examine the extent to which women themselves helped to define and police 'acceptable behaviour' by other women.

Regulation of townspeople's lives was affected by gendered perceptions of appropriate behaviour for men and women.[3] For women, this meant life should centre on concerns of household and family, rather than public life and politics. Women provided economic and other services essential to the survival of the household. However, 'within both the rhetoric of social order and the practicalities of male organizational institutions, women were nevertheless seen as subordinate and peripheral'.[4] Thus women should be responsible for the wellbeing of the household, but should carry out their activities quietly and unobtrusively, and always in obedience to the male head of the household. The problem was how to make precept fit practice, when successfully carrying out the activities necessary to maintain the household required assertive and independent behaviour.[5] 'Women trod a difficult line between conforming to their subordinate status in society and possessing enough forcefulness and independence to live successfully in precarious social and economic conditions.'[6]

Women generally accepted the prevailing beliefs about the household being the centre of their world. Indeed their legal status, unlike that of men, was defined by their marital status. Upon marriage, a woman's legal status became that of a minor, and she was under the authority of her husband. Full independent legal status was only regained if she was widowed. Moreover, unlike men, who often found their identity in the communal world of town politics, craft gilds or less formal brotherhoods of workers, women, denied full membership in such groups, rarely identified themselves by occupational status.[7]

However, 'care of the household' was a broader concept for women than it was for the authorities who enacted the regulations affecting their lives. The boundary between the 'private' world of the household and the 'public' world of the street might concern the town authoriteis, but in women's daily lives, it was so permeable as to be almost non-existent. Women's household concerns and activities went beyond the closed con- fines of their own house and out into the streets to embrace a community and culture where women not only carried out the activities necessary for looking after their own family but extended help, companionship, and criticism to the women of neighbouring households as well.

The sociability and public nature of women's lives were rarely commented upon by contemporaries, but glimpses of this world can be caught. Female servants gathered together doing the laundering in streams or lochs, women met at the common wells while collecting water for the household, or at bakehouses to have their bread baked, childbirth was attended by female attendants only, the markets brought together women for both buying and selling, and women gathered together in the taverns. 'Female sociability found little place in the conduct-books but it was central to female experience.'[8] Women also helped each other out in numerous informal ways which only rarely appear in the records, and then only when such conduct was seen as a problem. It was this female culture which could find itself at odds with narrower definitions of women's proper household role and could lead to everyday female activities being defined as 'criminal'.

The areas examined here all had close connections with the household. It was women's expected role to provide food and drink for the family. They were also expected to care for the physical health of family members. Single women who lived alone or with other women, and thus outside the ideal household model, were regarded with suspicion and suspected of prostitution. In general, women accepted the ideal and policed certain types of behaviour which were at odds with it. However, they also realised the impractical nature of the ideal of the meek, submissive woman when it came to coping with the realities of everyday life and caring for their households. The conflict between women's view of the household and the way it shaped the culture which they created and the narrower definition espoused by the authorities could result in the labelling of women's activities in support of the household as 'crimes'.

Women were not a homogenous group, although sometimes legislation aimed at women in general treated them in that way. Gendered expectations had a role to play here. Perceptions of the appropriate role for women were governed by attitudes about respectability – certain women, especially those of the elite, were considered to be 'good women' of whom a higher moral standard of behaviour, especially sexual behaviour, was expected. 'Good women' were also given extra protections against those who might be seen as a danger to them. Reputation was a valuable commodity which could however be lost; it was important to protect it even within one's own social group. Women, indeed, were among those who policed such ideals most carefully.

Providing the necessities of life

One of the basic duties of wives and mothers was to provide food, drink and other necessities for household members, although the money to buy these was expected to come largely from the male household head. Provisioning involved women in marketing, and necessitated their frequent presence on the streets, especially the marketplace, where goods were bought and sold. Indeed markets seem to have been very much 'women's places'.9 Women's importance can be seen in two pieces of legislation passed by the Aberdeen town council, almost a century apart. In 1438, during the worst harvest of the century, in order to conserve supplies, women were banned outright from purchasing meal in the market; only men could buy. As the need to conserve was desperate, the council must have expected this to make a huge difference, implying that women were major purchasers of meal. This impression is supported by legislation in the less troubled year of 1522, when it was decided that eight women, two from each quarter of the town, should meet each market day with the sellers of malt and meal and agree on the accepted price for the day. 'As the dominant buyers, they knew best the state of the market and the going price.'10

Marketing was an accepted sphere for female activity outside the household, but it was also an activity which was closely regulated and controlled. Women found themselves on the wrong side of the law in a number of ways, by breaking the statutes which governed transactions there, by attempting to circumvent the market in their buying and selling, and by contravening regulations controlling production outside the marketplace.

The market was held on certain days in specific places and between certain hours so that all townspeople might have equal opportunity to buy. There were statues governing the price and quality of goods, and baillies and other town officers such as flesh-apprisers and ale-tasters were empowered to enforce them. Goods were to be openly displayed, weights and measures were to be authorised by the town. Even the process of buying was subject to regulation. For example, when goods were purchased, but not paid for immediately, it was the custom to give a token sum or 'earnest money' to seal the bargain. The price of the goods, if not already set by the town, had to be agreed before this earnest money was given. In 1513 the town council of Aberdeen ruled that no-one was to try to pre-empt another purchaser by giving more earnest money than had already been agreed with the first buyer.11

On various occasions, usually at times of scarcity, warfare, or political upheaval, the amount which could be purchased by one person was restricted, turning what were common transactions for many women into crimes. For example, in the 1438 legislation mentioned above, men were only allowed to buy as much meal as would sustain their own household. There were also restrictions on other staple foodstuffs. These particular regulations were unusually strict in banning women completely. However, similar restrictions, allowing purchasers, both men and women, to buy only as much as would sustain their own household, were imposed at one time or another in many towns, usually as a short-term response to shortages.[12]

Such restrictions tended to hurt women more than men, as it was usually women who bought more than their household needed for its own subsistence. The problem with the market was that it did not meet the needs of all the town's inhabitants. It was designed first and foremost for the elite of the town, the burgesses, perhaps a third of the population at most, who could afford to buy wholesale and at the prices set by the council. There were many others, perhaps the majority, who scraped a living and could afford only to buy small amounts on a daily basis. These needs were met by women who bought and sold outside the marketplace.

Women commonly purchased extra supplies, either to sell again in smaller quantities to their neighbours who could not afford to buy wholesale at the market,[13] or to use to produce food and drink to sell to other families. These activities were often an essential component of women's contribution to the economy of the household. However, they were not viewed in this way by town officials suspicious of any unregulated buying and selling of food outside the market. The majority of these marketers were women.[14] Hucksters, as those who resold market goods were known, were grudgingly tolerated by the authorities when times were good, but their activities were among the first to be repressed when famine, plague or other disasters threatened the town. Even when they were allowed to function, they faced various restrictions. They might only be allowed to buy towards the end of the market day, when the needs of the burgesses had been satisfied, and the best produce had been sold; in Selkirk in 1528 hucksters could not buy foodstuffs until after four. They might be restricted to certain types of victual. In 1517 the Selkirk hucksters were prohibited from dealing in flesh, fish, victual, butter, cheese or salt.[15]

There were many points of contact between urban women and the country women who brought their produce to market. Many of their female customers were recent immigrants, drawn to the town through domestic service or marriage.[16] Such contacts could be used to 'forestall' the market, buying goods before they came to the marketplace and avoiding market tolls. The goods were then resold, either from the purchaser's house, or door-to-door. Jonet Howk, accused of forestalling barley in Dundee in 1521, was also charged with selling it from her house.[17] This type of selling suited women, as the tasks in which they engaged with other women meant they were well-informed about neighbouring families' needs.[18]

The authorities objected to these activities on two grounds. Financially, forestallers undercut the market, defrauding the town of market tolls and potentially causing shortages if they bought up large amounts of produce, while hucksters introduced an element of unfair competition in the purchase of goods. Moreover, such unregulated retail activities were not seen as a necessary part of women's lives by the authorities[19] and were viewed with suspicion. Thus a common activity in many women's daily lives faced constant risk of being defined as 'criminal' whenever the authorities thought it appropriate.

Women who sold outside the market could be found guilty of other unauthorised practices as well. Selling oatcakes was periodically banned, because the authorities wanted to preserve the supply of oats for the town baxters (bakers). Most 'cake baxters' were women, unable to join the baxters' guild and to invest capital in an expensive oven for baking bread. Oatcakes could be produced cheaply and easily with small quantities of oats baked over a hearth fire. The cake baxters' clients were the town's poor who could not afford the more expensive bread sold by baxters.[20] Women thus provided an essential item for the poor, but faced possible prosecution for doing so. Cake baxters were occasionally allowed to function freely, sometimes as a desperate measure in times of famine,[21] at other times in closely controlled numbers as in Stirling in 1525,[22] but generally their activities were frowned upon. Being charged with cake baking was one of the most common reasons women found themselves before the town courts.

There was one product which women were allowed, and even encouraged, to produce in greater quantities than they needed to sustain their household. Ale was one of the staples of the urban diet, along with bread. While the baking of bread was largely in the hands of men,[23] the brewing of ale was dominated by women. In Edinburgh and Aberdeen, for example, hundreds of women were involved in this activity at some point in their lives.[24] Every woman was expected to know how to brew; the commercial activity developed out of her household responsibilities. Because ale was such a crucial part of the townspeople's diet, brewing, like baking, was closely regulated and supervised. Unlike many other crafts, however, including the baxters, brewsters did not form guilds. Individual brewsters were directly under the supervision of municipal officials. Each brewster was required to call the town-appointed ale conner or taster whenever she had ale ready to sell, and abide by the price which he set.[25] In a sense, the brewster was creating a temporary marketplace in her home, subject to town regulation; such conditions allowed the authorities to permit this commercial activity by women.

While ale-brewing by women was accepted, the fact that it was so heavily supervised meant that its practitioners often came into conflict with the law. Most towns regularly declared a set price for bread and ale.[26] Breaking the price of ale was one of the most common offences committed by medieval women. In England, where there was similar legislation on prices, long lists of women appear regularly in the town and village court records charged with this offence. So regular are these lists that it has been argued that the fines acted in effect as a licensing system.[27] However, Nicholas Mayhew has argued convincingly that the punishments imposed on Scottish women for brewing offences were genuine penalties and not a licensing system. The lists do not appear regularly enough to have functioned as a licensing system. Moreover, punishments might go beyond a simple fine, to expulsion from the occupation for a year or more, and even the destruction of brewing equipment.[28] Aberdeen brewsters who disobeyed the set prices in 1435 were to have their brewing vessels taken away from them, while in Dunfermline in 1500 the bottoms of their cauldrons were to be struck out.[29]

Although brewing was practised by women of all social classes, the authorities at times attempted to underpin the social hierarchy by restricting the brewing of more expensive ale, or even of all ale, to women of higher social status. In 1442 the more expensive ale in Aberdeen could only be brewed by families of guild members, although later in the century this privilege was extended to all wives of burgesses. In early sixteenth-century Edinburgh, brewing of ale for sale was restricted to the wives of burgesses. These restrictions do not appear to have been terribly successful.[30] Despite the authorities' efforts, brewing, carried out in the private world of numerous households as part of women's normal household duties, was difficult to regulate effectively.

As Mayhew has shown, price regulation was sometimes challenged by women. Some asserted their opinions in the face of certain penalty. In 1540, when Gilbert Brabner's wife in Aberdeen was not only fined for selling ale at too high a price, but was also ordered to have it distributed free, she threw it away in anger and was not only fined again, but distrained for the value of the ale. Others attempted more discreet rebellion by taking away the set price marked on their doors by the ale-tasters, or using the same barrel but charging different prices for the ale.[31] In 1509 Bessy Layng went one step further, not only taking down the price written by the ale taster, but writing in another one herself.[32]

The frequency with which women were charged with price-breaking also suggests a certain degree of common resistance to the assize. Gemmill and Mayhew's study of medieval prices has suggested that ale prices in Aberdeen may have been set unrealistically low. Women who were fined for selling their ale at too high a price often sold at the same price as each other, a price more in line with those charged in other towns. One way around the assize was to risk charging a higher, more realistic price, and then, when caught, paying the resulting fine, perhaps by lowering production costs by economising on the quality of the ale for a period.[33] There is a hint of combined action in Dunfermline in 1492 when it was recorded that 'the community has forgiven the brewsters the fault of Yule'.[34] The fact that no individual names are given might imply that all the brewsters of the town acted together. In Dundee in July 1523 at least some brewsters seem to have been consulted by the council before it fixed the price of ale.[35]

Although brewing was an accepted activity for women, and there were sporadic attempts to confine it to women of the elite social groups, it did not in itself confer high status on its practitioners. Most women engaged in the activity only on a part-time basis, although a few appear to have made brewing a year-round pursuit.[36] There was a certain suspicion of ale-brewers, common to many of the food-purveyors on whom people depended. In the case of ale, there was the added problem that the product could impair the judgment of the purchaser, making it easier to suspect the worst of the seller.[37] The tavern and alehouse were popular sites for conviviality for both men and women, but alehouse keepers had to be assertive enough not only to deal with burgh officials but also with drunken customers and the problems they could cause. The path of business did not always run smoothly. When Kitty Blacot locked Thom Scharp out of her Dunfermline alehouse in 1503, he sued her for not giving him the drink for which he had paid.[38] Moreover, alehouses were often associated in the popular mind with dubious and criminal activities such as theft and prostitution. Working in an alehouse was not necessarily a good road to social respectability.

Caring for the health of the household

On certain occasions, especially times of crisis, activities which were normally an accepted part of women's responsibilities could become redefined as 'crimes'. The responses of the Edinburgh town council to outbreaks of plague in the early sixteenth century provide a good example of how this could happen. One area of women's lives that was affected was their responsibility for caring for the physical wellbeing of the members of their household. Women were expected to be the nurses and nurturers of their households, and in general the authorities supported and promoted this role. However, in times of plague, women's attempts to perform these functions led them into actions which became punishable by the court.

In October 1505, in an attempt to control the spread of plague, the Edinburgh town council ordered that any man or woman who had the rule and governance of a household, and who had a sick person within their house, must reveal the sickness to the baillies within 12 hours, under pain of burning on the cheek and banishing.[39] Women, used to caring for their families, and fearful of being cut off from society completely, often tried to hide the presence of sickness. Isobel Cattall, who had concealed her daughter's sickness for three days until she died, was banished with all her children under pain of death in 1530. George M'Turk and Molly Mudy his wife, as well as two other women of the household, were convicted of not revealing the sickness of their child to the officers until after it had died, and were condemned to be burned on the cheek and banished until the town allowed them to return. It seems that the two women, probably servants, conspired with the master and mistress of the household to conceal the sickness. One of them, Marion Sutherland, who had brought the sickness into the house, unknown to the others, was banished for life under pain of death.[40]

Attempts to isolate the disease led to statutes ordering houses to be closed[41] and forbidding communication with suspected households, thus shutting down one of women's main avenues of sociability. In 1505 it was ordered that 'no manner of person repair nor intercommune with any other person where any sickness happens without special license of the officers, under the pains as shall be thought expedient'.[42] The problems which enclosure could lead to were shown in 1530 when Isobel Bowy and Kate Boyd, both being shut up in their house as suspected of plague, drew on their network of female friends, taking feathers from a bed and giving them to Bessy Anderson to sell. It seems most likely that they were trying to raise money for provisions, but the council took a harsh view of their action which it saw as 'doing what was in them to infect the whole town'. Bowy and Boyd were banished for life, while Anderson was banished during the provost's will.[43]

Worse penalties awaited those who did not reveal their own sickness, and left the confines of their household. Jonet Cowane, a servant women who concealed the fact that she had the pestilence and who passed forth from her house to go on pilgrimage, presumably to ask a saint to restore her health, was sentenced to be burned on both cheeks and banished from the town forever.[44] The most severe penalty of all, however, was reserved for those who, being ill, went out and mingled among the townsfolk.

Marion Clerk, who had been ill for 10 days or more, went to mass
and to her sister's house, presumably for both spiritual and bodily aid.
When she was found out, she was convicted of attempting to spread the
pestilence, and was sentenced to be drowned.[45] Those who broke the
barrier between the household and the outside world in times of crisis
could pay with their lives.

The authorities also tried to prevent the movement of items such as cloth
which were suspected of harbouring infection; indeed the suspicion of
cloth was justified as clothing could harbour the fleas carrying the plague
bacillus, although this was not recognised at the time.[46] The prohibition
on cloth hit women especially hard, as this was a common item used for
acquiring loans, often from other women. In 1505, 'wedwives' (female
moneylenders) and female servants (who also lent money) were forbidden
to take any kind of cloth in pledge.[47] The penalties could be severe. Bessy
Symertoun, who concealed infected cloth in 1521, was branded on the
cheek and banished from the town. Katherine Heriot in October 1530 was
found to have stolen and concealed cloth, and thus brought 'contagious
sickness' into the town from Leith. She was sentenced to be drowned
immediately, while Margaret Baxter, who had received Katherine in her
house, was banished for life.[48]

Plague outbreaks also led to physical uprooting of households. Once
the disease had taken hold, it was common for towns to move their
infected citizens outside the walls. In Edinburgh, infected individuals and
families with infected members were sent to plague huts on the Borough
Muir. There they were to remain until it became clear that they were free
from infection; those who died were often buried in mass graves.[49] The
burden of caring for the household in such circumstances must have fallen
particularly hard on women, deprived of the financial resources normally
provided by their husbands and their own labour.

Living outside the household

Most of the women mentioned above were convicted for actions which
involved their families, but women without families also faced problems
with the authorities. The late fifteenth and early sixteenth centuries
witnessed increasing suspicion of those who lived alone, away from
the control of parents or masters. Paul Griffiths has defined the masterless young of early-modern England as those 'who were perceived
to have stepped outside the well-marked boundaries of the socialising
process by not being under the charge of an older householder and
who were labelled by magistrates as part of a definitional process of
criminal regulation, which was intended to publish and punish their

nonconformity'.⁵⁰ A similar definition seems to apply to the masterless young of Scotland.

Legislation prohibiting women from setting up independent households is found in England as early as the 1490s, but it was not long before similar legislation came to be enacted in many Scottish towns. Masterless young people were to 'pass to service', which for women meant finding employ-ment as domestic servants within a household. By 1530 the Edinburgh authorities ordered any landlords renting rooms to single women to expel them and that such women should be banished from the town.⁵¹ Living on one's own, if one was a woman, was becoming defined as a 'crime'.

Although fears of plague may have played a part in the timing of this legislation, it appears that the council also felt that it was becoming too easy for women to set up their own households. One route towards independence was the traditional female activity of brewing. Some female domestic servants gained experience in the business by brewing 'on their own adventure', that is, at their own expense while still employed as servants, giving part of the profits to their employers in return for use of the household brewing equipment. This skill was then put to good use after they left domestic service. As the council put it, 'there is no servant woman or nurse that gets in a good man's house through her service 5 or 6 merks [about £4] but she will take a house of her own and be a brewster or huckster'.⁵²

In order to make it more difficult for single women to brew, the council banned the common practice of hiring out brewing equipment, ordering that each brewster was to possess her own. In one stroke of legislation, the authorities managed to create a new crime for both the poorer women of the town and the wealthier women who might rent out the equipment. The legislation apparently did not stop the practice of hiring out equipment, but the seriousness with which the council regarded this new offence was underlined in 1553 when it warned anyone hiring out cauldrons for brewing that if the person renting it was found breaking the statutes of ale, the cauldron would be destroyed.⁵³ In other words, the person who owned the equipment was to bear part of the responsibility for its proper use.

It has been argued that the authorities' concern about women living independently was as much moral as economic, that it was feared that women on their own might easily slip into such morally questionable ways of earning their living as prostitution.⁵⁴ This certainly became a concern in Scotland after the Reformation of 1559–60. However, in the late Middle Ages, the attitude in Scottish towns seems to have been similar to that of most European towns. Prostitution was tolerated as a necessary evil, one which was best controlled by confining it within the quasi-household structure of a brothel. In 1426 Parliament had ordered that houses for 'common women' should be located on the edge of town.[55] At first sight this seems to be an attempt to control the trade by marginalising it geographically, but the statute explains that this was a precaution to reduce the peril of fire, suggesting the concern was more practical than moral. The spread of syphilis in the late 1490s may have helped lead to a hardening of attitudes; in 1497 the Aberdeen town council ordered that all 'light women' associated with the 'vice and sin of venery' leave off their occupation and pass to another trade or leave the town.[56] However, fears of the disease did not lead to an outright ban in most towns. Indeed in 1530 the Edinburgh magistrates saw only two possible futures for domestic servants leaving service – marriage or the brothel.[57] The second alternative was presumably intended for women who had been dismissed from service for pregnancy – the brothel was a way of controlling potentially unruly women and also provided a substitute household for the illegitimate child.

By the 1550s, however, probably under the influence of Reformation ideas about morality from the Continent and England, prostitution was regarded with increasing disfavour. Clothing regulations were passed so that prostitutes could be distinguished from 'honest men's wives'.[58] Again, as with the Flodden legislation of 1513, 'good women' were being distinguished from their less respectable sisters. Edinburgh, with its law courts, large numbers of clergy, and apprentices, had been recognised by the poet Dunbar in the early sixteenth century as a place where prostitution and illicit sexuality flourished,[59] but by the mid-sixteenth century the town council was becoming ashamed of this reputation. As part of an effort to curb it, they ordered in 1555 that only married men be accepted as burgesses, as unmarried men 'used themselves so unhonestly that the whole town has been shamed thereby'.[60] With the coming of the Reformation in 1559–60, efforts were made to stamp out prostitution altogether. What had been a legal, if not particularly approved of, method for many women to earn a living, now became a permanent crime to be rooted out and punished.

Fighting words

Prostitution, although tolerated by the medieval authorities, was regarded as an activity carried on by 'dishonourable women'. To a large extent, the definition of women's 'honour' as pre-eminently based on their sexual chastity, was accepted by women themselves. The imposition of standards of acceptable behaviour was not a one-way process, imposed on a passive populace from above. Authority had to be accepted by those over whom it was exercised in order to be effective.[61] As Laura Gowing has pointed out, women in their choice of insults tended to accept a double sexual standard which saw women's sexual honour as far more important than men's.[62] The insults used by women agaisnt other women were commonly sexual in nature – the most common term of abuse was 'whore' – calling into question their target's reputation for chastity. They were thus trying to uphold certain standards of sexual behaviour, although 'there was a fine line between upholding the moral order of the neighbourhood and participating in its destruction'.[63] Ironically, women's assertiveness in publicising their concerns often resulted in their finding themselves before the courts charged with the crimes of flyting (scolding or insulting) or defamation.

Although the ideal woman was portrayed as quiet or even silent, the realities of women's everyday lives meant that verbal assertiveness was a necessity. Buying and selling were activities which required a certain forwardness to carry them out successfully. The loud, jostling and competitive atmosphere of the marketplace where sellers called out their wares, and purchasers questioned the quality or disputed the price of the goods, easily gave rise to riotous and rude behaviour. There was a fine line between bargaining and insult. Disputes between buyers and sellers could turn violent either in word or deed or both. Michell Johnson, a fish-seller, and Maddy Jackson got into a major argument in Dunfermline in August 1503. Michell accused Maddy of damaging and discarding his fish without paying for them; he then accosted her and threw the platter she was carrying at the market cross. They both took each other to court, which found in favour of Maddy.[64] Physical assault was not restricted to men. Christian Inglis found herself before the Dunfermline court for accosting a man and striking his wife at the market cross in 1512.[65]

Women seem to have been especially associated with inappropriate verbal behaviour at the marketplace, perhaps because this was where women were most visible to the authorities. One of the poet Dunbar's complaints about Edinburgh was how the tone of the market was lowered by the 'fensum flytings of defame' (foul defamatory quarrels) of old women, especially fishwives.[66] The fishwives may have been regarded with special suspicion as most of them came from outside the town, bringing the fish their husbands caught from ports along the coast; they were not among the 'good women' of the town. Women fruitsellers were also especially noted for their independence and noisiness. Indeed one Edinburgh fruitseller showed little defence for hierarchy, not hesitating to demand payment from the King himself when she brought him cherries in 1497; the Treasurer records a payment to 'the wife who cried on [the King] for silver'.[67] In 1548 the Edinburgh town council ordered that no manner of woman, 'especially the fruit sellers', be found quarrelling on the High Street, otherwise they should be put in the jougs (an iron collar) for six hours.[68]

Most studies of scolding in other countries have argued that women were the main offenders in these types of crime. Certainly some Scottish men believed women had more of a propensity than men to verbal assault, whether by scolding or defamation. In some towns, women were specifically warned about the penalties they faced for scolding. In Selkirk, after a cuckstool was made in 1534, legislation followed four years later that 'evil-inclined women imputing infamity to their neighbour' were to be put on it.[69] However, 'Women were painted as harassers and haranguers by drawing on a powerful convention of "the scold", and we must be aware that the misbehaviour ascribed to such women may be evidence as much of that convention as it is of perceived or actual behaviour exhibited by the women concerned'.[70] In Edinburgh, women were not always singled out by the legislators. In 1503 the court judged that *persons* convicted of flyting and 'scaldrie' (scolding) were to be punished by public humiliation at the market cross.[71] Indeed in 1529 the town authorities blamed youths and fellows for causing disorder through their bickerings, and ordered their fathers and masters to control them.[72] Women were put on the cuckstool or in the stocks, but so were men.

In Peebles in 1471 women who insulted the respectable matrons of the town were punished by being forced to carry two stones in iron chains or a halter hanging on their shoulder to the four gates of the town.[73] Here, the main concern seemed to be with the reputation of the 'good women' of the town. As with the sixteenth-century legislation regulating the dress of prostitutes, it seems to have been mainly concern with the reputation of the good women of the town which led to some women being targeted. The distinction can be seen in a 1434 case from Aberdeen. Andrew Thomson, a flesher, was fined for assault on the wife of the taverner John Black, probably in the context of a drunken quarrel. Attacking the mistress of the tavern was not acceptable behaviour. He was fined and warned that if he ever committed such an assault, verbal or physical, against the 'honest women' of the town again, he would be banished.[74] The wording of the judgment implies that an assault against certain other women, perhaps the servants in the tavern, might not have brought such a severe threat.

Intemperate language could lead to an accusation of defamation by the person who was insulted, especially if the term 'whore' was used. The marketplace was a centre for the exchange of news and gossip, the site of meetings between folk of town and countryside. Gossip was (and is) a very powerful informal means of social control.[75] It was in the market that women 'fashioned reputations for themselves and others'.[76] Many defamation cases began with quarrels there. In an attempt to control such behaviour, the authorities sometimes imposed public penance rituals which also took place there, with the offender begging forgiveness of the victim at the market cross – many involved women, both as offenders and victims.[77] The publicity of such rituals ensured that those who might be most likely to commit such crimes were also the most likely to witness their punishment. However, by publicly vindicating the honour of the victims, the rituals also underlined the overwhelming importance of reputation.

Flyting and defamation were crimes which were associated with oral culture. The culture of women, who were much less likely than men to be literate, was overwhelmingly oral. It is significant that when the poet Robert Semple wished to criticise the politics of his day around 1560, he put his poems in the mouth of a market woman.[78] Maddie, a kale seller, pointed out how well-placed she was to hear about events as she sat in the market selling her kale. 'If men there walk, I hear their talk, and bears it well away.' Maddie may have been a male creation, but her real-life counterparts were to be found in any Scottish market. And it seems likely that despite government and church attempts to crack down on both written and verbal criticism in the post-Reformation period, the oral culture of the townswomen continued in its vitality, even if circumspectly.[79] Aspects of women's culture could be defined as crimes, but stamping out that culture completely was another matter altogether.

NOTES

1. *Extracts from the Records of the Burgh of Edinburgh [Edin Recs.],* (ed.) J.D. Marwick (Edinburgh, 1869–92), i, 143–4. The language of the sources in this paper has been translated from Middle Scots into modern English.
2. W.C. Dickinson. 'Introduction', in *Early Records of Aberdeen,* (ed.) W.C. Dickinson (Edinburgh, 1957).
3. Garthine Walker and Jenny Kermode, 'Introduction', in *Women, Crime and the Courts in Early Modern England,* (eds.) J. Kermode and G. Walker (London, 1994), 4.
4. Walker and Kermode, 'Introduction', 7.
5. Laura Gowing, *Domestic Dangers. Women, Words, and Sex in Early Modern London* (Oxford: Clarendon Press, 1996), 8; Susan Dwyer Amussen, *An Ordered Society. Gender and Class in Early Modern England* (Oxford, 1988), 119–21.
6. Lawrence Normand and Gareth Roberts, *Witchcraft in Early Modern Scotland* (Exeter, 2000), 61.
7. Walker and Kermode, 'Introduction', 7.
8. Bernard Capp, 'Separate Domains? Women and Authority in Early Modern England', in *The Experience of Authority in Early Modern England,* (eds.) P. Griffiths *et al* (Houndmills, 1996), 127–8.
9. Normand and Roberts, *Witchcraft,* 61.

10. Nicholas Mayhew, 'Women in Aberdeen at the end of the Middle Ages', in *Gendering Scottish History. An International Approach*, (eds.) T. Brotherstone *et al* (Glasgow, 1999), 146. The 1438 legislation is printed in Elizabeth Gemmill and Nicholas Mayhew, *Changing Values in Medieval Scotland. A study of prices, money, and weights and measures* (Cambridge, 1995), 78, Appendix I and discussed on p.63.

11. Aberdeen City Archives, Aberdeen Council Register, ix, 270. The process of purchasing goods in the market is discussed in Gemmill and Mayhew, *Changing Values*, 58–9.

12. For example, *Edin Recs*, i, 6, 53.

13. P.J.P. Goldberg, *Women, Work and Lifecycle in a Medieval Economy* (Oxford, 1992), 117–8.

14. In a list of those charged with such selling in Stirling, 25 out of the 27 people were women – the other two may also have been women, as their first names were blank. Stirling Council Archives, B66/15/1, Stirling Council Minutes, f.197r.

15. *The Burgh Court Book of Selkirk, 1503–45* [*Selkirk Recs*], (ed.) J. Imrie *et al* (Edinburgh, 1960–69), i, 93, 41.

16. I.D.Whyte and K.A. Whyte, 'The Geographical Mobility of Women in Early Modern Scotland', in *Perspectives in Scottish Social History*, (ed.) L. Leneman (Aberdeen, 1988), 83–106.

17. Dundee City Archives, Book of the Church, f.45v.

18. M. Wiesner Wood, 'Paltry Peddlers or Essential Merchants? Women in the Distributive Trades in Early Modern Nuremberg', *The Sixteenth Century Journal*, 12 (1981), 7, 10.

19. Grethe Jacobsen, 'Women's Work and Women's Role: Ideology and Reality in Danish Urban Society, 1300–1500', *The Scandinavian Economic History Review*, 31 (1983), 12.

20. Mayhew, 'Women in Aberdeen', 147.

21. Gemmill and Mayhew, *Changing Values*, 42.

22. In February the town permitted six cake baxters to work, but in April it increased the number to eight. Stirling Council Minutes, ff 109r, 118r.

23. There were some women baxters in most towns, although their numbers were usually small. Dundee Book of the Church, f.92r; *Selkirk Recs*, i, 33, ii, 148,220–1; *Charters and Documents Relating to the Burgh of Peebles* [*Peebles Recs*], (ed.) W. Chambers (Edinburgh, 1872), 147, 150.

24. Mayhew, 'Women in Aberdeen', 146–7; E. Ewan, '"For Whatever Ales Ye": Women as Consumers and Producers in Late Medieval Scottish Towns', in *Women in Scotland c.1100–c.1750*, (eds.) E. Ewan and M. Meikle (East Linton, 1999), 129–30.

25. *Selkirk Recs*, ii, 118.

26. *The Burgh Records of Dunfermline* [*Dunfermline Recs*], (ed.) E. Beveridge (Edinburgh, 1917), 19, 46, 101; *Edin Recs*, i, 12,62,75; *Peebles Recs*, 128, 147, 166; Stirling Council Minutes, ff 2v, 7v, 13r; *Early Records of Aberdeen*, 39, 41, 46, 53–4.

27. J. Bennett, *Ale, Beer and Brewsters in England: women's work in a changing world 1300–1600* (New York, 1996) 4, 161–3.

28. Nicholas Mayhew, 'The Status of Women and the brewing of Ale in Medieval Aberdeen', *Review of Scottish Culture*, 10 (1996–7), 18; Mayhew, 'Women in Aberdeen', 147–50. For a transcription and analysis of a 1509 list of

brewsters from Aberdeen, see N. Mayhew, 'The Brewsters of Aberdeen in 1509', *Northern Studies*, 32 (1997), 71–82.

29. *Extracts from the Council Register of the Burgh of Aberdeen* [*Aber Extracts*], (ed.) J. Stuart (Aberdeen, 1844–8), i, 390–1; *Dunfermline Recs*, 104.
30. Ewan, 'For Whatever Ales Ye', 130.
31. Gemmill and Mayhew, *Changing Values*, 29, 51–2.
32. Mayhew, 'Women in Aberdeen', 150.
33. Gemmill and Mayhew, *Changing Values*, 53
34. *Dunfermline Recs*, 33.
35. Dundee Book of the Church, f.150v.
36. E. Ewan, 'Mons Meg and Merchant Meg: Women in Later Medieval Edinburgh', in *Freedom and Authority: Scotland c.1050–c.1650*, (eds.) T. Brotherstone and D. Ditchburn (East Linton, 2000), 137.
37. J. Bennett, 'Misogyny, Popular Culture and Women's Work', *History Workshop Journal*, 31 (1991), 178–82.
38. *Dunfermline Recs*, 132.
39. *Edin Recs*, i, 106.
40. *Edin Recs*, ii, 30, 35.
41. For example, *Aber Extracts*, i, 427–8 (21 Aug 1500).
42. *Edin Recs*, i, 106.
43. *Edin Recs*, ii, 42.
44. *Edin Recs*, ii, 35–6.
45. *Edin Recs*, ii, 43.
46. T.C. Smout, 'Coping with Plague in Sixteenth and Seventeenth-Century Scotland', *Scotia* 2/1 (April 1978), 21–3.
47. *Edin Recs*, i, 106–7.
48. *Edin Recs*, i, 124; ii, 42.
49. Smout, 'Coping with Plague', 25–6.
50. Paul Griffiths, 'Masterless Young People in Norwich, 1560–1645', in *Experience of Authority*, 147.
51. *Edin Recs*, ii, 40.
52. *Edin Recs*, ii, 24–5, 27.
53. *Edin Recs*, ii, 177–8.
54. R. A. Houston, 'Women in the economy and society of Scotland 1500–1800', in *Scottish Society 1500–1800*, (eds.) R.A. Houston and I.D. Whyte (Cambridge, 1988), 132–3.
55. *The Acts of the Parliaments of Scotland*, (eds.) T. Thomson and C. Innes (Edinburgh, 1814–75), ii, 12 c.23.
56. *Aber Extracts*, i, 397.
57. *Edin Recs*, ii, 27.
58. *Edin Recs*, ii, 248.
59. William Dunbar, 'Ane mureland man of vplandis mak', in *The Poems of William Dunbar*, (ed.) P. Bawcutt (Glasgow, 1998), no.2, p.39, 11. 54–5.
60. *Edin Recs*, ii, 216.
61. 'Introduction', in *Experience of Authority*, 1–2.
62. Gowing, *Domestic Dangers*, especially Chapter 3.
63. Walker and Kermode, 'Introduction', 14.
64. *Dunfermline Recs*, 134.
65. *Dunfermline Recs*, 188.

66. William Dunbar, 'Quhy will ze, merchantis of renoun', in *Poems*, (ed.) Bawcutt, no. 55, p.174, 11.10–11

67. *Accounts of the Lord High Treasurer of Scotland*, (eds.) T. Dickson and J.B. Paul (Edinburgh, 1877–1916), i, 348.

68. *Edin Recs*, ii, 148.

69. *Selkirk Recs*, ii, 140, 198.

70. Walker and Kermode, 'Introduction', 18.

71. *Edin Recs*, i, 97.

72. *Edin Recs*, ii, 8.

73. *Peebles Recs*, 167.

74. Aberdeen Council Register, iv, f.8.

75. Amussen, *Ordered Society*, 129–31.

76. Normand, *Witchcraft*, 61.

77. E. Ewan, '"Many Injurious Words": Defamation and Gender in Late Medieval Scotland', in *History, Literature and Music in Scotland, 700–1560*, (ed.) R.A. McDonald (Toronto, forthcoming).

78. Robert Semple, 'Maddeis Proclamatioun', in *Satirical Poems of the Time of the Reformation*, (ed.) J. Cranstoun (Edinburgh, 1891–3), i, 149, 11. 23–4.

79. For the continuation of ballads as a woman's tradition, see Deborah Symonds, *Weep Not for Me: Women, Ballads and Infanticide in Early Modern Scotland* (University Park, PA, 1997); Catherine Kerrigan, 'Reclaiming history; the ballad as a woman's tradition', *Etudes Ecossaises*, 1 (1992), 343–50.

FURTHER READING

Aberdeen City Archives, Aberdeen Council Registers, vols iv, ix.

Central Region Archives, B66/15/1, Stirling Council Minutes.

Dundee City Archives, Book of the Church.

Amussen, Susan Dwyer (1988), *An Ordered Society: Gender and Class in Early Modern England*, Oxford: Basil Blackwell.

Bawcutt, P. ed. (1998), *The Poems of William Dunbar*, Glasgow: Association for Scottish Literary Studies.

Bennett, J. (1991), 'Misogyny, Popular Culture and Women's Work', *History Workshop Journal*, 31.

Bennett, J. (1996), *Ale, Beer and Brewsters in England: women's work in a changing world 1300–1600*, New York: Oxford University Press.

Beveridge, E. ed. (1917), *The Burgh Records of Dunfermline*, Edinburgh: William Brown.

Capp, Bernard (1996), 'Separate Domains? Women and Authority in Early Modern England', in Griffiths, P. *et al* (eds.), *The Experience of Authority in Early Modern England*, Houndsmills: Macmillan, 117–45.

Chambers, W. ed. (1872), *Charters and Documents Relating to the Burgh of Peebles*, Edinburgh: Scottish Burgh Records Society.

Cranston, J. ed. (1891–3), *Satirical Poems of the Time of the Reformation*, Edinburgh: Scottish Text Society.

Dickinson, W.C. ed. (1957), *Early Records of Aberdeen*, Edinburgh: Scottish History Society.

Dickson, T. and Paul, J.B. eds. (1877–1916), *Accounts of the Lord High Treasurer of Scotland*, Edinburgh: HM General Register House.

Ewan, E. (1999), 'For Whatever Ales Ye: Women as Consumers and Producers in Late Medieval Scottish Towns', in Ewan, E. and Meikle, M. (eds.), *Women in Scotland c.1100-c.1750*, East Linton: Tuckwell Press, 125–36.

Ewan, E. (2000), 'Mons Meg and Merchant Meg: Women in Later Medieval Edinburgh', in Brotherstone, T. and Ditchburn, D. (eds.), *Freedom and Authority: Scotland c.1050-c.1650*, East Linton: Tuckwell Press, 131–42.

Ewan, E. (forthcoming), 'Many Injurious Words: Defamation and Gender in Late Medieval Scotland', in McDonald, R.A. (ed.), *History, Literature and Music in Scotland, 700–1560*, Toronto: University of Toronto Press.

Gemmill, E. and Mayhew, N. (1995), *Changing Values in Medieval Scotland: A study of prices, money, and weights and measures,* Cambridge: Cambridge University Press.

Goldberg, P.J.P. (1992), *Women, Work and Life Cycle in a Medieval Economy*, Oxford: Clarendon Press.

Gowing, Laura (1996), *Domestic Dangers: Women, Words and Sex in Early Modern London*, Oxford: Clarendon Press.

Griffiths, Paul (1996), 'Masterless Young People in Norwich, 1560–1645', in Griffiths, P. *et al* (eds.), *The Experience of Authority in Early Modern England*, Houndmills: Macmillan, 146–86.

Houston, R.A. (1988), 'Women in the economy and society of Scotland 1500–1800', in Houston, R.A. and Whyte, I.D. (eds.), *Scottish Society 1500–1800*, Cambridge: Cambridge University Press.

Imrie, J. *et al* (eds.) (1960–69), *The Burgh Court Book of Selkirk 1503–45*, Edinburgh: Scottish Record Society.

Jacobsen, Grethe (1983), 'Women's Work and Women's Role: Ideology and reality in Danish Urban Society 1300–1500, *The Scandinavian Economic History Review*, 31.

Kerrigan, Catherine (1992), 'Reclaiming history: the ballad as a woman's tradition', *Etudes Ecossaises*. 1.

Marwick, J.D. (1869–92), *Extracts from the Records of the Burgh of Edinburgh*, Edinburgh: Scottish Burgh Records Society.

Mayhew, Nicholas (1996–7), 'The Status of Women and the Brewing of Ale in Medieval Aberdeen', *Review of Scottish Culture*, 10, 16–21.

Mayhew, Nicholas (1997), 'The Brewsters of Aberdeen in 1509', *Northern Studies*, 32, 71–81.

Mayhew, Nicholas (1999), 'Women in Aberdeen at the end of the Middle Ages', in Brotherstone, T. *et al* (eds.), *Gendering Scottish History. An International Approach*, Glasgow: Cruithne Press, 142–55.

Normand, Lawrence and Roberts, Gareth (2000), *Witchcraft in Early Modern Scotland*, Exeter: University of Exeter Press.

Smout, T.C. (1978), 'Coping with Plague in Sixteenth and Seventeenth-Century Scotland', *Scotia*, 2 (1), April, 19–33.

Stuart, J. (ed.) (1844–8), *Extracts from the Council Register of the Burgh of Aberdeen*, Edinburgh: Scottish Burgh Records Society.

Symonds, Deborah (1997), *Weep Not for Me: Women, Ballads and Infanticide in Early Modern Scotland*, University Park, PA: Penn State Press.

Thomson, T and Innes, C. (eds.) (1814–75), *The Acts of the Parliaments of Scotland*, Edinburgh: HM General Register House.

Walker, G., and Kermode, J. (1994), Introduction, in Kermode, J. and Walker, G. (eds.), *Women, Crime and the Courts in Early Modern England*, London: UCL Press, 1–25.

Whyte, I.D. and Whyte, Kathleen (1988), 'The Geographical Mobility of Women in Early Modern Scotland', in Leneman, L. (ed.), *Perspectives in Scottish Social History*, Aberdeen: Aberdeen University Press.

Wiesner Wood, M. (1981), 'Paltry Peddlers or Essential Merchants? Women in the Distributive Trades in Early Modern Nuremberg', *The Sixteenth Century Journal*, 12.

EIGHT

Twisted by Definition: Women Under Godly Discipline in Seventeenth-Century Scottish Towns

Gordon DesBrisay

Transgression is in the eyes of the beholder.[1] When early-modern women acted out, they did so within a social and religious context in which secular and church leaders construed all women as essentially or at least potentially transgressive. To say that early-modern authorities regarded women as a lesser and inherently disruptive sex – twisted by definition – is to restate the obvious, but Scottish historians of late have played down the impact of that ideology just where we might expect it to have had the greatest practical effect. The crusade for 'godly discipline', the great Calvinist war on sin, was the single most distinctive feature of Scottish life for the better part of two hundred years.[2] Kirk sessions across the country disciplined their parishioners for all sorts of misconduct, but almost everywhere the emphasis was almost always on sins of the flesh: in the seventeenth century cases of fornication and adultery normally accounted for about sixty percent of a session's disciplinary business.[3] Of course it takes two to fornicate, and in recent years historians have emerged from the archieves to report that early-modern Scottish men (those below the landed classes, at least) were nearly as likely as women to be convicted by the kirk of a sexual offence.[4] Secular and ecclesiastical law explicitly called for the equal treatment of the sexes in such cases, and it was, in fact, common practice for men and women to be assessed the same fines and the same penance for the same sexual offences.[5] It has also been pointed out that the kirk pursued absconding fathers at no cost to unwed mothers and helped to broker arrangements for child support, and that these things were very much to the women's advantage.[6] Although I do not dispute any of these findings, I believe that they paint an incomplete picture that stops short of capturing the actual experience of women under godly discipline. I cannot, therefore, share in the oft-stated conclusion that, whatever its excesses in other regards, godly discipline in Scotland was at least gender-blind, a view stated most firmly perhaps by Michael Graham, who has argued that 'by holding individuals – men as well as women – primarily responsible for their own behaviour, [the kirk] militated against the maintenance of any double standard in the area of sexual ethics.'[7]

Reports of the death of the double standard strike me as premature.[8] Scottish men were just as convinced as their English and European brethren that women were the root of temptation, and the burgesses among them were especially apprehensive about the small army of female servants occupying their cities.[9] Early-modern towns routinely hosted more women than men thanks to the influx of countrywomen arriving to work as domestics, and the sex-ratio of Scotland's larger towns may have been especially lopsided: in the 1690s there were only 76 men for every 100 women in Edinburgh, and as few as 71 per 100 in Aberdeen.[10] Although urban householders understood that the mainly young and overwhelmingly single women living under their roofs, native and newcomer alike, needed to be protected from sexual predators, they were equally convinced that these women were carriers of a socially corrosive sexuality that, if left unchecked, could corrupt individuals, disrupt households, and bring God's wrath upon the entire community. This attitude came to the fore in moments of civic crisis. In the aftermath of war, plague, famine, or other of God's unfavourable judgements, calls to purge a town of (inevitably sexual) sin always seemed to involve purging women.[11] But even in less fraught times, a negative vision of women underpinned much of the daily work of godly discipline, and helped to uphold the double standard in at least two important and related ways. First, a whole constellation of restrictive practices concerning employment, housing, wages, and credit circumscribed the lives of unmarried women, especially domestic servants, in ways that did not apply as forcefully to men, and which fed back into the broad stream of godly discipline. Second, although court records can seem to suggest a pattern of equal treatment of the sexes, differential penalties were often applied to men and women accused of fornication or adultery, and even when they were not, equal penalties had differential effects because most of the women involved were so disadvantaged relative to men. Not only, then, would I plead for the continued relevance of the sexual double standard in early modern Scotland, but I would suggest that the war on sin was first and foremost a war on women: it was not that men got off 'Scot-free', but that their treatment overall amounted to collateral damage in relation to the judicial pounding inflicted on women.[12]

From the moment a single woman arrived in a seventeenth-century Scottish city she was meant to be tethered by a number of restrictions that did not apply to her male counterparts. Although young single men were expected to live with a master, they were not normally banned from living alone or with only their peers for company, as young women in

Scottish and many European cities were.[13] Only widows and respectable spinsters and their female servants were allowed to live without benefit of a male head of household. Most women arrived in towns with a job lined up or a recommendation in hand, but those who came on spec had only a few days to move in with a suitable employer, or move on.[14] In medieval Scotland this injunction had also applied to young men, but by the seventeenth century only women's domestic arrangements were at issue. There were various reasons for singling out single women. One that usually went unstated was to limit employment options for women so as to help secure for employers a steady supply of low-cost domestic help.[15] The reason most often given by city fathers, and which was echoed all over western Europe, was that unsupervised single women were at risk of becoming either victims or agents of immorality, with an emphasis on the latter.[16]

Civic authorities went to some lengths to try to screen undesirables out of the servant pool. Town officers were meant to check all incoming 'strangers and servants' for a written testimony of good character from the minister of their last parish of residence.[17] In Aberdeen, officials were ordered to take special note of arriving wet nurses, almost invariably unwed mothers, who were not to be hired until they had completed or arranged to complete their penance for what the kirk called 'thair harlatrie and fornicationes'.[18] It is important to stress that no special precautions were taken against incoming fathers of bastard children. In Edinburgh, a city-run employment agency was established in 1697, not just to screen incomers and match employers and servants, but to keep a running tab of servants' 'faults or misdemeanors'.[19] Faults and misdemeanors came in all shapes and sizes, of course, but it was the spectre of illicit sex that most haunted city fathers across the country. They fussed continually, for example, over tapsters, female servants who sold ale in the street or door-to-door, and who were proverbially inclined towards sexual 'uncleanness'.[20] Tapsters enjoyed a freedom of movement and an access to alcohol and money that put them in a special category of risk, but even rank-and-file female domestic servants were considered a threat to the moral health of the community unless properly quarantined in respectable, preferably male-headed, households.[21] Thus, in Glasgow in 1670 the magistrates reported a 'great outcry' against the 'ill practis that is risen among us' of female servants who had 'desertit their service, out of honest mens houssis, and hes tak up houssis of their awine, quher some twa some thrie of them dwellis togither' in what the authorities could only imagine were bordellos, where 'they doe quhat thei can to bring the plague of God in this citie'. Officers were ordered to expel these women and to 'inhibit all weomen who have bein servantis to tak up privat houssis'.[22]

Once they had found a position and moved in, domestic servants in Scotland were bound to employers by six-month contracts, although they could be dismissed at any time. As elsewhere, they were paid room and board and a small cash wage. In Aberdeen, the maximum wages and tips for female domestics were set by the town council, and, if tax returns are anything to go by, it seems that employers were only too happy to abide by this low wage ceiling.[23] A low-paid male day-labourer in that city could expect to earn about £70 Scots a year in the latter half of the seventeenth century, out of which he had to house and feed himself and any dependents: the cash portion of a senior Aberdeen domestic's annual wage in this period worked out to just £10 Scots, suggesting that room and board accounted for by far the lion's share of her pay.[24] The calibre of room and board obviously varied considerably from household to household, as did working conditions and the sorts of work undertaken. There were plenty of incentives for a servant to try to trade up to a better employer when her contract expired, but money (assuming she had actually been paid what she was owed to date) was probably not one, at least in Aberdeen.[25]

Being paid mainly in room and board had its advantages. When food prices soared, as in the great famine of the 1690s, servants fed by their employers were much better off than those wage-only workers who had to fend for themselves.[26] That degree of security, however, only lasted as long as the job. It was not just that employers could turn servants out in hard times, but that even the most frugal servant could not save room and board.[27] Only the cash portion of a servant's wages could be saved, and that cannot have been easy when the cash added up, as it did in Aberdeen, to less than 7d. Scots a day – not quite enough for a humble loaf of oat bread or a single imperial pint of ale.[28] Most female servants worked about ten years before they married, and it must have taken years of disciplined saving to put a reasonable sum aside for a dowry or a rainy day.[29]

For many a female domestic in Scotland, that rainy day came when she found herself pregnant. It was when a servant became pregnant that she really needed money, not just to tide her over a spell of unemployment that usually began almost as soon as her employer learned of her condition (normally in the second trimester), and not just to help with the expenses of bearing and supporting an infant, but, most pressingly, to pay her fine for fornication or adultery so that she could avoid the worst rigours of godly discipline. In Scotland, about five percent of children were born out of wedlock, a much higher proportion than in England or most other western European countries of the seventeenth century. In Aberdeen, illegitimacy levels at times approached fifteen percent.[30] Well over ninety percent of unwed mothers in the cities were servants when they conceived – hardly surprising given that the vast majority of single women of childbearing age were in service.[31]

Once an illicit pregnancy became known to the authorities, the offending parties were required to undergo both civil punishment and church penance. Ordinarily, both strands of godly discipline were administered by the local kirk session, the parish consistory on which the burgh magistrates almost always served.[32] The session's first concern was to secure a confession from the woman, who was expected to acknowledge her own sin and name the father. There was little point denying the fact of pregnancy, and nearly all women confessed promptly and gave up the names that made it possible for the kirk to prosecute their male partners. Men were expected to confess, too, and most did so when confronted.[33] Confession was the necessary first step on the road to purging the sin and reconciling with the community.[34] Having confessed and offered 'tockens of . . . unfaigned repentance' to the ministers and elders in private, the offending parties were permitted to proceed to public penance, which for first-time offenders convicted of fornication (i.e. neither party being married) culminated in three Sunday appearances before the congregation, during which they were subjected to gawks, jibes, leers, and prayers, and were expected to offer in return further evidence of contrition and remorse.[35] Repeat offenders made extra appearances, and adulterers (i.e. one or both parties being married) could be required to spend twenty-six Sundays on the stool of repentance, barefoot and dressed in sackcloth. Once the prescribed penance had been completed, the penitent was publicly absolved of the sin and welcomed back as a full member of the congregation.[36]

Church penance seems to have been administered to women and men fairly even-handedly, but that was only one aspect of the two-pronged process of godly discipline: with regard to civil punishments the treatment of the two sexes could diverge sharply. This despite the apparent gender-blindness of Scottish secular and church law, which explicitly prescribed the same fines for men and women: £10 Scots for fornication, £40 for adultery.[37] But, as suggested above, this was a false equality given the disparity of income between the sexes, the particular vulnerabilities of female servants in general and female guestworkers in particular, and the prevailing attitudes towards women.[38] Offenders had less than a week to pay their fines, and those who could not or would not pay were clapped in prison, subjected to painful public shaming rituals, and, usually, banished from the town. This could and did happen to men, but it was far more likely to happen to women. In cases of adultery, which almost invariably involved the unequal pairing of a married male householder and an unmarried female domestic servant, the contrast between the treatment of men and women was stark: because the £40 fine was so steep, one in four adulterous men convicted in Aberdeen proved unable to pay and were made to suffer accordingly, as compared to fully three in four of the women they impregnated. Offenders of either sex who could not pay could be imprisoned, carted, whipped, and ritually banished by the hangman, but only women could be made to endure the additional indignities of head shaving, branding, or being strapped to the dockside crane and ducked in the icy waters of the harbour.[39]

The Aberdeen authorities pegged most fines for fornication and adultery at the statutory maximum, which meant that most of the twenty-odd female domestics convicted of fornication there each year had less than a week to pay £10, a sum that matched or exceeded their annual cash earnings. Because the alternatives to paying a fine were so shameful and unpleasant, it seems safe to assume that anyone who could pay, would pay. The wonder is that most women convicted of fornication (as opposed to adultery) managed to come up with the money.[40] Those who had been working a few years might draw on their savings, but others had to borrow. Some had families or friends or lovers nearby to turn to, while others borrowed against future earnings (especially those who had turned their predicament to opportunity by lining up relatively well-paid work as wet nurses) or found other ways to tap into the sticky web of credit that extended to the very lowest reaches of Scottish society.[41]

Many men must have had to borrow to pay their fines on time, but the higher proportions of bodily punishments meted out to women suggests that borrowing tended to be more difficult for them, as one might expect given their low earning potential. Many female domestics in sudden need of cash to pay a fine were from out of town, and lacked community ties of the sort one might bank on. Lenders who did not know them and felt no responsibility for them would need assurances they would be repaid, and pregnant young women who had suddenly lost their jobs and their reputations cannot have been very good risks. But creditworthiness, then as now, was not always a simple matter of pounds, shillings, and pence. Small claims court records confirm that there were hundreds of potential lenders in a town like Aberdeen, and it is likely (though here I must argue from silence, albeit a silence that strikes me as pointed) that a refusal to lend money could also be a moral judgement, an expression of the community's lack of sympathy for a particular woman's situation, a tacit ratification of the authorities' actions against her.[42] Given that women who could not pay were usually driven out of town after they were punished, creditworthiness was a reliable indicator as to whether anyone wanted her to stay.

The case of Janet Walker and John Schiphard illustrates several of these points. Walker was a domestic servant in Aberdeen who in the winter of 1638/39 was found to be pregnant by Schiphard, the local postmaster.[43] He was evidently well known around town, and was certainly well known to the kirk session, because this was his third conviction for fornication. His fine should have been set at £30, but 'in respect of his povertie' the session lowered the amount to £20, with a warning that next time he would be banished. He still could not pay his fine, but a friend stepped forward to pledge 'caution' or bail, and John Schiphard left the session house a free man. No such slack was cut Janet Walker, even though it was her first offence. She was probably young (and therefore short of savings) and from out of town (and therefore short of accessible creditors), because the session calculated that she 'wanted meanes' to pay a £10 fine and was in no position to borrow that much.[44] Rather than lower the fine as it did for John Schiphard, the session sentenced her to a month in the new workhouse. Nobody stepped forward to buy her out of trouble, the way Schiphard's friend had done for him. She eventually scraped together £2.9s. – enough to have paid her entire fine in Glasgow, but sufficient only to spare her a final week of incarceration in the Aberdeen Correction House.[45] Janet Walker disappears from the records at this point, probably because she left Aberdeen. If she did leave, it would at least have been under her own power, since it was her first offence. Women found to be three-time losers like John Schiphard could usually expect to be carted, whipped, and escorted out of town by the hangman.

The workhouse Janet Walker was sent to, the Aberdeen Correction House, was meant to set indigent 'volunteers' and obstinate sinners to profitable, soul-cleansing work carding and spinning wool.[46] Like most workhouses, it soon proved to be an expensive failure. But the kirk session had invested heavily in it, and shortly after it opened ruled that:

> all those persones who hereafter shall hapin to fall in the sin of fornication within this burgh wanting meanes to pey thair penalties shall be injoyned to the Correction house . . ., thairin to remain for the space of ane moneth and to work for thare meat during that space, thairefter to be presentit to the [market] croce and to sit in the brainkes [i.e. stocks] on ane Setterday with thair heid clipped according to custom.[47]

As with other aspects of godly discipline, the gender-neutral language used here is deceptive, for the 'persones' the kirk had in mind were plainly female. The first thirty prisoners sent by the kirk session to the Correction House were all women, most of them pregnant ex-servants unable to pay their fines for fornication or adultery: the session did threaten to send one man there for a sexual offence, but, as with John Schiphard, a friend promptly stepped up to pay his fine.[48] Just as carding and spinning were women's work, shaving the head was a ritual of shaming and purification that applied exclusively to women. Simply to unbind a woman's hair in public was shaming, and for the authorities to then cut it off was a further violation laden with sexual meaning. It was an ordeal in which, as an historian of early-modern France put it, 'the connection between purity, piety, chastity, honor, and hierarchical order was visibly demonstrated'.[49] Not only were men spared this ordeal, but there was no equivalent shaming ritual inflicted only on the male body.

Cases of adultery and rape tended to set the sexual double standard in sharpest relief, and an unusual but revealing Aberdeen case from 1680 involved both offences. Jean Stevin was a servant in a town sergeant's house where a married sailor from Leith named Thomas Kentie was a guest.[50] According to Jean Stevin, around midnight Kentie decided to check on his ship, and Stevin's employer ordered her to light his way down to the shore. The ship was not there. Kentie had Stevin lead him to the end of the pier and then up into Garvock's Wynd, where he extinguished the torch, tore the cap off her head as she struggled, bloodied her face, and, as she later testified, 'did ravishe her, there being none to rescue her that tyme of night'. Immediately upon returning home, 'she shew her master & mistres how that man hade abused her Butt did not tell them that he hade carnall dealing with her'.[51] That only came out some months later, when her pregnancy became apparent. Kentie evidently fled on the night in question and was never seen again: the Aberdeen ministers tried in vain to interest their Leith counterparts in the case, and periodic snooping by visiting Aberdonians or their agents likewise failed to turn up any leads. After six years the Aberdeen kirk session, in a rare admission of defeat, finally struck Kentie's name from its books.[52]

Jean Stevin's case was highly unusual on two counts: she claimed she was raped, and the man was never caught.[53] In Thomas Kentie's absence the kirk session never directly addressed the issue of rape, but there is circumstantial evidence to suggest that civic and church authorities regarded Stevin as something of a victim in this case, or at least as being of diminished responsibility. The magistrates reduced her fine for adultery from £40 to £20, and when she still had difficulty paying they took the unusual step of reducing it by a further third: they clearly did not wish to bring the full force of the law against her. The kirk session, for its part, reduced her penance from twenty-six Sunday appearances in sackcloth to sixteen. The wider community also seems to have offered Jean Stevin a vote of confidence. After she gave birth, but while still under church censure, two prominent employers in succession (one of them the provost of Banff) hired her as a live-in wet nurse, a plum position of intimacy and trust.[54] Wet-nursing was the best option for many single mothers in seventeenth-century Scotland. The job paid relatively well (in Aberdeen the cash wage was £20 a year, double what ordinary domestics received) and wet nurses could probably expect to be better fed and better treated than ordinary servants. An added benefit was that employers could arrange with the kirk session to have their nurse's penitential appearances before the congregation suspended until after the client child had been weaned: both of Jean Stevin's employers requested and were granted this exemption. Suspensions of disciplinary proceedings worked to a wet nurse's advantage – the passage of time probably lessened the notoriety of her case when she did resume her penance – but the point of the exemption was to distance the employers from her scandal and to spare their child the tainted milk that nursing women exposed to emotional upsets were thought to produce.[55] Any advantage to the woman actually under church censure was purely accidental, as indicated by the fact that unwed mothers were never granted a suspension for their own sake or for that of their own illegitimate children. Indeed, the fathers of illegitimate children could sometimes claim a stay of penance for themselves even though the women who bore their children could not: in June 1676 the Aberdeen kirk session agreed to postpone the adulterer James Ranken's penance for the remainder of the salmon-fishing season after he explained that his work kept him out on the Dee until midnight on Saturdays (any later would constitute a breach of Sabbath) and that this 'might occasione ane drowsines to fall upon him the tyme of divyne Worshipe'.[56] A single mother up all night with a colicky baby would just have to take that risk.

Jean Stevin rewarded the magistrates, ministers, elders, and employers for their trust by proving to be a model penitent. Unlike many women in her circumstances, she did not try to run away, and if she indulged in the sorts of passive resistance (feigning ignorance, illness, or tears, for example) that so wearied the elders and deacons in other cases, they appear not to have noticed. As soon as her employers' children were weaned, she turned up in church faithfully every week until her penance was completed. On 2 October 1682, twenty-seven months after her initial appearance before the kirk session, she was duly absolved of the sin of adultery.[57] In a highly unusual sign of reconciliation, she turned up on Aberdeen's poor rolls just a few months later.[58]

For all the apparent sympathy and support directed her way, Jean Stevin was still convicted of adultery on the basis of her having become pregnant after being raped by a married man. Indeed, she must have known all along that the issue of rape would have no bearing on her own status as an adulteress – a fact that no doubt gave her story added credence.[59] Her unquestioned guilt had to do in part with pre-modern legal practice in which guilt or innocence was chiefly a matter of circumstance rather than agency.[60] But surely it also reflects a systemic bias against women so pronounced that even when the courts were willing to acknowledge rape, they still held the woman culpable.[61] The mixed signals sent in this case – by the authorities who mitigated her punishment, by elite employers who took her in, by Jean Stevin herself when she confessed to adultery even as she said she was raped – reveal a degree of confusion on all sides regarding the treatment of women in general, and domestic servants in particular. After all, when disaster struck Jean Stevin, she was living under the roof of a respectable master (an officer of the law, no less) and following his orders. As we have seen, the tightly regulated urban labour market for single women, with its employment and housing restrictions that pushed them into domestic service in a patriarchal household and its low wages that helped keep them there, was justified in part by the need to protect these women from sexual peril. The system plainly failed to protect Jean Stevin, and we can perhaps detect a degree of collective guilt in her subsequent treatment, because here was godly discipline on its best behaviour, with the authorities responding as flexibly and compassionately as they knew how. Yet still they could not imagine that a single woman might be a wholly innocent victim in a sexual encounter, and Jean Stevin herself appears to have accepted the necessity, or at least the inevitability, of her punishment.

The fact that the Aberdeen authorities did their poor best to go easy on Jean Stevin only emphasises how strict their dealings with most female sex offenders were, and how unfair the supposedly even-handed treatment of men and women really was. The Aberdeen custom of prescribing the maximum fine in most cases of fornication or adultery was especially hard on the low-paid domestic servants who everywhere comprised the bulk of the women charged with sexual offences.[62] But all across Scotland men and women tended to be assessed similar fines, and everywhere prevailing wage differentials meant that such fines inevitably bore more heavily on women. Women were also more likely to suffer the consequences of not being able to pay their fines, and were sometimes made to endure bodily mortifications for which there were no male equivalents. And women were far more likely than men to be expelled from a town, in many cases to be sent back whence they came. In the end this element of disposability, of a sense that any woman who could or would not conform to the standards of godly discipline could be replaced for the same low price by another who might, underpinned the entire economy of domestic service in early-modern Scottish towns, an economy so tightly integrated

with the processes of godly discipline as to be virtually inseparable
from it.

NOTES

1. Earlier versions of this essay were presented to the Sixteenth Century Studies
   Conference in Cleveland, and the Scottish Studies Conference at the University
   of Guelph. I would especially like to thank Susan Blake and Marybeth Carlson
   for their comments.
2. See especially R. Mitchison and L. Leneman, *Sexuality and Social Control: Scotland 1660–1780* (Oxford, 1989); M. F. Graham, *The Uses of
   Reform: 'Godly Discipline' and Popular Behaviour in Scotland and Beyond,
   1560–1610* (Leiden, 1996); and L. Leneman and R. Mitchison, *Sin in the
   City: Sexuality and Social Control in Urban Scotland 1660–1780* (Edinburgh,
   1998).
3. M. Graham, 'Social Discipline in Scotland, 1560–1610', in R. A. Mentzer, ed.,
   *Sin and the Calvinists: Morals Control and the Consistory in the Reformed
   Tradition* (Kirksville, MI, 1994), 136–139; G. Parker, 'The "Kirk By Law
   Established" and the Origins of "The Taming of Scotland"', in L. Leneman,
   ed., *Perspectives in Scottish Social History: Essays in Honour of Rosalind
   Mitchison* (Aberdeen, 1988), 9; G. DesBrisay, '"Menacing Their Persons
   and Exacting on Their Purses": The Aberdeen Justice Court, 1657–1700',
   in D. Stevenson, ed., *From Lairds to Louns: Country and Burgh Life in
   Aberdeen, 1600–1800* (Aberdeen, 1986), 78–81; S. J. Davies, 'The Courts
   and the Scottish Legal System, 1600–1747: The Case of Stirlingshire Crime
   and the Law', in V. A. C. Gatrell, B. Lenman and G. Parker, eds., *The Social
   History of Crime in Western Europe Since 1500* (London, 1980), 123–125.
4. Graham, *Uses of Reform*, 286–287. On the defiance of the gentry and other
   men accused of paternity, see L. Leneman and R. Mitchison, *Sexuality and
   Social Control*, 202–208; the same authors' 'Acquiescence in and Defiance
   of Church Discipline in Early Modern Scotland', *Records of the Scottish
   Church History Society*, 25 (1993), 25; and M. F. Graham, 'Equality Before
   the Kirk? Church Discipline and the Elite in Reformation-era Scotland', *Archiv
   für Reformationsgeschichte*, 84 (1993), 296–298.
5. L. Leneman and R. Mitchison, 'Girls in Trouble: The Social and Geographical
   Setting of Illegitimacy in Early Modern Scotland', *Journal of Social History*,
   21 (1988), 483; G. DesBrisay, '"Menacing Their Persons"', 85–88. Men and
   women were prescibed the same fines for fornication in the famous 1567 Act
   of the Scottish Parliament. *APS* iii. 25, c.14 (1567).
6. Mitchison and Leneman, *Sexuality and Social Control*, 25, 152–153, 238.
7. M. F. Graham, 'Women and the Church Courts in Reformation-Era Scotland',
   in E. Ewan and M. Meikle, eds., *Women in Scotland, c 1100-c. 1750* (East
   Linton, 1999), 195–196; and Graham, *The Uses of Reform*, 289. Graham
   acknowledged that some women felt the disciplinary 'sting . . . in ways that
   men could not', much as Rosalind Mitchison and the late Leah Leneman
   concluded that although men 'had an easier course to run', in general
   the kirk brought 'steady pressure . . . towards equality of treatment for
   the two sexes'. Mitchison and Leneman, *Sexuality and Social Control*,
   237. Robert M. Kingdon made a similar case for Calvin's Geneva, where

aspects of the notorious double standard laws are said 'to represent a significant step toward a gender-neutral single standard'. *Adultery and Divorce in Calvin's Geneva* (Cambridge, Mass, 1995) 117, but see the comments of Joel F. Harrington in 'The Forest for the Trees: Society and the Household in Early Modern Europe', *The Historical Journal* 41 (1998), 1165. My point is that gestures toward equality rang hollow in practice. The confusion on this point is reflected in an excellent article by Julian Goodare in which he endorses the idea that the sexual double standard was relatively muted in Scotland before concluding that 'The vigorous assault on sexual offences that characterized the Scottish Reformation was also, inevitably, a move towards the criminalization of women'. J. Goodare, 'Women and the Witch-Hunt in Scotland', *Social History*, 23 (1998), 296, 307.

8. Regarding the ongoing viability of the sexual double standard in early modern England, see L. Gowing, *Domestic Dangers: Women, Words, and Sex in Early Modern London* (Oxford, 1996), 3–5, 65. Bernard Capp sets out to modify, rather than overturn, our understanding of the double standard by stressing the vulnerability of men to accusations of sexual impropriety. He still concludes, however, that in England '[t]here is no doubt that the double standard was deeply embedded in the culture of the age and that it placed women at a massive disadvantage'. 'The Double Standard Revisited: Plebeian Women and Male Sexual Reputation in Early Modern England', *Past and Present* 162 (1999), 98.

9. See for example U. Rublack, *The Crimes of Women in Early Modern Germany* (Oxford, 1999), 13–15.

10. J. de Vries, *European Urbanization: 1500–1800* (London, 1984), 178; I.D. Whyte and K.A. Whyte, 'The Geographical Mobility of Women in Early Modern Scotland', in L. Leneman, ed., *Perspectives in Social History: Essays in Honour of Rosalind Mitchison* (Aberdeen, 1988), 83–106; H. M. Dingwall, *Late 17th-Century Edinburgh: A Demographic Study* (Aldershot, 1994), 28; Dingwall, 'The Power Behind the Merchant? Women and the Economy in Late Seventeenth-Century Edinburgh', in E. Ewan and M. Meikle, eds., *Women in Scotland c.1100–c.1750* (East Linton, 1999), 153–154; G. DesBrisay, 'City Limits: Female Philanthropists and Wet Nurses in Seventeenth-Century Scottish Towns', *Journal of the Canadian Historical Association*, 8 (1997), 39. Unless otherwise noted, all references to Aberdeen refer exclusively to the royal burgh of New Aberdeen.

11. Between October 1659 and September 1660, in the wake of the English army's withdrawal, the Aberdeen magistrates expelled or threatened to expel thirty-one single women (some with children), two married women, and just two married men thought to have been overly familiar with soldiers or to have 'no way of living'. Aberdeen City Archives (ACA), Aberdeen Justice Court Book 1(1).

12. Julian Goodare makes this point with regard to the Scottish witch-hunt, which he regards as 'an attack on women *as women*; in a sense, it got a little out of hand in attacking men'. (His italics.) 'Women and the Witch-Hunt in Scotland', 308.

13. R.A. Houston, 'Women in the Economy and Society of Scotland, 1500–1800', in R.A. Houston and I.D. Whyte, eds., *Scottish Society 1500–1800* (Cambridge, 1989), 132–133.

14. See for example R. Renwick, ed., *Extracts from the Records of the Burgh of Peebles, 1652–1714* (Glasgow, 1910), 25.
15. Houston, 'Women in the Economy and Society of Scotland,' 133–134.
16. L. Leneman and R. Mitchison, 'Girls in Trouble', 483–497; C. C. Fairchilds, 'Female Sexual Attitudes and the Rise of Illegitimacy: A Case Study', in R. I. Rotberg and T. K. Rabb, eds., *Marriage and Fertility: Studies in Interdisciplinary History* (Princeton, 1980), 163–204.
17. R.A. Houston, 'Geographical Mobility in Scotland, 1652–1811: The Evidence of Testimonials', *Journal of Historical Georgraphy*, 11 (1985), 380–384.
18. NAS CH2/448/24 (Aberdeen St Nicholas Kirk Session Register, 10 May 1697).
19. Dingwall, *Late 17ᵗʰ-Century Edinburgh*, 48–49; R.A. Houston, *Social Change in the Age of Enlightenment: Edinburgh, 1660–1760* (Oxford, 1994), 153–154.
20. NAS CH2/131/3 (Edinburgh General Sessions Register, 2 July 1694); M. Wood, *Extracts from the Records of the Burgh of Edinburgh, 1655–1665* (Edinburgh, 1940), 144–145; Houston, 'Women in the Economy', 133; Houston, *Social Change in the Age of Englightenment*, 80. Theft and inebriation were also risks associated with tapsters: a statute in Aberdeen accorded them top servants' wages 'because they have advantage upon that which they handle'. ACA Aberdeen Council Register Vol. 57 (18 November 1696).
21. See for example ACA Aberdeen Justice Court Book, I(1) (9 July 1660); J.D. Marwick, ed., *Extracts from the Records of the Burgh of Glasgow, A.D. 1630–1662* (Edinburgh, 1881), 282, 301.
22. J.D. Marwick and R. Renwick, eds., *Extracts from the Records of the Burgh of Glasgow, A.D. 1663–1690* (Edinburgh, 1905), 126–128.
23. J. Stuart, ed., *List of Pollable Persons Within the Shire of Aberdeen, 1696* (2 vols., Aberdeen, 1844), ii, 595–692.
24. G. DesBrisay, 'Wet Nurses and Unwed Mothers in Seventeenth-Century Aberdeen', in E. Ewan and M. Meikle, eds. *Women in Scotland, c.1100–c.1750* (East Linton, 1999), 214. Male day-labourers earned 6s.8d. Scots a day in Aberdeen from about 1630 through 1700, and could typically expect to work an average of four days a week through the year, or about 203 days, which would yield £67.6s. Scots. A.J.S. Gibson and T.C. Smout, *Prices, Food and Wages in Scotland, 1550–1780* (Cambridge, 1995), 284. If the labourer had a family, his wife and older children might bring in additional cash in various ways, most notably spinning wool.
25. Moving to Edinburgh where the pay was generally better was an option for some. Dingwall, *Late 17ᵗʰ-Century Edinburgh*, 118–120. Servants in richer households might have expected to receive more money in the way of tips, but it should be noted that Aberdeen's wage rate included a standardised amount for 'bounty' or tips. ACA Aberdeen Council Register, Vol. 57 (18 November 1696).
26. Houston, *Social Change in the Age of Enlightenment*, 89.
27. Some servants did probably supplement their income, however, doing a little work on the side (spinning, delivering packages, etc.), selling the mistress's old clothes or scraps from her table, or simply stealing from their masters. P. Earle, *The Making of the English Middle Class: Business, Society and Family Life in London, 1660–1730* (Berkeley, 1989), 219.

28. Calculations based on figures in Gibson and Smout, *Prices, Food and Wages*, 370. The price of a loaf of oat bread was fixed at 8d. in Aberdeen, though the weight of the loaf varied with the harvest. Wheat bread cost 12d. a loaf. The price of the best ale in late seventeenth-century Aberdeen was fixed at 24d. (2s.) per Aberdeen pint, which was 1.8 litres, or just over three of today's imperial pints.

29. Most women entered service in their early to mid teens, and married (and left service) in their mid twenties.

30. For the most recent discussion of these figures, see Leneman and Mitchison, *Sin in the City*, 69–80. Children conceived out of wedlock but born in it (a small proportion, much lower than in England) are not included in these estimates.

31. DesBrisay, 'Wet Nurses and Unwed Mothers', 212–213.

32. Aberdeen was unusual in that after 1657 secular punishments were administered separately by the Justice of the Peace Court. Since the J.P.s were the magistrates of the town council who, as elsewhere, also sat on the kirk session, the secular and ecclesiastical branches of godly discipline still worked hand-in-glove, much as in other towns where the entire business was overseen by the kirk session. See DesBrisay, 'Wet Nurses and Unwed Mothers', 213.

33. Mitchison and Leneman, *Sexuality and Social Control*, 200–208.

34. DesBrisay, 'Wet Nurses and Unwed Mothers', 214; H. Schilling, '"History of Crime" or "History of Sin"? Some Reflections on the Social History of Early Modern Church Discipline', in E.I. Kouri and T. Scott, eds., *Politics and Society in Reformation Europe: Essays for Sir Geoffrey Elton on the Occasion of his Sixty-Fifth Birthday* (Basingstoke, 1987), 296–303.

35. NAS CH2/448/4 (Aberdeen St Nicholas Kirk Session Register, December 31, 1639); J. Stuart, ed., *Selections From the Records of the Kirk Session, Presbytery, and Synod of Aberdeen* (Aberdeen, 1846), 62–3, 136. Ministers and elders understood that only God knew if a penitent was truly sincere, but they insisted upon unambiguous outward signs of acquiescence and sincerity. On this point, see J.C. Scott, *Domination and the Arts of Resistance: Hidden Transcripts* (New Haven, 1990), 204–205.

36. NAS CH2/448/4 (Aberdeen St Nicholas Kirk Session Register, December 31, 1639); DesBrisay, 'Wet Nurses', 213–214.

37. See n.5, above. Acts of 1655 and 1661 granting justices of the peace authority in cases of fornication and double standard stipulated that fines were to be 'levied not only of the Man, but also of the Woman, according to her quality, and degree of her Offence'. *APS* vi, 835; vii, 310. This would seem to have allowed a latitude in sentencing that magistrates seldom invoked, at least in Aberdeen. DesBrisay, '"Menacing Their Persons"', 85–88.

38. In a pioneering article, Keith Thomas argued that in English divorce law 'it might seem as if the double standard went into abeyance. But such an impression would be misleading, for in practice it [was] usually only the husband who was in a position to take advantage of this . . . [T]he reasons for this were economic'. 'The Double Standard', *Journal of the History of Ideas* 20 (1959), 200.

39. DesBrisay, '"Menacing Their Persons"', 87–88.

40. Ninety percent of the women offered a chance to pay a fine did so within a week. ACA Aberdeen Justice Court Accounts.

41. See L. Ewen, 'Debtors, Imprisonment and The Privilege of Girth', in L.

Leneman, ed., *Perspectives in Scottish Social History: Essays in Honour of Rosalind Mitchison* (Aberdeen, 1988); I. D. Whyte and K. A. Whyte, 'Debt and Credit, Poverty and Prosperity in a Seventeenth-Century Scottish Rural Community', in R. Mitchison and P. Roebuck, eds., *Economy and Society in Scotland and Ireland: 1500–1939* (Edinburgh, 1988); and C. Muldrew, 'The Culture of Reconciliation: Community and Settlement of Economic Disputes in Early Modern England', *The Historical Journal*, 39 (1996).

42. ACA Aberdeen Baillie Court Records, vol.xiv (1687–1691): C. Muldrew, *The Economy of Obligation: The Culture of Credit and Social Relations in Early Modern England* (Basingstoke, 1998), 7: Scott, *Domination and the Arts of Resistance* (New Haven, 1990), 140–152.

43. NAS, CH2/448/4 (Aberdeen St Nicholas Kirk Session Register, December 16, 1638, and January 20, 1639).

44. In Aberdeen fines had to be paid within one week, making it difficult for those who might have drawn on creditors back home to reach them in time.

45. See for example NAS CH2/173/1 (Barony Kirk Session of Glasgow Register, June 3, 1677).

46. J. Stuart, ed., *Extracts From the Council Register of the Burgh of Aberdeen 1625–1642* (Edinburgh, 1871), 106–112.

47. NAS CH2/448/4 (Aberdeen St Nicholas Kirk Session Register, March 11, 1638).

48. NAS CH2/448/4. Men were sometimes sent to the Correction House, but not by the kirk session, and not (so far as we can tell) for sexual offences. Exasperated householders sent the occasional wayward son or back-talking male servant there to teach them a lesson.

49. J.R. Farr, 'The Pure and Disciplined Body: Hierarchy, Morality and Symbolism in France During the Catholic Reformation', *Journal of Interdisciplinary History*, 21 (1991), 404. See also Graham, *Uses of Reform*, 49–50.

50. NAS CH2/448/17–18 (Aberdeen St Nicholas Kirk Session Register, July 12, 1680-October 2, 1682).

51. NAS CH2/448/17 (Aberdeen St Nicholas Kirk Session Register, 12 July 1680).

52. Kentie's name was added to a list of fugitives, however, so that there would be a record in case he showed up. NAS CH2/448/18 (Aberdeen St Nicholas Kirk Session Register, undated, summer of 1686).

53. Mitchison and Leneman, *Sexuality and Social Control*, 194–196.

54. Stevin was hired first by Provost Stewart of Banff, and then by the wife of John Forbes, an Aberdeen burgess. NAS CH2/448/17 (Aberdeen St Nicholas Kirk Session Register, 24 & 30 January, 1681); NAS CH2/448/18 (Aberdeen St Nicholas Kirk Session Register, 3 October 1681).

55. DesBrisay, 'City Limits', 55–58.

56. NAS CH2/448/14 (Aberdeen St Nicholas Kirk Session Register, 5 June, 1676).

57. NAS CH2/448/18 (Aberdeen St Nicholas Kirk Session Register, 2 October, 1682).

58. ACA Aberdeen St Nicholas Kirk Session Accounts, March 1683. In an ongoing study of poor relief in Aberdeen I have found very few confirmed cases of women convicted there of fornication turning up later on the poor rolls, let alone while the memory of their 'fall' was still fresh.

59. Although there was no escaping the double standard charge, it was clearly

in Jean Stevin's interest to win over the court of public opinion. A good
reputation was critical in terms of employment, credit, marriageability, and
her future prospects generally. Leneman and Mitchison noted that when kirk
sessions evaluated statements they often took the woman's sexual and overall
reputation into account, but never the man's. 'Acquiescence in and Defiance
of Church Discipline', 19.

60. B. Lenman and G. Parker, 'The State, the Community and the Criminal Law
in Early Modern Europe', in V. A. C. Gatrell, B. Lenman and G. Parker,
eds., *The Social History of Crime in Western Europe Since 1500* (London,
1980), 31.

61. Leneman and Mitchison noted that even where the courts acknowledged
that a woman had been raped she was still punished on the grounds that
it was her responsibility to make sure such a thing did not happen. *Sin in
the City*, 61.

62. Women facing church censure fled Aberdeen more readily than other places,
probably as a result of the high fines and harsh penalties levied there. Leneman
and Mitchison, 'Acquiescence in and Defiance of Church Discipline', 20.

FURTHER READING

MANUSCRIPTS:
Aberdeen City Archives (ACA)
ACA Aberdeen Baillie Court Records, Vol. xiv
ACA Aberdeen Council Register Vol. 57
ACA Aberdeen Justice Court Book 1(1)
ACA Aberdeen Justice Court Accounts
ACA Aberdeen St. Nicholas Kirk Session Accounts
National Archives of Scotland (NAS)
NAS CH2/448/4–24 (Aberdeen St. Nicholas Kirk Session Register)
NAS CH2/173/1 (Barony Kirk Session of Glasgow Register)
NAS CH2/131/3 (Edinburgh General Sessions Register)

PRINTED PRIMARY SOURCES:
Acts of the Parliaments of Scotland. Edited by T. Thomson and C. Innes. Edinburgh,
1814–75.
Marwick, J.D., ed. *Extracts from the Records of the Burgh of Glasgow, A.D.
1630–1662.* Vol. 12, Scottish Burgh Records Society. Edinburgh: Scottish Burgh
Records Society, 1881.
Marwick, J.D., and Robert Renwick, eds. *Extracts from the Records of the Burgh of
Glasgow, A.D. 1663–1690.* Vol. 16, Scottish Burgh Records Society. Edinburgh:
Scottish Burgh Records Society, 1905.
Renwick, Robert, ed. *Extracts from the Records of the Burgh of Peebles, 1652–1714.*
Vol. 24, Scottish Burgh Records Society. Glasgow: Scottish Burgh Records
Society, 1910.
Stuart, John, ed. *List of Pollable Persons Within the Shire of Aberdeen, 1696.* 2
vols. Aberdeen: William Bennett, 1844.
Stuart, John, ed. *Selections From the Records of the Kirk Session, Presbytery, and
Synod of Aberdeen.* Vol. 15, Spalding Club. Aberdeen: Spalding Club, 1846.
Stuart, John, ed. *Extracts From the Council Register of the Burgh of Aberdeen,*

1625–1642. Vol. 8, Scottish Burgh Records Society. Edinburgh: Scottish Burgh Record Society, 1871.

SECONDARY WORKS:

Capp, Bernard. 'The Double Standard Revisited: Plebeian Women and Male Sexual Reputation in Early Modern England.' *Past and Present* 162 (1999): 70–100.

Davies, Stephen J. 'The Courts and the Scottish Legal System, 1600–1747: The Case of Stirlingshire Crime and the Law.' In *The Social History of Crime in Western Europe since 1500*, edited by V.A.C. Gatrell, Bruce Lenman and Geoffrey Parker, 120–154. London: Europa, 1980.

DesBrisay, Gordon. '"Menacing Their Persons and Exacting on Their Purses": The Aberdeen Justice Court, 1657–1700.' In *From Lairds to Louns: Country and Burgh Life in Aberdeen, 1600–1800*, edited by David Stevenson, 70–90. Aberdeen: Aberdeen University Press, 1986.

DesBrisay, Gordon. 'City Limits: Female Philanthropists and Wet Nurses in Seventeenth-Century Scottish Towns.' *Journal of the Canadian Historical Association* 8 (1997): 39–60.

DesBrisay, Gordon. 'Wet Nurses and Unwed Mothers in Seventeenth-Century Aberdeen.' In *Women in Scotland, c.1100–c.1750*, edited by Elizabeth Ewan and Maureen Meikle, 210–221. East Linton: Tuckwell Press, 1999.

de Vries, Jan. *European Urbanization: 1500–1800*. London: Methuen, 1984.

Dingwall, Helen M. *Late 17th-Century Edinburgh: A Demographic Study*. Aldershot: Scolar Press, 1994.

Dingwall, Helen M. 'The Power Behind the Merchant? Women and the Economy in Late Seventeenth-Century Edinburgh.' In *Women in Scotland, c.1100–c.1750*, edited by Elizabeth Ewan and Maureen Meikle, 152–162. East Linton: Tuckwell Press, 1999.

Earle, Peter. *The Making of the English Middle Class: Business, Society and Family Life in London, 1660–1730*. Berkeley: University of California Press, 1989.

Ewen, Lorna. 'Debtors, Imprisonment and The Privilege of Girth.' In *Perspectives in Scottish Social History: Essays in Honour of Rosalind Mitchison*, edited by Leah Leneman. Aberdeen: Aberdeen University Press, 1988.

Farr, James R. 'The Pure and Disciplined Body: Hierarchy, Morality and Symbolism in France During the Catholic Reformation.' *Journal of Interdisciplinary History* 21 (1991): 391–414.

Fairchilds, Cissie C. 'Female Sexual Attitudes and the Rise of Illegitimacy: A Case Study.' In *Marriage and Fertility: Studies in Interdisciplinary History*, edited by Robert I. Rotberg and Theodore K. Rabb. Princeton: Princeton University Press, 1980.

Gibson, A.J.S., and T.C. Smout. *Prices, Food and Wages in Scotland, 1550–1780*. Cambridge: Cambridge University Press, 1995.

Goodare, Julian. 'Women and the Witch-Hunt in Scotland.' *Social History* 23 (1998): 288–308.

Gowing, Laura. *Domestic Dangers: Women, Words, and Sex in Early Modern London*. Oxford: Clarendon Press, 1996.

Graham, Michael F. 'Equality Before the Kirk? Church Discipline and the Elite in Reformation-era Scotland.' *Archiv für Reformationsgeschichte* 84 (1993): 289–309.

Graham, Michael. 'Social Discipline in Scotland, 1560–1610.' In *Sin and the Calvinists: Morals Control and the Consistory in the Reformed Tradition*, edited by Raymond A Mentzer, 129–157. Kirksville, MI: Sixteenth Century Journal Publishers, 1994.

Graham, Michael F. *The Uses of Reform: 'Godly Discipline' and Popular Behaviour in Scotland and Beyond, 1560–1610.* Vol. LVIII, *Studies in Medieval and Reformation Thought.* Leiden: E.J. Brill, 1996.

Graham, Michael F. 'Women and the Church Courts in Reformation-Era Scotland.' In *Women in Scotland, c 1100-c. 1750,* edited by Elizabeth Ewan and Maureen Meikle, 187–198. East Linton: Tuckwell Press, 1999.

Harrington, Joel F. 'The Forest for the Trees: Society and the Household in Early Modern Europe.' *The Historical Journal* 41 (1998): 1161–1172.

Houston, R.A. 'Geographical Mobility in Scotland, 1652–1811: The Evidence of Testimonials.' *Journal of Historical Geography* 11 (1985): 379–394.

Houston, R.A. 'Women in the Economy and Society of Scotland, 1500–1800.' In *Scottish Society, 1500–1800,* edited by R. A. Houston and I. D. Whyte, 118–147. Cambridge: Cambridge University Press, 1989.

Houston, R.A. *Social Change in the Age of Enlightenment: Edinburgh, 1660–1760.* Oxford: Clarendon Press, 1994.

Kingdon, Robert M. *Adultery and Divorce in Calvin's Geneva.* Cambridge, Mass: Harvard University Press, 1995.

Lenman, Bruce, and Geoffrey Parker. 'The State, the Community and the Criminal Law in Early Modern Europe.' In *The Social History of Crime in Western Europe since 1500,* edited by V.A.C. Gatrell, Bruce Lenman and Geoffrey Parker, 1–48. London: Europa, 1980.

Leneman, Leah, and Rosalind Mitchison. 'Girls in Trouble: The Social and Geographical Setting of Illegitimacy in Early Modern Scotland.' *Journal of Social History* 21 (1988): 483–497.

Leneman, Leah, and Rosalind Mitchison. 'Acquiescence in and Defiance of Church Discipline in Early Modern Scotland.' *Records of the Scottish Church History Society* 25 (1993): 19–39.

Leneman, Leah, and Rosalind Mitchison. *Sin in the City: Sexuality and Social Control in Urban Scotland, 1660–1780.* Edinburgh: Scottish Cultural Press, 1998.

Mitchison, Rosalind, and Leah Leneman. *Sexuality and Social Control: Scotland 1660–1780.* Oxford: Basil Blackwell, 1989.

Muldrew, Craig. 'The Culture of Reconciliation: Community and Settlement of Economic Disputes in Early Modern England.' *The Historical Journal* 39 (1996): 915–942.

Muldrew, Craig. *The Economy of Obligation: The Culture of Credit and Social Relations in Early Modern England.* Basingstoke: Macmillan Press, 1998.

Parker, Geoffrey. 'The "Kirk By Law Established" and the Origins of "The Taming of Scotland"'. In *Perspectives in Scottish Social History: Essays in Honour of Rosalind Mitchison,* edited by Leah Leneman, 1–32. Aberdeen: Aberdeen University Press, 1988.

Rublack, Ulinka. *The Crimes of Women in Early Modern Germany. Oxford Studies in Social History.* Oxford: Clarendon Press, 1999.

Schilling, Heinz. '"History of Crime" or "History of Sin"? Some Reflections on the Social History of Early Modern Church Discipline.' In *Politics and Society in Reformation Europe: Essays for Sir Geoffrey Elton on the Occasion of his Sixty-Fifth Birthday,* edited by E I. Kouri and T Scott. Basingstoke: Macmillan, 1987.

Scott, James C. *Domination and the Arts of Resistance: Hidden Transcripts.* New Haven: Yale University Press, 1990.

Thomas, Keith. 'The Double Standard'. *Journal of the History of Ideas* 20 (1959): 195–216.

Whyte, I.D., and K.A. Whyte. 'Debt and Credit, Poverty and Prosperity in a Seventeenth-Century Scottish Rural Community.' In *Economy and Society in Scotland and Ireland: 1500–1939*, edited by Rosalind Mitchison and Peter Roebuck, 70–80. Edinburgh: John Donald, 1988.

Whyte, Ian D. and K.A. Whyte. 'The Geographical Mobility of Women in Early Modern Scotland.' In *Perspectives in Social History: Essays in Honour of Rosalind Mitchison*, edited by Leah Leneman. Aberdeen: Aberdeen University Press, 1988.

NINE

Maternal Monsters: Murdering Mothers in South-West Scotland, 1750–1815

Anne-Marie Kilday

According to Laila Williamson:

> Infanticide is a practice present-day westerners regard as a cruel and inhuman custom, resorted to by only a few desperate and primitive people living in harsh environments. We tend to think of it as an exceptional practice, to be found only among such peoples as the Eskimos and Australian Aborigines, who are far removed in both culture and geographical distance from us and our civilised ancestors. The truth is quite different. Infanticide has been practised on every continent and by people on every level of cultural complexity, from hunters and gatherers to high civilisations, including our own ancestors. Rather than being the exception, then, it has been the rule.[1]

Certainly, with regard to the present-day episodes of infanticide brought to our attention, albeit rarely, by the media, this crime can be accurately described as '. . . an enduring phenomenon in the history of humankind'.[2] Throughout Europe in the early-modern period, and during the eighteenth century in particular, although the killing of a new-born infant by its mother was considered '. . . a crime at the base idea of which the human mind revolts',[3] it was also deemed to be a tragically common occurrence.[4]

There are three key features related to the incidence of infanticide in Scotland, during the period 1750–1815, which warrant its separate attention from other crimes against the person.[5] Firstly, the legal statute which defined indictments for the crime of child murder was unique in Scots Law in that it substituted the usual presumption of innocence of the accused party with that of guilt.[6] Secondly, after the crime of assault of authority, child murder was the most frequently indicted offence against the person levelled against women. In addition, it is a crime set apart from that of the assault of authority, as whereas that crime was predominantly committed by women acting with others, infanticide was a crime overwhelmingly committed by women acting alone. Thirdly, child murder was a '. . . specifically female crime'.[7] Although a few men were involved as accessories, it was preponderantly women who acted as principals in these offences.

Therefore, by initially studying the legal context for the crime of child murder, followed by an investigation into the incidence of Justiciary Court indictments for this crime, and then going on to look at the defendants themselves in terms of their general characteristics, the methods they employed in the committal of the offences and by offering suggestions as to the motives involved, it is hoped that an insight will be gained into this crime. Moreover, this 'insight' should in turn enable the testing of Laila Williamson's argument that infanticide was the 'rule' rather than the 'exception',[8] and indicate the accuracy of her hypothesis in relation to the south-west Scottish experience of child murder.

Although, as R.W. Malcolmson argues, 'in many pre-Christian and non-Christian societies infanticide was widely practised as a method of controlling population size, and it was condoned by the value system of these societies',[9] evidence of a less tolerant attitude toward the act of child murder exists in abundance. Such an attitude can be traced back as far as four thousand years ago with a collection of Babylonian laws known as The Code of Hummurabi which provided that '. . . if a nurse or mother allowed a suckling to die in her hands and substituted another, her breast should be amputated'.[10] Closer to home, however, it was not until the late sixteenth century that most European states singled out infanticide for severe punishment.[11]

The climate of opinion necessary to instigate a Europe-wide moral and legislative opposition to child murder was caused by the confluence of two aspects of contemporary thinking. The first was a craving for the protection of infant life. As Malcolmson points out in relation to eighteenth-century England, there was a '. . . general hostility to any sort of interference with the natural course of human generation'[12] and it was widely held that if religious and legal institutions conjunctly offered what he termed '. . . a vigorous proscription of 'violence' against foetal or newborn life'[13] this would result in the more effectual defence of 'innocent blood'.

The second aspect of contemporary thinking, and indeed the one which was the real concern of the moralists of the day, was the apparent need to control the sexual morality of the populace. According to the historians P.C. Hoffer and N.E.H. Hull, 'as the sixteenth century drew to a close, authorities grew increasingly fearful of the sexual immorality and criminal tendencies of the increasingly numerous wandering poor'.[14] Such a concern was also manifest in the Scottish church of the period, as increasing

numbers of defendants were brought before the kirk session to answer
charges of fornication.[15] As Rosalind Mitchison and Leah Leneman argue,
'the Scottish Church in the early modern period displayed extreme distaste
for physical intimacy between the sexes: it usually labelled any such dem-
onstration 'scandalous carriage' and penalised it'.[16] Over time, however,
this 'distaste' and 'concern' were transferred from the actual act of fornication itself to the frequent end product of such activity: illegitimacy. Indeed,
it was the preoccupation with attempts to manage the rate of illegitimacy
which ultimately resulted in the statutory changes to Scots Law at the end
of the seventeenth century, and it was this 'new' legislation which formed
the basis for the indictments of the women accused of infanticide brought
before the Justiciary Court between 1750 and 1815.[17]

The twenty-first act of the second session of the first parliament of King
William and Mary, entitled 'An Act Anent the Murdering of Children',
directed juries to capitally convict women accused of infanticide regardless
of whether there was any direct evidence of murder. According to Baron
Hume, 'the circumstances selected for this purpose are, that the woman
have concealed her pregnancy during the whole period thereof, and have
not called for help to her delivery, and that the child is found dead, or is
missing'.[18] The wording of the statute clearly illustrates the presumption of
guilt directed against defendants accused of the charge of infanticide. As a
result of this, according to various Scottish legal commentators, '. . . many
inhuman convictions took place'[19] and '. . . many capital sentences did
certainly pass, and . . . were executed, in pursuance of verdicts which
proceeded on the statutory evidence only'.[20]

Aside from contemporary society's apparent preoccupation with the
preservation of infant life and the perceived need to curb sexual immorality, motives for the toughening of the legal attitude towards child murder
must be seen in the context of the witch-hunt which occurred throughout
Europe during the sixteenth- and seventeenth-century period.[21] As Hoffer
and Hull demonstrate with regard to early modern England and New
England:

> The law and conscience of Europe in the sixteenth and seventeenth
> centuries vented its force upon old women and unwed mothers . . .
> The witch, like the poor, wandering unwed mother, lived at the edge
> of society. Both had an aura of sexual license about them, The crimes
> of both were concealed, and often were directed against children . . .
> When fears of one rose, accusations of the other increased
> correspondingly.[22]

Certainly, infanticide, like witchcraft, was widely considered to be 'unnatural', as it encouraged '. . . a contradiction of normal maternal feelings'.[23] In

addition, as the act of '. . . taking the life of a newborn infant . . . deprived its soul of an eternally blissful afterlife,'[24] as the victim would not have been baptised, it is relatively easy to see why the connection is made by historians between these two female-dominated 'crimes'. The relationship between the two areas as far as Scotland is concerned is not clear, and the realms of such a comparison lie outwith this present study. Nevertheless, even if it were merely a coincidence that the vigorous approach adopted by the authorities to the Scottish witch-craze[25] occurred at the same time that the law courts were readily accepting and enforcing the new rigorous statute concerning infanticide, this concurrence should certainly not be overlooked or simply dismissed.

After the immediate passing of the 1690 statute, the pursuit of capital convictions of women charged with child murder and concealment of pregnancy was remorseless. As Baron David Hume suggested when writing in the late eighteenth century:

> Such indeed, was the facility of conviction laid open by the statute, as had at one time betrayed both prosecutor and Judges into a degree of slovenliness, and indecent haste, in trials for child murder, to which I find nothing to be compared in any portion of our criminal proceedings. Of this I need mention no stronger illustration than the practise, which was far from uncommon, of carrying on several trials for child murder, in one sitting, and with the same assize, who inclosed, and returned their verdicts *simul et semel*, on the several indictments.[26]

The intensification of interest in conviction rates for infanticide in the Scottish courts was becoming less by the 1750s: 'As the misogynistic Puritan influence that inspired infanticide laws wore off in the eighteenth century, their very severity made them more and more unenforceable in an increasingly understanding climate of opinion'.[27] As J.M. Beattie further suggests: 'Over the course of the eighteenth century the view gradually strengthened that it was wrong to threaten the death of the mother when direct proof of her killing her baby was not available . . .'[28] Evidence of the establishment of a more humanitarian attitude (perhaps as a reflection of contemporary Enlightenment thinking) in the Scottish legal system by the middle of the eighteenth century can be found in the readiness of prosecutors to consent to female defendants' petitions for banishment furth of the country, rather than attempting to achieve a capital conviction.

In addition, the defences offered by the women accused of infanticide were being more readily accepted by the court. If a woman could disprove that the death of her child was in any way premeditated, the jury would find the charges against her not proven. Principal among the attempts of indicted women to do this was the defence of a stillbirth, and it was left to the testimony of autoptical surgeons through the use of the scientific test of hydrostasy to give credence to such a claim. Pioneered in seventeenth-century Germany, the hydrostasy test was based on the theory that '. . . unaerated lungs would sink in water; but if the child had breathed they would float'.[29] Although the test was considered relatively basic and flawed, as it was argued that the lungs could be adversely affected by the gases of decomposition,[30] and it was met with a great deal of scepticism by English law courts (with Lionel Rose citing one judge who referred to it as '. . . scientific humbug'[31]), it appears to have been widely used in Scotland up to the 1790s, in cases where a woman had not petitioned for banishment.[32]

Other forms of defence attempting to prove an absence of premeditation included accidental death, temporary insanity and even the preparation of linen for the child after birth. This last form of defence was less convincing as such clothing arrangements could easily be contrived after the act of infanticide or even beforehand by a cold-blooded woman intent on killing her child and avoiding punishment. Daniel Defoe described it as a '. . . transparent stratagem'[33] but the Scottish courts still accepted it as a sign that the act of child murder was not planned.

The apparent wish of the law courts to avoid the conviction of women charged with infanticide by the end of the eighteenth century stands in stark contrast to their policy in the early years of the 1700s. By the early 1800s, however, it was being noted by the moralists of the day that the leniency of the law in this respect reflected an '. . . utter indifference'[34] to the victims of these types of offences. Lionel Rose explains that 'Historically, the value of infant life is determined by the forces of supply and demand, and contemporary attitudes to the inevitability of death. Dead babies were quickly replaceable when the birth rate was high; and an ignorance of the means to prevent death bred a helpless, resigned mentality . . . which compounded the cheapening of infant life'.[35] In order to affect this 'mentality', and yet avoid reverting to the severity of the act of 1690, '. . . it was thought advisable to repeal that statute, and to substitute in its stead a qualified and more temperate enactment'.[36] Under the new statute of the 49th. Geo. III c. 14 passed in 1809, if a mother '. . . shall conceal her being with child, during the whole period of her pregnancy, and shall not call for, or make use of help or assistance in the birth, and if the child shall be found dead, or be amissing, she shall be imprisoned for a period not exceeding two years'.[37] According to Hume, 'as modified by this law, a concealment of pregnancy, and a failure to call for help in the birth, are not to be viewed as grounds of suspicion of a *wilful murder*, but rather as a species of *culpable homicide*, – a criminal neglect of the safety of the child, – whereby it has come to perish in or upon the birth, for want of the due and timeful assistance'.[38] This statute is the last legislative change that affects the study of women brought before the Justiciary Court for child murder and concealment of pregnancy between 1750 and 1815.

It is clear from this legal context that although the severe statutory provisions were in place, to be used against those accused of infanticide, by the 1750s and then increasingly through the century into the early decades of the 1800s, the Scottish legal system was less willing to implement such provisions against accused individuals. It is now pertinent to ask how necessary these legal statues were in relation to the south-west Scottish experience of infanticide and to explore the incidence of indictments that fell into this unique category of crimes against the person.

It must be stressed from the outset that data provided on infanticide by any historian, for any area, over any period of time, cannot be an accurate presentation of the number of infant murders related to his or her study but rather an account of the incidence of cases brought to court. Although this statement can be applied to any of the crimes for which both men and women were brought before the Justiciary Court in relation to south-west Scotland between 1750 and 1815, it is especially true of the crime of child murder, which in the words of Dr Maria Piers was '. . . often veiled or even invisible'.[39]

Clearly, the highly masked nature of this offence, coupled with the obvious lack of testimony from the subsequent victim, makes infanticide '. . . one of the most secretive of all crimes'.[40] Indeed, the very statute charged against those accused of infanticide, as has been shown, emphasised the act of 'concealment'. The number of women who were successful in hiding their pregnancy, the actual act of infanticide itself and the related incriminating evidence can therefore never fully be known. The so-called 'Dark Figure' of enigmatic statistics is considered by historians and criminologists alike to be more a problem for the crime of child murder than for any other offence.[41]

The deficiency of the statistics related to infanticide is compounded by the fact that in the cases that *were* brought to court, the degree of proof necessary to charge a suspect in the first instance was somewhat derisory. The discovery of the dead body of an infant in a neighbourhood, the mere appearance of a 'swell' in a local woman's belly, or the recollection as part of neighbourhood gossip of a cry heard from a particular house in the night during an apparent illness was enough for suspicions to be aroused,[42] and it was clear that the semantics of the relevant statute encouraged such suspicions to be reported. The evidence and testimony of midwives and doctors which led to indictments were also 'erroneous' according to contemporary commentators such as the surgeon Christopher Johnson for the reasons already suggested and because they '. . . frequently failed in the performance of their duty . . .'[43] when an indictment was craved by the majority against a given suspect.

Clearly, then, the extent to which those accused of child murder were the real mothers of the victims must also be doubted. Having said all this, even though inadequacies of the data relevant to infanticide clearly exist, they are apparent to all historians of this crime, and as long as they are recognised they do not devalue the available evidence so as to render any study of this offence worthless. It is this evidence which will now be analysed in relation to the incidence of child murder.

The work done by historians of infanticide in England in the seventeenth and eighteenth centuries appears to confirm the statement made by R.W. Malcolmson that '. . . criminal indictments for infanticide . . . were never very numerous'.[44] J.A. Sharpe calculates that, between 1620 and 1680, 83 women were accused of child murder at the Essex assizes,[45] and R. W. Malcolmson himself shows that 'only sixty-one cases were tried at the Old Bailey between 1730 and 1774'.[46] Professor Beattie claims that over a 95-year sampling survey of the Surrey assizes between 1660 and 1800, only 62 women were indicted for the murder of their newborn children during that entire period.[47] Considering the rigorous legislative measures which were in place in an attempt to eradicate this crime, it is perhaps surprising that not more women were indicted, especially in the period of Sharpe's study when the English equivalent of the later Scottish statute concerning infanticide was passed in 1624.[48] Yet none of the three historians attempts to explain the relatively low incidence of infanticide apparent from their data, preferring to concentrate on the lack of male involvement in the perpetration of this crime, as being its most important characteristic. What of the incidence of infanticide elsewhere in Europe?

The evidence available from eighteenth-century France on the subject of child murder is somewhat more confusing than that presented by the contemporary English experience of the crime. In France, by an edict of Henri II in 1556 (which was not abolished until 1791), women '. . . who failed to register their pregnancies would be regarded as murderesses if their newborn infants died without baptism and proper burial'.[49] Dr Maria Piers vividly describes eighteenth-century France as '. . . the scene of infanticide of unprecedented magnitude'[50] where, as a result of massive over-population, mothers '. . . disposed of human beings, as an exterminator might dispose of rodents'.[51] However, she gives no statistical evidence to reinforce her conclusions. Dr Piers's findings contrast sharply with the work of J.R. Ruff in his study of the Sénéchaussées of Libourne and Bazas between 1696 and 1789. Ruff came across only three indictments for infanticide during that entire period. He explains its low incidence as being due to the readiness of contemporary unmarried French women to go through their pregnancies, give birth, and then pursue the father of their bastard offspring through the civil courts for substantial maintenance awards.[52] It is unclear which of the two commentators provides the more accurate account in relation to the subject of infanticide incidence as they both exist at such extremes of opinion. So, before coming to the south-west Scottish experience, the frequency of child murder in one other European country, Ireland, must be considered.

The Irish parliament did not officially ratify the infanticide act passed in England in 1624 and in Scotland in 1690 until 1707, but it would appear from the evidence available that such legislation was definitely warranted by that time. James Kelly, in his study of infanticide recorded in the predominantly Dublin-based Irish newspapers between 1721 and 1800,[53] reveals high incidence of infanticide, certainly in comparison with England and Ruff's analysis of the French experience, and this is reinforced by Brian Henry who claims that over a mere fifteen-year period in the eighteenth century, between 1780 and 1795, some 34 infanticides were committed in Dublin city alone.[54] Both Kelly and Henry contend that the '. . . stern sexual code of morality'[55] prevalent in Ireland at this time forced many unmarried women into acts of child murder and concealment of pregnancy in order to avoid the ignominy and public condemnation that was analogous to illegitimacy, for both the mother and her child. Indeed, it would seem to be clear that certainly in relation to England and France, this 'code' was more influential in Ireland than elsewhere in Europe.

The English, French and Irish experiences of infanticide in the early-modern period, and the eighteenth century in particular, appear far from homogeneous. Where, though, does the south-west Scottish experience fit into the pattern of incidence of child murder?

Between 1750 and 1815, 140 women were brought before the Justiciary Court charged with child murder and the concealment of pregnancy said to have been committed in the south-west of Scotland. These indictments accounted for nearly a quarter of all charges of crimes against the person, and indeed infanticide was second only to assault of authority in terms of being the most frequently indicted offence of that category. Furthermore, if the total number of indictments for infanticide brought against south-west Scottish women during this period is added on to the total number of indictments for homicide, accusations of women causing wilful death increase triplefold to a level almost as great as that charged against men.[56] In addition, bearing in mind the element of the 'Dark Figure' in statistics for this offence in this particular, it appears logical to consider the 'true' extent of infanticide in south-west Scotland as being considerably *more* substantial than the Justiciary Court evidence suggests.

Even bearing in mind the limitations of comparing the findings of one criminological study to another, the available evidence for south-west Scotland clearly adds another dimension to the European trends of infanticidal evidence, as, although not as prolific as in Ireland or France (if we are to agree with Piers), accusations of child murder levelled against women relating to south-west Scotland were certainly more prevalent than those charged in England or in the Sénéchaussées of Libourne and Bazas during the same period.

Even though there are significant variations of incidence in indictments for infanticide between these European countries, the key characteristics of the defendants themselves are very similar both over time and geography, and it is these features which will now be studied.

The first common characteristic of those accused of child murder and concealment of pregnancy was that the overwhelming majority of them were women who had committed the crime on their own newborn infants and had done so acting alone. Only five of the 140 cases brought before the Justiciary Court involved the use of an accomplice. Two of these were women and three were men. There was indeed no instance of a man being the sole defendant in an infanticide case throughout the entire period. Of the five accomplices, three were declared fugitate by the court, along with their co-accused principals, for not appearing to answer to the charges against them, and little is subsequently known of the circumstances of their cases.

Of the two remaining cases, Jean Baillie (Principal) and her 'master' Alexander Baird (Accomplice) appeared before the West Circuit Court, charged that on 12th December 1776, after Jean Baillie:

> . . . brought forth a living Male Child which was come to the full term in her house in Woodhead in the parish of Monkland and County of Lanark, [she] . . . did immediately Murder the said child by cutting the throat thereof with a knife or other Sharp instrument And in order to Conceal the crime, the said Alexander Baird having put the body of the Child into a Pock [pouch] carried out the same . . . and buried it at the back of a hedge near the Minister's Manse of Old Monkland.[57]

Then, in 1792, Sarah McDougall (Principal) was indicted along with her mother, Mary McPherson (Accomplice), at the South Circuit Court, charged that on 4th June 1792:

> . . . at Blackbyars Park in the Parish of Maybole and County of

Ayr, . . . you the said Sarah McDougall did bring forth a living
Female Child which was come to the full term [after which] . . . with
the aid or assistance of your mother the said Mary McPherson you
did then and there wickedly, feloniously and inhumanly Murder the
infant by drowning it in a small Run of Water in a Glen or Hollow
in the said park, or in some other way did deprive the Child of life.[58]

These two examples both confirm the second common characteristic of
women accused of infanticide: the principals involved were unmarried.
As Hoffer and Hull explain, 'unwed infanticide suspects played a role,
not just as targets for frustration and anger, but as a living definition of
the boundary of unacceptable deviance'.[59] They '. . . had ignored social
norms and official pronouncements too flagrantly'.[60] One hundred and
thirty-three, or some 95%, of the women indicted before the Justiciary
Court for south-west Scotland between 1750 and 1815 for this offence
were spinsters, five were relicts (widows) and only two were married. J.A.
Sharpe attempts to explain this anomaly by arguing that:

Infanticide within marriage would, of course, have been difficult to
detect, a consideration which suggests that the sample of infanticidal
mothers tried at the assizes was probably a distorted one. Even so,
an unwanted child born to married parents could be more effectively,
and less obtrusively, got rid of by a period of deliberate neglect
rather than infanticide proper. This latter course would have a
greater appeal to the unmarried mother anxious, in a period when
considerable odium was laid upon pregnancy outside marriage, to
dispose quickly of a source of shame and inconvenience.[61]

The evidence uncovered for south-west Scotland in this respect suggests
a relatively high level of illegitimacy in that area. The work of Rosalind
Mitchison and Leah Leneman appears to confirm this hypothesis.[62] The
figures of illegitimacy levels for Scotland as a whole show a downward
trend from the 1660s through to the 1720s, after which fluctuate, with
no obvious trend in their pattern being apparent (in stark contrast to the
pronounced rise in corresponding eighteenth-century English statistics for
illegitimacy).[63] The one significant exception, when the general trends
were broken down, was the south-west of Scotland which showed a
markedly upward trend in illegitimacy levels from the 1750s.[64] This
distinctiveness of the south-west of Scotland in relation to bastard-bearing
was still prominent by the time of civil registration in 1855; where during
the early 1860s the illegitimacy ratio for the whole of Scotland was 9.73%,
for England as a whole it was between 6 and 7%,[66] but in the south-west
of Scotland the figure was more than 13%.[67]

T.C. Smout attributes the high illegitimacy levels in south-west rural Scotland in the nineteenth century to the fact that unmarried pregnancy conferred no stigma on the mother or child in such areas due to an absence of the 'social restraints' in existence elsewhere in the country.[68] Furthermore, he argues, for a woman pregnant with an illegitimate child in rural Lowland Scotland there was '. . . no pressure . . . to commit any crime in order to conceal her lapse from virtue'.[69] This was because '. . . amongst her own class there was no feeling of indignation aroused in consequence of what they would call her 'misfortune'.[70] Rather, she would be supported by them both emotionally and financially. Smout's explanation, however, does not seem to correspond with the evidence of south-west Scotland in terms of infanticide indictments at the Justiciary Court, as almost three-quarters of them derived from rural area crimes. If, as Smout argues, there was absolutely no social stigma attached to illegitimacy, why were so many women accused of committing infanticide in rural areas?

Mitchison and Leneman offer a slightly different explanation for the levels of significant illegitimacy in south-west Scotland. They state that in various instances throughout history the area displayed an overt resistance to 'authority'. Citing traits such as an '. . . irreconcilable Covenanting sentiment'[71] and the existence of an '. . . organised form of resistance to agricultural innovation and reorganisation'[72] manifest in the Levellers' Revolt of 1724, Mitchison and Leneman argue that dissent was endemic in the south-west of Scotland. They go on to claim that this 'dissent' was not only directed towards the government or landowners, but also the church.[73] The unusual level of resistance to church discipline in the south-west of Scotland suggests that women from that area would be less likely to use the moral guidelines prescribed by the church authorities in their sexual behaviour compared to women elsewhere. Men, too, appear to have played a part in dissent towards church authority, for in terms of confessing illegitimate parenthood before the kirk session during the 1660–1780 period, 'in the south-west the percentage of men rapidly admitting responsibility was markedly lower than in most parts of Scotland'.[74] The contention of Mitchison and Leneman, therefore, is that illegitimacy levels were higher in south-west Scotland on account of a more truculent attitude to the moral doctrines of the church in that area. However, the extent to which such an attitude was harboured among the women indicted for infanticide before the Justiciary Court is not apparent from the evidence.

Another reason put forward for the higher illegitimacy levels of south-west Scotland in the period which may be tentatively linked to the relatively high levels of infanticide indictments before the Justiciary Court was the

'. . . continuous presence of soldiers in Dumfries, either in billets there or passing through to England or Ireland'.[75] Although of course it is debatable whether this area was any more vulnerable in this respect than any other, due to the nomadic nature of military service, it must be supposed that many young women were abandoned by their suitors and perhaps the fathers of their illegitimate offspring when it was time for the battalion to move on. This hypothesis is only speculation, however, as the Justiciary records rarely reveal who was responsible for the defendant's initial 'condition' in infanticide indictments.

What is more readily apparent is the third and final common characteristic of the women brought to court under such charges: they were predominantly employed as domestic servants. In south-west Scotland, between 1750 and 1815, 74% of the 140 females indicted for child murder were in employment, and of these some 90% were employed in domestic service. The high incidence of participation in this type of offence by these women in contemporary England led one commentator to contend that the servant-girl was '. . . very vulnerable to unmarried motherhood, from which it might be inferred that she was correspondingly prone to infanticide'.[76] As Professor J.M. Beattie explains, 'it is hardly surprising that many of the women accused . . . were domestic servants, for women in service were, on the one hand, most commonly in their early child-bearing years and on the other, in close and constant contact with men, both members of the family they worked for and their fellow servants'.[77] In addition, as Peter Linebaugh contends for London in the eighteenth century, illegitimate pregnancy '. . . meant disaster . . . to domestic servants, most of whom were hired on condition of remaining both single and childless'.[78] The loss of reputation to a household employing an unmarried pregnant servant would rarely be tolerated and would inevitably result in dismissal without a reference. The pressure on such women to conceal their pregnancies and thereafter rid themselves of the cause of ruin to their character and economic livelihood in the form of their bastard offspring can be easily understood.[79] Just how this criminal act was carried out will now be examined in order to gain an impression of the 'type' of south-west Scottish woman charged with infanticide before the Justiciary Court in the mid-eighteenth and early nineteenth-century period. Was she relatively passive or fundamentally aggressive in her committal of this category of crime against the person?

As 53 of the 140 women brought before the Justiciary Court during the period relevant to this study were either declared fugitate or had petitioned for banishment, specific details of their alleged offences with respect to exactly how they were carried out were not provided in their indictments. This was probably because they would not be facing a trial, and therefore evidence and witness testimony was deemed unnecessary. Of the remaining 87 accused, as has been shown, there was often no substantive or direct evidence of any kind linking them to the actual crime itself. Frequently the evidence used to indict in the first instance could be described as '. . . flimsy', risible, and '. . . not even strong enough to warrant the description 'circumstantial' . . .'[80] For instance, in less than 10% of cases was the victim's body found in the living quarters or immediate surroundings occupied by the accused. Whether falsely charged or otherwise, however, if the cause of death of the victim and the *modus operandi* employed in the original act was in any way brutal, a conviction would be imminent regardless.

According to Samuel X. Radbill, 'the methods used in infanticide have not changed much throughout history. Blood is rarely shed'.[81] Radbill's comments appear to be confirmed by other studies of the means employed by women in carrying out infanticide. R.H. Helmholz, in his study of the Province of Canterbury during the fifteenth century, concluded in this respect that '. . . overlaying was the principal means of infanticide'.[82] Both Wrightson in relation to seventeenth-century England and Kelly on eighteenth-century Ireland contend that 'Forms of asphyxia (strangulation, suffocation or drowning) . . . predominated over more violent methods'.[83]

The profile of those accused of infanticide in south-west Scotland between 1750 and 1815 is somewhat different. One Justice of the Peace for Dumfries in 1778 described such women as 'Monsters of the vilest kind'.[84] In 19% of the cases, no discernible 'marks of violence' were discovered on the body of the victim.[85] Six percent of the fatalities were suffocated, 7% were strangled, 5% were drowned, but in a significant 63% of the indictments brought to trial, blood was shed, with 48% of the infants being killed by attacks with a sharp instrument and 15% battered to death. This evidence suggests, therefore, that the women accused of infanticide in south-west Scotland appear to have committed this crime in a much more 'violent' manner than other studies of this offence would have predicted.

It is clear, for example, even in the *modus operandi* considered to be less aggressive, that the women involved were not averse to substantial degrees of violence. Janet McGuffog, indicted before the South Circuit Court in 1787, for instance, was accused of having given birth to a fully developed son whom she '. . . did immediately strangle with such ferocity that it did turn blae [blue] and by which means the neck bones of the said Child became but splinters'.[86] Similarly Mary Thomson, also indicted at the South Circuit Court in 1802, was charged with giving birth to a fully developed female child in a field near Irvine in Ayrshire whom she '. . . did then and there strangle with the aid of its own umbilical cord [chord] . . . the pressure of which caused the Child's windpipe to separate'. The child was found later by a farmer who testified in court that '. . . one of its Eyes was out and a piece cut off its tongue, as he thought, picked out by Birds of Prey'.[87] Also, Mary Speir (alias Fellow) was indicted at the West Circuit Court in 1804 charged with having 'stopped' her newly-born daughter's mouth with '. . . earth, grass roots and corn roots', and this mixture '. . . had been thrust into the throat and was so hard stoped [stopped] there that it had keept [kept] open the Child's mouth'.[88] Similar 'violent' methods of asphyxiation were employed by Janet Gardener (West Circuit Court, 1751),[89] Agnes Marshall (West Circuit Court, 1770),[90] Grizel Ninian (alias McLean) (South Circuit Court, 1772)[91] and others.

Even though the violence of their ultimate intentions could never be doubted, there were of course women accused of infanticide who adopted less aggressive methods of asphyxiation. However, their incidence before the Justiciary Court in relation to south-west Scotland was relatively rare. An example of such behaviour was that displayed by Elizabeth Frazer who was indicted at the West Circuit Court in 1804 charged that '. . . after being delivered of a Male Child come to the full time, on the twenty first of August in the year of our Lord one thousand eight hundred and four, in a house in Bridgetoun in the Barony of Glasgow and County of Lanark' she '. . . did then and there wickedly and feloniously bereave of life and Murder her Said Child by tying it up in a Linen bag . . . alongst with a Smoothing iron for the purpose of Making it sink, and Afterwards throwing it into a well'.[92]

By far the most common *modus operandi* employed by women accused of child murder in relation to south-west Scotland between 1750 and 1815 was attacking the infant with a sharp instrument, usually a knife or razor. Thirty women were indicted for cutting the throat of their child, including Sarah Quarrier (South Circuit Court, 1752),[93] Jean Stewart (South Circuit Court, 1755),[94] Christian Kerr (South Circuit Court, 1767),[95] Janet Hislop (West Circuit Court, 1777),[96] Elizabeth Buntine (West Circuit Court, 1788)[97] and Isobel Perston (West Circuit Court, 1798).[98] Indeed, Jean Allison's indictment at the West Circuit Court in 1805 was typical in this respect. She was charged that '. . . having given birth to a fully developed Female Child', she did '. . . immediately thereafter most barbarously, wickedly and inhumanely cutt [cut] the Child's throat from Ear to Ear with a razor in a gret [great] Effusion of Blood, with such force as causing the windpipe thereof to sever in two'.[99]

Stabbings made up the remaining attacks on newborn children with sharp instruments. Pitchforks, penknives, lances and nails were most commonly used in this type of offence.

A substantial number of south-west Scottish women were also accused of battery between 1750 and 1815. Janet Cooper (South Circuit Court, 1768)[100] and Lilias Miligan (South Circuit Court, 1774)[101] were indicted for '. . . dashing' their infants' skulls off the ground. Elizabeth Swinton (West Circuit Court, 1791)[102] was accused of '. . . dashing' her child on a tree trunk, Hannah Main (West Circuit Court, 1793)[103] allegedly killed her new-born son with a hammer, and Catharine MacDonald (West Circuit Court, 1797),[104] after using a '. . . spead [spade]' to attack her child in which its '. . . left leg above the knee was torn off . . . its right leg was disjointed and its nose flatted [flattened]', fed the child's remains to a neighbourhood dog.

The evidence in the Justiciary records emphasises categorically the readiness of south-west Scottish women to resort to violent means when committing infanticide. Of course it could be argued that these crimes only came to court in the first instance, and to the Justiciary Court in particular, due to their exceptionally violent nature. There may have been many more less violent crimes of infanticidal 'overlaying' and suffocation which went undetected by the authorities.

Motives for committing infanticide, as with all other crimes brought before the Justiciary Court between 1750 and 1815, are difficult to establish. Certainly, no definitive evidence can be cited, because the trial proceedings were geared to achieving a conviction rather than an understanding of why the crime was committed. However, the nature of the tangible information that *is* available in relation to other areas of the crime of child murder does allow a fair degree of convincing conjecture with regard to provocation.

The first area of motivation to be examined is why women in south-west Scotland during the mid-eighteenth and early nineteenth centuries predominantly chose infanticide as the means of ridding themselves of their unwanted newborn offspring rather than the other options apparently open to them at this time.

Although provisions for a nationwide adoption service and improvements in abortion techniques to reduce the risk of fatal complications in the procedure for the mother did not exist until the mid-nineteenth century,[105] it is perhaps surprising that south-west Scottish women rarely resorted to the relatively simple act of 'exposure' as a means to infanticide.

Exposure, or 'dropping' as it was commonly called, meant the abandoning of a newborn infant in a relatively public place such as '. . . on a church porch, in a basket at a market place or on the doorstep of a rich man's house . . .',[106] presumably so that it would be found and cared for. Although described by Frank McLynn as being '. . . frequent . . .'[107] and by R.W. Malcolmson as being '. . . fairly common . . .'[108] in eighteenth-century England, only five south-west Scottish women were indicated for the crime of infanticide through exposure between 1750 and 1815. McLynn goes some way to explain this by suggesting that the risk of detection was too great. As he puts it, 'to jettison a child necessitated moving immediately from the place of abandonment without having to worry about the baby's crying'.[109]

One of the five women charged with exposure before the Justiciary Court, Ann Parker (otherwise Ann Hepple), a midwife from Glasgow, was indicted at the West Circuit Court in 1806 accused of '. . . the Crime of exposing an Infant child, not her own, by laying it down in a common or public stair'.[110] The nature of the charge suggests an early example of a practice common in Glasgow and Edinburgh by the late nineteenth century:[111] baby-farming, also known as 'wet-nursing'.

According to Pollak, 'baby farmers were women to whom unmarried mothers turned over their newly born infants, ostensibly to have the children cared for and brought up against the payment of a lump sum. Actually there was a quiet understanding that the children should be made to die inconspicuously. Neglect and insufficient food soon weakened the children so that they succumbed easily to diseases, and the overburdened practitioners in the urban and rural districts, where these baby farms were '. . . located, seldom had time enough to probe carefully into the death causes of the children'.[112] The fact that monetary payment was involved in this kind of arrangement may have prevented many contemporary mothers from using such measures. However, it may well also have been the case that, as Pollak suggests, baby-farming *was* relatively widespread, although during the 1750 to 1815 period it was masked or undetected.

As far as motivation for the crime of infanticide itself was concerned, the rationale was not created immediately before the actual act of post-natal killing but rather originated after conception when efforts to conceal the pregnancy were first attempted. Although it must be accepted that in some cases the failure to disclose pregnancy was not '. . . a deliberate decision . . . made with criminal intent',[113] it would seem to be the case that for the women indicted for child murder before the Justiciary Court the motives for concealment of pregnancy were similar to those for infanticide.

One of the suggested principal motives for infanticide amongst the majority of unmarried women, as has been shown, was the need for the '. . . avoidance of the social stigma of being considered 'of easy virtue' and of having produced a bastard'.[114] The contemporary '. . . opprobrium'[115] associated with an illegitimate pregnancy reinforced by moralistic and religious commentators alike would seemingly not only tarnish the reputation of the woman directly involved and damage her prospects of a 'good' marriage, but might also apparently affect the status of the rest of her family amongst the wider community in which she lived. This disgrace became manifest if a woman was brought before the Kirk-Session suspected of an illegitimate pregnancy. She was charged to account for her condition, name the man responsible and if found guilty would be fined and ordered to make 'appearances' before the entire congregation.[116] Bearing this in mind, therefore, it is perhaps not surprising that the guilt and shame involved in an unmarried pregnancy are suggested as key incentives for women to terminate the life of the cause of such derogation.

As has also been shown, another potent factor in the committal of infanticide is economic. Falling pregnant during employment, especially as a domestic servant, meant dismissal and a loss of earnings. This forfeiture of income was then compounded by the spectre of severe financial hardship caused by the additional mouth to feed, clothe and care for. As Daly and Wilson comment, 'if the history of infanticide reveals anything, . . . it is surely that acts of desperation are principally the products of desperate circumstances'.[117] South-west Scottish women, eager to maintain their independence and security by earning a wage, and uncertain how to deal with the threat that an illegitimate child would pose to their future economic status, may well have considered concealment of pregnancy and child murder the only options open to them.

Lionel Rose suggests another possible motive for women to commit infanticide which is also related to economics. A pregnant woman would pay a few pennies a week into a fund set up in case anything happened to her child during the labour and delivery processes in order to enable her to pay for its funeral. Rose contends that women were deliberately killing their infants at birth, claiming the money (plus interest accrued) from the burial insurers, giving the child an inexpensive funeral and reaping the profits made. However, although Rose suggests that such practices were widely used in Glasgow during the nineteenth century,[118] surely in order for the women to successfully claim the money due to them, the death of the child must have appeared natural to the insurers or the premium would not have been paid out.[119] Yet, as the evidence for this study has already indicated, there were relatively few apparent 'natural' deaths in comparison with obviously violent ones, suggesting that this type of motivation was probably not as common in this region as Rose insists. Furthermore, as the women involved in this practice would necessarily have had to reveal themselves to be pregnant, it may have been more common amongst married women, who, like 'natural' deaths, accounted for relatively few indictments in the present investigation.

Another reason for infanticide, one that appears more plausible given the violent nature of child murder in the cases brought before the Justiciary Court in relation to south-west Scotland between 1750 and 1815, is the attitude of the accused towards her victim. Many instances must have occurred of women who had naively accepted a proposal of marriage on condition that they submitted to the pre-nuptial sexual desires of their suitors, but on discovering themselves to be pregnant were promptly abandoned by their 'betrothed', and as a result the women took their revenge upon what they saw as the reason for their abandonment – their newborn infant.[120]

This inducement to the act of infanticide involves a fair degree of psychological dissociation. The evidence of the brutality involved in the committal of that crime in south-west Scotland between the mid-eighteenth and early nineteenth centuries does indeed suggest that types of temporary insanity (perhaps induced by alcohol consumption), whether in the form of psychogenic infanticide or paranoid delusional hallucinations, may well have been 'unconscious' incitements for women to murder their newborn offspring.[121]

The only statement that can be made with relative conviction regarding the motivation behind women's participation in this type of offence, as with their participation in other crimes against the person, is that no common or simple explanation is discernible from the evidence. As Hoffer and Hull conclude:

> Motivation for the crime of infanticide was as varied as the personalities . . . of the women who attempted it and the situations in which they found themselves. External pressures like social ostracism, shame, loss of employment and reputation, and forcible intercourse, were certainly motives for the crimes, but before any individual would undertake it, these influences had to pass through the filter of individual character and perception. Outside forces created stress, but response to stress was not uniform. When fear and anger were overwhelming enough to cause the perpetrator to view the child as a thing, a cancer or a foreign object, or to make the perpetrator believe that such injustices as led to conception and would follow from successful birth were unsupportable, the crime might follow . . . Infanticidal mothers . . . frustrated at their own lives and unable to reach back into their own childhoods for resources to nurture the growth of the new lives entrusted to them, . . . struck out at the cause of their misery.[122]

In conclusion, it is impossible to say whether or not the incidence of infanticide in south-west Scotland in the mid-eighteenth and early nineteenth centuries was, to quote Laila Williamson, the 'exception' rather than the 'rule'[123] due to the element of the 'Dark Figure' previously discussed. Nevertheless, the evidence available from the indictments for infanticide seems to suggest that the Scottish experience of this unique crime differs in certain respects from what were considered to be its normal attributes. In this respect, the Justiciary Court records from south-west Scotland between 1750 and 1815 contribute to the understanding of infanticide as a wider European or indeed global phenomenon. It remains to be seen whether this contemporary regional experience is magnified by a nation-wide incidence of infanticide, to the levels of '. . . annual holocaust'[124] in the killings of newborn children predicted by the legislative authorities back in the early seventeenth century.

NOTES

1. L. Williamson, 'Infanticide: An Anthropological Analysis', in M. Kohl (ed.), *Infanticide and the Value of Life*, quoted in M. Tooley, *Abortion and Infanticide* (Oxford, 1983), p. 317.
2. J. Kelly, 'Infanticide in Eighteenth Century Ireland', in *Irish Economic and Social History*, Vol. 19 (1992), p. 5. Unfortunate evidence to substantiate this claim came during the writing of this paper, when a teenage English girl was charged with the murder of her newborn child on 24th August 1999.
3. B. Henry, *Dublin Hanged: Crime, Law Enforcement and Punishment in Late Eighteenth Century Dublin* (Dublin, 1994), p. 38.
4. See for example the evidence presented in A. Macfarlane, *The Justice and the Mare's Ale: Law and Disorder in Seventeenth Century England* (Oxford, 1981).
5. The primary evidence presented in this study will focus its attention on the south-west area of Scotland and will pertain to the period 1750–1815.
6. Act 1690, c. 21. The English equivalent was also unique for similar reasons: Act 1624 (21 Jas I, c. 27). For further discussion, see C. Damme, 'Infanticide: The Worth of an Infant under Law', in *Medical History*, Vol. 22 (1978), pp. 1–24.
7. J.A. Sharpe, *Crime in Early Modern England, 1550–1750* (New York, 1984), p. 109.
8. L. Williamson, quoted in M. Tooley, *Abortion and Infanticide*, p. 317.
9. R.W. Malcolmson, 'Infanticide in the Eighteenth Century', in J.S. Cockburn (ed.), *Crime in England, 1550–1800* (London, 1977), p. 208.
10. S.X. Radbill, 'A History of Child Abuse and Infanticide', in R.E. Helfer and C.H. Kempe (eds.), *The Battered Child* (Chicago, 1968), p. 13.
11. For further discussion, see J.A. Sharpe, *Crime in Early Modern England*, pp. 60–61.
12. R.W. Malcolmson, 'Infanticide in the Eighteenth Century', p. 208.
13. R.W. Malcolmson, 'Infanticide in the Eighteenth Century', p. 208.
14. P.C. Hoffer and N.E.C. Hull, *Murdering Mothers: Infanticide in England and New England, 1558–1803* (New York, etc., 1984), p. 12.
15. For further discussion, see K.M. Boyd, *Scottish Church Attitudes to Sex, Marriage and the Family, 1850–1914* (Edinburgh, 1980).

16. R. Mitchison and L. Leneman, *Sexuality and Social Control: Scotland 1660–1780* (Oxford, 1989). p. 9.

17. The Justiciary Court was the court which dealt with the most serious offences committed in early-modern Scotland.

18. Baron D. Hume, *Commentaries on the Laws of Scotland, Respecting Crimes*, Vol. 2 (Edinburgh, originally 1797, 1844 edition, 1986 reprint), Chapter VI, p. 291.

19. A. Alison, *Principles of the Criminal Law of Scotland*, Vol. 1 (Edinburgh, originally 1832, 1989 edition), Chapter III, p. 153.

20. D. Hume, *Commentaries*, Chapter VI, p. 292.

21. For a fuller discussion of the link between infanticide and witchcraft, see A. O'Connor, 'Women in Irish Folklore: The Testimony Regarding Illegitimacy, Abortion and Infanticide', in M. MacCurtain and M. O'Dowd, *Women in Early Modern Ireland* (Edinburgh, 1991) and J. Pentikäinen, *The Nordic Dead-Child Tradition, Nordic Dead Child-Beings* (Helsinki, 1968).

22. P.C. Hoffer and N.E.C. Hull, *Murdering Mothers*, p. 28.

23. K. Wrightson, 'Infanticide in Earlier Seventeenth Century England', *Local Population Studies*, No. 15 (1975), p. 11.

24. A. O'Connor, 'Women in Irish Folklore', p. 309.

25. For further discussion, see C. Larner, *Enemies of God: The Witch-hunt in Scotland* (London, 1981).

26. D. Hume, *Commentaries*, Chapter VI, p. 292. Relating specifically to a case from 1709.

27. L. Rose, *The Massacre of the Innocents: Infanticide in Britain, 1800–1939* (London, etc., 1986), p. 2.

28. J.M. Beattie, *Crime and the Courts in England, 1660–1800* (Oxford, 1986), p. 124.

29. L. Rose, *The Massacre of the Innocents*, p. 72.

30. For further discussion of the medical tests carried out in relation to infanticide victims, see C. Johnson, 'An Essay on the Signs of Murder in New Born Children', *Edinburgh Medical and Surgical Journal*, Vol. 10 (July 1814), p.394 and P.J. Martin, 'Observations on Some of the Accidents of Infanticide', *Edinburgh Medical and Surgical Journal*, Vol. 26 (July 1826), pp. 34–37.

31. L. Rose. *The Massacre of the Innocents*, p. 72.

32. In 79% of cases (or 72 out of 91 indictments), where petitioning for banishment was not forthcoming, still-birth was claimed. Every one of these cases employed the hydrostasy test. In only six instances (8%) was this defence accepted and the accused acquitted.

33. Daniel Defoe, *Augusta Triumphans: or the Way to Make London the Most Flourishing City in the Universe* (1728), quoted in F. McLynn, *Crime and Punishment in Eighteenth Century England* (London, 1989), p. 113.

34. L. Rose. *The Massacre of the Innocents*, p. 75.

35. L. Rose, *The Massacre of the Innocents*, p. 5.

36. D. Hume, *Commentaries*, Chapter VI, p. 292.

37. A. Alison, *Principles of the Criminal Law*, p. 153.

38. D. Hume, *Commentaries*, Chapter VI, p. 293.

39. M.W. Piers, *Infanticide* (New York, 1978), p. 9.

40. J. Kelly, 'Infanticide in Eighteenth Century Ireland', p. 5. See also O. Pollak, *The Criminality of Women* (Philadelphia, 1950), p. 22.

41. See for example J.A. Sharpe, *Crime in Seventeenth Century England – A*

County Study (Cambridge, 1983); J.A. Sharpe, *Crime in Early Modern England, 1550–1750* (London, 1984); J.M. Beattie, *Crime and the Courts in England, 1660–1800* (Oxford, 1986); R.W. Malcolmson, 'Infanticide in the Eighteenth Century', in J.S. Cockburn (ed.), *Crime in England, 1550–1800* (London, 1977); O. Pollak, *The Criminality of Women* (Philadelphia, 1950); P.C. Hoffer and N.E.C. Hull, *Murdering Mothers: Infanticide in England and New England, 1558–1803* (New York, etc., 1984), etc.

42. See J.M. Beattie, *Crime and the Courts*, p. 117.
43. C. Johnson. 'An Essay on the Signs of Murder', p. 394.
44. R.W. Malcolmson, 'Infanticide in the Eighteenth Century', p. 191.
45. J.A. Sharpe, *Crime in Seventeenth Century England*, p. 135.
46. R.W. Malcolmson, 'Infanticide in the Eighteenth Century', p. 191.
47. J.M. Beattie, *Crime and the Courts*, pp. 114–115.
48. 21 Jas I, c. 27.
49. J.R. Ruff, *Crime, Justice and Public Order in Old Regime France: The Sénéchaussées of Libourne and Bazas, 1696–1789* (Kent, 1984), pp. 169–170.
50. M.W. Piers, *Infanticide*, p. 56.
51. M.W. Piers, *Infanticide*, p. 79.
52. See J.R. Ruff, *Crime, Justice and Public Order*, p. 170.
53. J. Kelly, 'Infanticide in Eighteenth Century Ireland', p. 6.
54. B. Henry, *Dublin Hanged*, p. 37.
55. J. Kelly, 'Infanticide in Eighteenth Century Ireland', p. 7.
56. As 57 south-west Scottish women were indicted for homicide, and 140 were accused of infanticide, the total number of women who were charged with committing a crime where the death of a victim had resulted was 197. The corresponding figure for south-west Scottish men was 212, a difference between the two sexes of only 15.
57. NAS (National Archives of Scotland) J.C. 26 / 212.
58. NAS J.C. 26 / 266.
59. P.C. Hoffer and N.E.C. Hull, *Murdering Mothers*, p. 31.
60. P.C. Hoffer and N.E.C. Hull, *Murdering Mothers*, p. 31.
61. J.A. Sharpe, *Crime in Seventeenth Century England*, p. 136.
62. It must be borne in mind that Mitchison and Leneman's study does not extend over the same geographical area as that examined in the Justiciary records, i.e. it does not consider parishes in the Lanarkshire, Renfrewshire and Dunbartonshire regions. For further discussion, see L. Leneman and R. Mitchison, 'Scottish Illegitimacy Ratios in the Early Modern Period', *Economic History Review*, 2nd. Series, Vol. XL, no. 1 (1987), pp. 61–63 and R. Mitchison and L. Leneman, *Sexuality and Social Control*, pp. 244–245.
63. R. Mitchison and L. Leneman, *Sexuality and Social Control*, p. 146.
64. R. Mitchison and L. Leneman, *Sexuality and Social Control*, p. 147.
65. R. Mitchison and L. Leneman, *Sexuality and Social Control*, p. 9.
66. R. Mitchison and L. Leneman, *Sexuality and Social Control*, p. 10.
67. R. Mitchison and L. Leneman, *Sexuality and Social Control*, p. 10.
68. For further discussion, see T.C. Smout, 'Aspects of Sexual Behaviour in Nineteenth Century Scotland', in A.A. MacLaren (ed.), *Social Class in Scotland: Past and Present* (Edinburgh, 1976), p. 80.
69. T.C. Smout, 'Aspects of Sexual Behaviour', p. 71.
70. T.C. Smout, 'Aspects of Sexual Behaviour', p. 71.
71. R. Mitchison and L. Leneman, *Sexuality and Social Control*, p. 146.

72. R. Mitchison and L. Leneman, *Sexuality and Social Control*, p. 243.
73. For further discussion, see R. Mitchison and L. Leneman, *Sexuality and Social Control*, p. 145.
74. R. Mitchison and L. Leneman, *Sexuality and Social Control*, pp. 145 and 205.
75. M.M. Stewart, '"In Durance Vile": Crime and Punishment in Seventeenth and Eighteenth Century Records of Dumfries', *Scottish Archives: The Journal of the Scottish Records Association*, Vol. 1 (1995), p. 72. M.W. Piers argues that similar circumstances caused an increase in both illegitimacy and the spread of sexually transmitted diseases throughout eighteenth-century France. See M.W. Piers, *Infanticide*, pp. 59–61.
76. J.A. Sharpe, *Crime in Early Modern England*, p. 137.
77. J.M. Beattie, 'The Criminality of Women', *Journal of Social History*, Vol. 8 (1975), p. 84.
78. P. Linebaugh, *The London Hanged: Crime and Civil Society in the Eighteenth Century* (London, 1991), p. 147.
79. For further discussion, see R.W. Malcolmson, 'Infanticide in the Eighteenth Century', pp. 192–193 and p. 203, and R. Sauer, 'Infanticide and Abortion in Nineteenth Century Britain', *Population Studies: A Journal of Demography*, Vol. 32 (1978), p. 85.
80. F. McLynn, *Crime and Punishment*, p. 113.
81. S.X. Radbill, 'A History of Child Abuse and Infanticide', p. 9.
82. R.H. Helmholz, 'Infanticide in the Province of Canterbury during the Fifteenth Century', in R.H. Helmholz (ed.), *Canon Law and the Law of England* (London, etc., 1987), p. 160.
83. See K. Wrightson, 'Infanticide in Earlier Seventeenth Century England', p. 15 and J. Kelly, 'Infanticide in Eighteenth Century Ireland', p. 18.
84. NAS J.C. 26 / 216: Archibald Malcolm in Duncow of Kirkmahoe. The appellation 'monsters' in relation to women accused of infanticide appears to have been quite common amongst eighteenth-century commentators. Joseph Addison described such women as '. . . monsters of inhumanity . . .' (see R.W. Malcolmson, 'Infanticide in the Eighteenth Century', p. 198.) See also L. Stone, *The Family, Sex and Marriage in England, 1500–1800* (London, 1977), p. 475 and J. Kelly, 'Infanticide in Eighteenth Century Ireland', p. 19.
85. This figure includes five women who had allegedly committed the crime of infanticide through the use of exposure. For further discussion, see pp. 21–22 of the article.
86. NAS J.C. 26 / 246.
87. NAS J.C. 26 / 314.
88. NAS J.C. 26 / 322.
89. NAS J.C. 26 / 144, No. 2650–2678.
90. NAS J.C. 26 / 191.
91. NAS J.C. 26 / 196.
92. NAS J.C. 26 / 322.
93. NAS J.C. 26 / 146, No. 2722–2741.
94. NAS J.C. 26 / 155.
95. NAS J.C. 26 / 183.
96. NAS J.C. 26 / 212.
97. NAS J.C. 26 / 251.
98. NAS J.C. 26 / 294.

99. NAS J.C. 26 / 326.
100. NAS J.C. 26 / 186.
101. NAS J.C. 26 / 201.
102. NAS J.C. 26 / 263.
103. NAS J.C. 26 / 270.
104. NAS J.C. 26 / 290.
105. For further discussion, see R.W. Malcolmson, 'Infanticide in the Eighteenth Century', p. 187 and pp. 207–208.
106. F. McLynn, *Crime and Punishment*, p. 112.
107. F. McLynn, *Crime and Punishment*, p. 112.
108. R.W. Malcolmson, 'Infanticide in the Eighteenth Century', p. 188.
109. F. McLynn, *Crime and Punishment*, p. 112.
110. NAS J.C. 13 / 34.
111. See L. Rose, *The Massacre of the Innocents*, pp. 82–84. For further discussion of this type of employment, see E.C. Sanderson, *Women and Work in Eighteenth-Century Edinburgh* (Basingstoke and New York, 1996), pp. 49–53.
112. O. Pollak, *The Criminality of Women*, pp. 19–20.
113. R. Mitchison and L. Leneman, *Sexuality and Social Control*, p. 212.
114. F. McLynn, *Crime and Punishment*, p. 111.
115. R. Sauer. 'Infanticide and Abortion', p. 85.
116. For further discussion, see R. Mitchison and L. Leneman, *Sexuality and Social Control*, p. 136.
117. M. Daly and M. Wilson, *Homicide* (New York, 1988), p. 69.
118. See L. Rose, *The Massacre of the Innocents*, p. 148.
119. For further discussion, see L. Rose, *The Massacre of the Innocents*, Chapters 15 and 16; S.X. Radbill, 'A History of Child Abuse and Infanticide', p. 8; and R. Sauer, 'Infanticide and Abortion', pp. 87–88.
120. For further discussion, see L. Rose, *The Massacre of the Innocents*, p. 24; J.R. Ruff, *Crime, Justice and Public Order*, p. 169; R.W. Malcolmson, 'Infanticide in the Eighteenth Century', p. 204; and L. Stone, *The Family, Sex and Marriage*, p. 613.
121. For further discussion of this, see P.C. Hoffer and N.E.C. Hull, *Murdering Mothers*, pp. 145–158.
122. P.C. Hoffer and N.E.C. Hull, *Murdering Mothers*, pp. 157–158.
123. L. Williamson, 'Infanticide', quoted in M. Tooley, *Abortion and Infanticide*, p. 317.
124. L. Rose, *The Massacre of the Innocents*, p. 36.

FURTHER READING

J.M. Beattie, *Crime and the Courts in England, 1660–1800* (Oxford, 1986).
J.M. Beattie, 'The Criminality of Women', *Journal of Social History*, Vol. 8 (1975).
C. Damme, 'Infanticide: The Worth of an Infant under Law', in *Medical History*, Vol. 22 (1978).
P.C. Hoffer and N.E.C. Hull, *Murdering Mothers: Infanticide in England and New England, 1558–1803* (New York, 1984).
J. Kelly, 'Infanticide in Eighteenth Century Ireland', in *Irish Economic and Social History*, Vol. 19 (1992).

R.W. Malcolmson, 'Infanticide in the Eighteenth Century', in J.S. Cockburn (ed.), *Crime in England, 1550–1800* (London, 1977).

R. Mitchison and L. Leneman, *Sexuality and Social Control: Scotland, 1660–1780* (Oxford, 1989).

M.W. Piers, *Infanticide* (New York, 1978).

S.X. Radbill, 'A History of Child Abuse and Infanticide', in R.E. Helfer and C.H. Kempe (eds.), *The Battered Child* (Chicago, etc., 1968).

L. Rose, *The Massacre of the Innocents: Infanticide in Britain, 1800–1939* (London, etc., 1986).

J.R. Ruff, *Crime, Justice and Public Order in Old Regime France: The Sénéchaussées of Libourne and Bazas, 1696–1789* (Kent, 1984).

J. Sharpe, *Crime in Early Modern England, 1550–1750* (London, 1984).

M. Tooley, *Abortion and Infanticide* (Oxford, 1983).

K. Wrightson, 'Infanticide in Earlier Seventeenth Century England', *Local Population Studies*, No. 15 (1975).

TEN

From Demon to Victim:
The Infanticidal Mother in Shetland, 1699–1899 *

Lynn Abrams

The crime of infanticide has held a fascination for historians. The crime itself is almost uniquely female – very few men are prosecuted either as perpetrators or accomplices – and the revulsion felt towards the act itself, together with the severity of the punishment, has created a lasting appeal. Infanticide has particularly engaged the interest of feminist historians of the early-modern period, largely on account of the insights it can offer into the attitudes towards women in a community.[1] This was a time when the infanticidal woman stood adjacent to the witch as the archetypal demonic force in contemporary discourse. During the seventeenth and eighteenth centuries, the murdering mother was regarded as an unnatural monster, one who denied her maternal instinct, the perpetrator of a premeditated homicide.[2] Across Europe, including Scotland where the 1690 Act Anent Child Murder in Scotland treated infanticide as a capital crime, the prevalence of the death sentence for convicted women reflected this harsh attitude.

Historians of the late-modern period, on the other hand, have paid only limited attention to this crime. By the nineteenth century the infanticidal mother was more likely to be considered sympathetically, as a victim of circumstance rather then the perpetrator of an evil act. In Scotland the statue of 1809, which interpreted the concealment of pregnancy and failure to call for assistance at the birth as culpable homicide warranting no more than two years in prison, signalled a sea-change in the way the legal system dealt with suspected women. This chapter is concerned with the consequences of this shift in legal attitudes in Shetland, a place where pre-modern beliefs and practices arguably survived longer than anywhere else in Britain. It is about the regulation of women in an island community at a time when 'modern' attitudes towards the infanticidal mother on the part of the legal system existed in a tension with community discipline, especially the measures adopted by the church and its court, the kirk session.[3] In what follows we shall see how the softening of the law on infanticide in 1809 was not immediately paralleled by a shift in popular attitudes and practices until around the 1860s in Shetland. The investigation surrounding a suspicion or allegation that a woman had concealed a pregnancy and murdered her child sharply illuminates the web of observation, discipline and control that was spun around women in these most female of islands.

Between 1690 and 1918, hundreds of Scottish women were indicted for the crime of infanticide.[4] It is likely that many more were investigated on suspicion of murdering a newborn child, but their cases did not reach the courts on account of the difficulties in gathering sufficient evidence to convict a woman. In Shetland, just 40 cases of alleged child murder or concealment of pregnancy survive for the period between 1699 and 1920. Only 17 women were tried in the sheriff court and only three of these are known for certain to have served jail sentences, the lengthiest being 15 months. The remainder of the cases exist only as precognitions (witness statements taken by the procurator fiscal) and it is unclear whether or not these proceeded to a prosecution.[5] The crime of child murder, or the alternative and lesser charge of concealment of pregnancy, appears then to have been an extremely rare occurrence in Shetland.[6]

Shetland is a prime locality in which to investigate the consequences of this shift in the way the infanticidal mother was perceived and dealt with. In the nineteenth century Shetland was a relatively isolated community in terms of its geography and its insularity from modernising influences. In 1800 Shetland was a primarily rural society of around 22,000 inhabitants, dependent upon an economy dominated by fishing and crofting. The kirk session acted as the primary disciplinary body; there were no police, even in the main town of Lerwick, and few doctors. The menfolk of the islands travelled extensively beyond Shetland as seamen, and the islands were a point of transit for whalers, fishermen and smugglers of all nationalities who alighted there to drink, to trade and to engage in dalliance with Shetland women.[7] But the inclination of Shetland women to leave the islands was limited and the opportunities to do so were few. Throughout the nineteenth century women outnumbered men in the islands to an exceptional degree. In 1861 the sex imbalance peaked at 143 women to every 100 men, a consequence of the absences and dangers associated with the major form of employment for men – fishing – and the preponderance of men amongst migrants. Hence the marriage rate in the islands was significantly lower than the Scottish average – there were 7.1 marriages per 1000 of the population in Scotland in 1871 compared with just 4.9 in Shetland – and the average age at marriage was significantly higher. The never-married woman was ubiquitous here; female-headed households numbered up to 27 per cent in 1881 and a large proportion of households contained unmarried female relatives.[8] In these circumstances, in a marriage market that favoured men, it was in the interests of Shetland men to maintain control over their womenfolk.

Moreover, the discourse of domesticity and female piety which, in the rest of Britain, had been acculturated at all levels of society by the early nineteenth century, took much longer to reach Shetland. Thus, at least until the 1850s, the early-modern discourse on womanhood which emphasised control of an unruly female sexuality and the potential dangers posed by the single woman still informed the actions of the kirk session, and this came into conflict with the legal system which had taken on board the new view of womanhood as virtuous and maternal. In these islands, then, we can move back and forth across the threshold between the pre-modern and modern world view.

The analysis is based on material drawn from 39 cases of alleged concealment of pregnancy or child murder in Shetland between 1699 and 1920.[9] The infanticidal women were almost all young and single, employed in a variety of labouring and service occupations typical in the islands. Just three of the women were married and one was a widow, but all were pregnant with an illegitimate child. The average age was 26 and all but three resided in the rural parts of the islands. We know little about the circumstances of their pregnancies. Two made rape allegations but the majority had engaged in a sexual relationship with a man they hoped to marry, as in the case of Jemima Nicolson who claimed she had told her lover that she was pregnant but 'he always tried to reason me out of it . . . that it was a mere whim with me fancying that I was with child and that I said it merely with the view of getting him to marry me'.[10] Others had conceived after a fleeting sexual encounter, sometimes with a master or employer, but more often with a work acquaintance or seaman who swiftly departed the islands.[11]

The circumstances and details of the crimes in these cases bear remarkable similarities to those described by historians in other countries and at other times. Although the social and economic conditions prevailing in Shetland were exceptional, the circumstances in which these women found themselves were not. Most of the women, though, either lived with their parents and/or were employed in one of the typical occupations available to Shetland women: they were crofters and farm labourers, knitters, fish gutters and straw plaiters, in no better or worse economic situation than other unmarried women in the islands. It is possible, though, that such women were victims of expectations based on an outmoded set of courtship patterns. They anticipated that pregnancy would lead to marriage whereas it is clear that the men involved felt no such responsibility to their lovers.[12] This was especially so after 1850 when the kirk session virtually ceased pursuing cases of fornication owing to the reluctance of men and women to come forward and submit to a rebuke. Here in Shetland, as in much of Protestant Europe, illegitimacy was not uncommon although far from pervasive. In fact the illegitimacy rate was much lower here – less than 4 per cent in the 1870s – than the Scottish average of 9.5, and commentators frequently remarked upon the 'high degrees of affection and constancy' amongst both sexes. 'Although from their modes of life, the freest intercourse prevails, yet in the country parishes, deviations from chastity are by no means frequent', observed Arthur Edmondston in 1809.[13] Community censure was part and parcel of the system by which sexuality was regulated, and illegitimate children were incorporated into the community. The treatment of the alleged perpetrators of infanticide, on the other hand, suggests that women suspected of this crime in Shetland were caught between the old world and the new.

Margaret and Gina: 'perpetrator' and 'victim'

Two exemplary cases serve to characterise the shift from blame to sympathy in the treatment of women suspected of infanticide. On 17 January 1699, Margaret Magnusdaughter, servant in the house of Erasmus Irvine in the parish of Tingwall in Shetland, appeared in the Shetland sheriff court accused of the murder of her newborn child. Also present in court were the father of the child – the aforementioned Erasmus Irvine – who was accused of 'concealling & conneving of in . . . the murder of the chyld', Barbara Marwick, an Orkney woman, and John Mowat. The latter pair had allegedly supplied Margaret Magnusdaughter with a drink to bring forth an abortion and thus stood trial for not divulging Margaret's 'cruell enterprise'. If found guilty, all four defendants could be sentenced to death for committing 'so horrabill & deteastable a crime a[s] murthering ane poor innocent infant, a lyf in the mothers belly not come to the light of the world'.[14]

Margaret Magnusdaughter was already well known in her parish as a 'trelaps furnicatrix', that is, she had appeared three times before the kirk session for fornication. In November of 1698 the session heard rumours that she was with child and that Margaret had approached John Mowat and Barbara Marwick for an abortifacient. Summoned once more before the kirk elders, Margaret denied everything, but her protestations of innocence fell on the deaf ears of the session members who gave little credence to the words of a woman they described as a 'baise and vyld strumpet'. Margaret appeared again before the session in January 1699 when she eventually confessed to having been pregnant but stated the father was a strange man who had lodged in her master's house and who had now left the country. Under pressure, however, she acknowledged that Erasmus Irvine was the true father, that she had not told anyone of her condition, that she had not called for any assistance during the birth but that she alone 'brought furth that abortion', and that Irvine had taken the child away. Erasmus Irvine likewise broke down under interrogation and confirmed this version of events, admitting that he had 'receaved the chyld from her and wrapt it in a linning cloth and privatly under cloud & silence of night conveyed the same away and buried it on the east syd of the barn'. He estimated the child to be as big 'as thow could put it in thy mittine', but later estimated it to be a seven-month child and already dead when he received it. Justice William Menzies judged Margaret Magnusdaughter, Erasmus Irvine and Barbara Marwick to be murderers (there was insufficient evidence to implicate Mowat). Citing not the law but the Old Testament, he declared: 'whear slaughter is counted the slaughterer shall be szeased upon and if found forthnight feallanie he shall dy'.

Margaret was not a sympathetic defendant on account of her notorious lifestyle and her evident disdain for the morals and the disciplining of the kirk. Yet neither was she a cold-blooded murderer who did away with her newborn baby with evil intent. Indeed she might be regarded as a victim of a one-night stand with Irvine and of his desperation to be rid of an illegitimate child. It had been Irvine who had gone to great trouble and considerable expense to obtain an abortifacient when Margaret was 'five weeks with quick child', with the story that she required a cure for a swelling in her womb and pain in her breast. Margaret was convicted of concealing a pregnancy and failing to call for help at the birth and thereby leaving herself open to the accusation of child murder under the terms of the 1690 Act Anent Child Murder, despite the fact that the circumstances of the child's death were unclear.[15]

The case of Margaret Magnusdaughter is the earliest recorded infanticide case in Shetland. The latest recorded case in the islands occurred in 1920. By the end of the period attitudes towards infanticidal women had markedly changed. As Anne-Marie Kilday argues in her chapter of this volume, there was a toughening of the law against child murder in the sixteenth and seventeenth centuries (Margaret Magnusdaughter's case fell just nine years after the introduction of the notorious 1690 statute which presumed the guilt of the defendant and convicted women against whom there was no direct evidence), but during the eighteenth century Scottish judges were tempering the harshness of the law with less severe penalties than death or banishment. By the nineteenth century, however, the infanticidal mother was handled more sympathetically. Thus, when Gina Skaar, a 23-year-old Norwegian domestic servant, was found guilty of concealment of pregnancy by the Shetland sheriff court in 1899, the outpouring of public sympathy for the girl contrasted markedly with the punitive attitude adopted towards Margaret Magnusdaughter.[16] The sheriff in the Skaar case accepted, to a degree, the mitigating circumstances presented by the woman's defence counsel – that she did not speak the language, was far from home and separated from relatives and friends, 'especially females in whom she might have confided and consulted' – and sentenced her to just nine months' imprisonment rather than the maximum two years. Nonetheless, public opinion was far more willing to interpret Gina as a victim, as the correspondence in the local press indicated:

> When . . . the long months of sickening apprehension and suffering, and the acute physical agony both of body and mind, are taken into consideration, and the mean conduct of the male participant, whom I will not call a man . . . it might be thought that any woman under such circumstances has suffered enough . . . The girl has done wrong, no doubt, but she has suffered for it . . . we do not kill the fatted calf for the female prodigal in such cases; we reserve this entirely for the male.[17]

The author of this letter in *The Shetland News* proceeded to hope that Gina would be released from prison and, following a petition signed by a number of residents of her parish of Mossbank, the sentence was reduced to six months.[18]

By the time Gina Skaar was prosecuted, popular and official attitudes towards infanticide and the means by which the suspect was treated had markedly changed since 1699. Skaar was the beneficiary of a more modern view which regarded the infanticidal woman as a victim of circumstance, a woman not wholly responsible for her actions. According to the Scottish surgeon and 'midwife' William Hunter in 1783, infanticidal mothers were not dangerous, deviant women; indeed he argued that women 'who are pregnant without daring to avow their situation . . . are generously less criminal than the world imagine'.[19] For Hunter, who had attended numerous births and who claimed to have a unique insight into the mind of the parturient mother, these female murderers were not the very antithesis of the maternal female as some liked to portray them; indeed he believed that a woman was incapable of murdering her own child. Rather it was fear, shock and exhaustion that blocked a woman's maternal instinct. For Hunter, women who committed infanticide did so when in a virtually unconscious state.[20] The context within which Hunter and other like-minded contemporaries were writing is significant. By the end of the eighteenth century a discourse on the presumption of natural maternal affection was widespread. The maternal woman was elevated and revered and motherhood was idealised as the zenith of a woman's emotional and spiritual fulfilment. It was this attitude that informed nineteenth-century legal and medical reactions to infanticide.

By the twentieth century, medical or scientific explanations for the act of infanticide were predominant. In England the 1922 Infanticide Act permitted a woman to claim as a defence the fact that the balance of her mind was disturbed as a result of giving birth. In 1938 this was extended to permit cases where a mother was diagnosed as suffering from puerperal or lactational insanity.[21] More recently psychiatrists have sought to understand both pregnancy denial and infanticide. Using the term 'splitting', perinatal psychiatrists explain how such women dissociate themselves from reality. They deny their own knowledge of their condition, and this denial may even result in the suppression of the physical symptoms of pregnancy and thereby explain the oft-stated declaration that no pain was felt upon childbirth.[22] What unites the maternalist views of Hunter in the eighteenth century with present-day psychiatrists is the common belief that infanticidal women are neither deviant nor dangerous, but rather women who are desperately trying to conform to an idealised model of womanhood which their illegitimate pregnancy threatens to undermine.

The narratives constructed by the women themselves and witnesses support this position. Each woman reached the position of denial informed by individual circumstances, and the historian cannot reach far beyond the surviving legal texts in order to explain motivation. However, the infanticide narrative does provide an insight into the gender dynamics of Shetland communities. The rest of this chapter will reconstruct the intimate and the everyday experiences of the women accused of concealment and infanticide in nineteenth-century Shetland and in doing so will explore three key issues. Firstly, it will consider what the observation of a woman's body in these cases tells us about interpretations of bodily signs and symptoms specifically in relation to pregnancy and childbirth. Secondly it will look at how cases of infanticide can provide an insight into community controls, networks and hierarchies of knowledge. And thirdly it will demonstrate how women who denied their pregnancy and who gave birth in secret and silence isolated themselves from traditional supportive rituals and practices designed to protect mother and child, and close observation of a woman by members of her community.

Women's bodies

The female body was (and is) a site of contradictory and competing knowledges. Until the twentieth century pregnancy was not easily diagnosed and could never be certain. The pregnant woman, her female relatives and neighbours, mere acquaintances, midwives and doctors, all provided often conflicting interpretations of bodily signs and symptoms. Women's bodies were regarded as unstable; physical processes and signs were ambiguous.²³ And it was not until the very end of the nineteenth century that medical diagnoses pronounced by medical doctors were given greater weight than the observations and interpretations of women themselves. Indeed, doctors throughout the century appear to have concurred with the uncertainty of diagnosis and the range of interpretations of symptoms adopted by their patients. The symptoms normally associated with a pregnancy today – cessation of menstruation, a swelling belly, enlarged breasts, swollen legs, sickness, tiredness and even food cravings – were all open to a number of interpretations. Dropsy, a cyst or boil, a 'swelling' of the stomach – all of these were commonly cited as explanations for a woman assuming the appearance of a woman with child. Hard physical labour, psychological trauma, a cold or a fall could all explain interrupted menstruation.

In 1859 Jemima Nicolson was suspected of having concealed her pregnancy. Rumours of her being with child circulated amongst her neighbours on the island of Unst, but no-one would admit to being certain of her condition. Charles Mouat, a 61-year-old Elder of the Free Church, admitted he had heard the rumour and thought she looked stouter than usual but admitted that 'the new fashion of women's dresses' meant 'it was impossible to say'. Lawrence Edmondson, the island's doctor, told how Jemima had visited him with a stomach complaint and that he had given her a tonic for dyspepsia. Her hitherto irreproachable character meant that he never suspected Jemima of being pregnant. Her sister-in-law Charlotte, on the other hand, a woman who herself was pregnant and who lived in the same house as Jemima, had her suspicions but even she could not be certain:

> Sometimes I fancied she looked stouter than usual and at other times I thought I had been mistaken. I sometimes spoke to her sister Jane about her and we did think at times that there might be truth in the rumour, but we never could come to any decided opinion . . . Jemima has ever since I came to the house appeared strong and healthy and wrought well and actively.²⁴

Elizabeth Williamson, the sister of Christina Williamson who was investigated for concealment of pregnancy in 1857, was similarly ambivalent about her sister's state of health. Although she was aware of rumours that Christina was pregnant, she declared that she never spoke to her sister on the subject. 'I had frequent opportunities of seeing her both dressed and undressed but I cannot say I observed any change in her figure or appearance . . . she maybe was rather fuller than she ought to have been.'²⁵ It was clear that Christina's belly was swollen but Elizabeth professed not to know what had been the matter with her sister. Even at the end of the nineteenth century pregnancy was still surrounded with much uncertainty, with symptoms easily confused with other complaints. Margaret Johnston was known to suffer from erysipelas (inflammation of the skin) which frequently confined her to the house. In the summer of 1893 rumours abounded that Margaret was showing signs of pregnancy but few were willing to believe the stories. 'I noticed that she was swelled', remarked one witness. 'I thought it awful of the people to say it. I knew she was subject to erysipelas and was often confined to the house with it . . . I could not say she was with child. Any other thing might have caused the swelling.'[26] Another neighbour concurred: 'I remember the report about accused but I could not believe it was true . . . she just as it were crept along like one who had a severe illness'.[27]

One might have expected the woman accused of concealing a pregnancy and the murder of a child to deny under interrogation that she knew she was pregnant, as deliberate concealment was a crime in itself. Yet the protestations of the accused are often striking in their veracity. Their tendency to emphasise ignorance of their true condition took advantage of the uncertainty that so often surrounded a diagnosis of pregnancy or illness. In 1815, 34-year-old Margaret Fraser was tried in the sheriff court for child murder. She had been delivered of a female child alone and had wrapped the child and concealed it in her bed for ten days. Margaret only admitted she had delivered a still-born child when a neighbour called to ascertain the truth of the rumour and squeezed Margaret's breasts and nipples until milk was forthcoming. Margaret Fraser had been aware of the rumours about her but she consistently rejected the inference that she was with child. Moreover, as she explained in her statement, despite having been raped whilst she was in service in Lerwick, she had no thought that her 'illness' could have arisen from this encounter. On her return to her father's house at Walls she 'felt herself sickish and unwell':

> that in particular a suppression of her monthly courses took place,
> but she never once surmised that her illness arose from pregnancy
> and she applied to several persons in Walls for medicines to remove
> the suppression of her menses; that this ailment still continued and
> that she increased in size so much that she became alarmed and
> supposed that it was a swelling or some dropsical complaint that she
> was labouring under; that at last she was so ill from pains from what
> she considered the swelling in the lower part of her belly that she
> feared it to be a boil about breaking, that at the end of about three
> days from the time at which these severe pains seized her she was
> delivered of a female child and until then she never once knew or
> thought she had been pregnant.[28]

While it is surprising that a 34-year-old woman did not associate her 'illness' with pregnancy, in the case of 17-year-old Janet Deyell the protestations of all concerned that no-one had any idea that she was pregnant are more convincing. According to her mother, Janet had just started to menstruate but her periods were irregular. She suffered stomach pains and had a furred tongue but Margaret Deyell put this down to 'a disordered stomach'. Janet's mother noticed a change in her daughter's figure – 'I noticed her breasts increasing but looking to her age I thought she was just developing into womanhood':

> She continued to work every day although complaining occasionally.
> On Monday she carried peats all day. On Tuesday she wrought all
> day at the hill filling peats . . . On Wednesday she was carrying peats
> all day . . . and came home quite well but complaining of being tired.
> On Thursday morning she complained of a severe pain in the back
> and I kept her bed in the morning. I thought her menstruation was
> to recommence . . . I then got Wilhelmina Thomson and her mother
> Barbara Williamson and Isabella Williamson to see my daughter.
> I thought my daughter was suffering from inflammation and the
> women thought the same . . . She grew worse but about 5 o'clock
> the pain left. The women were still in the house then. Between 6
> and 7 after the women left I went to the bed and said 'Janny is the
> pain fairly away?' She said 'yes mother but there is a child born' . . .
> When she said a child was born I lifted the blanket and saw the
> child but could not lay my hand on her. I called out "my God" and
> ran out.[29]

It is clear that there was no agreed meaning ascribed to a range of symptoms which might or might not signify a pregnancy. As Ulinka Rublack has argued for early-modern Germany, 'the criminalization of "hidden pregnancies" therefore tried to impose a unified meaning upon a deeply ambiguous situation'.[30] Different interpretations were ascribed to physical changes in the body which, according to the context in which these symptoms were understood, could mean either pregnancy or something else such as a growth, a swelling, a temporary blockage or even weight gain. A woman's age and experience – as in the case of Janet Deyell – her reputation, and the vehemence of her denial of pregnancy, all determined the way in which her physical symptoms were understood by community members and by the courts. Margaret Fraser was said to be 'extremely religious'.[31] Gina Skaar's mistress was inclined to believe her servant's denial of pregnancy despite the evidence before her own eyes that Gina was 'growing bigger and bigger' because 'she had been such a good servant and had always been so trustworthy'.[32] Agnes Hawick was said to be a 'very quiet and apparently pious girl', so much so that her fellow servant was not inclined to believe the rumours she heard about Agnes having an abortion.[33]

The 'illness narrative' constructed by these women during the course of their pregnancy and again in court privileged a woman's interpretation of her body. This was not merely a defence tactic employed by accused women. Legal officials engaged with these narratives, with all their uncertainties and ambiguities. Even doctors were willing to believe women's interpretations, at least until the end of the century. This may explain why so many cases failed to be prosecuted. Proof of pregnancy in the absence of a child was hard to come by. Thus, from the accused woman's perspective, the privileging of a pre-modern, unscientific understanding of the female body could be empowering at a time when the elevation of the pious, spiritual mother was beginning to assume greater importance.

The disciplining of women

Notwithstanding the uncertainty surrounding the symptoms of pregnancy, some individuals were clearly privileged with greater knowledge of women's bodies. Until the 1850s women who had already borne children, and midwives, possessed a degree of power in the criminal system otherwise dominated by legal and religious men. Prosecutors, sheriffs and church elders used women's knowledge and insight in an attempt to gain evidence and understanding of a female world of pregnancy and childbirth. It was only later that medical doctors came to usurp the knowledge and power of women in the community.

Pregnancy and childbirth were the domain of women. Married women most likely welcomed the interest shown in their bodies by other women, and they understood that the openness required of them was a form of protection for themselves and their babies. Men were not part of this culture. Indeed, men were so often absent from their homes and communities that they were unreliable witnesses to a woman's changing appearance. The father of Mary Twatt, accused of child murder in 1853, acknowledged that his daughter was in poor health but commented that he did not know the cause. 'I did not speak to her mother or herself about this but I often wondered at her gradually wasting countenance which was previously to be full and blooming. I had no suspicion of her being in the family way nor did I ever hear such a rumour.'[34] It was only when Mary had delivered a child that her father understood the cause of her ill health. Called home from his fishing booth by his wife, James Twatt was 'so taken by surprise and shocked' that he left the house and called on a neighbour who described him as being 'in great distress and crying' and 'in great agony of mind'.[35] In 1908 James Clark, husband of Williamina Clark, only discovered his wife was pregnant when he returned having been away at sea for more than a year. When told by an acquaintance, he said, 'I did not believe it and did not speak to my wife about it'.[36]

Church ministers and elders, on the other hand, regarded the observation and control of women's sexual comportment as a central part of their disciplinary role. Meetings of the kirk session spent considerable time on matters concerning fornication and adultery, at least until mid-century in rural areas, a little earlier in urban Lerwick, and ministers regularly reminded their parishioners from the pulpit of the consequences of sexual misconduct including the punishment for concealment and child murder.[37] Session elders were often among the first on the scene following the rumour of a dead child, but whereas during the eighteenth century elders would have requested to see a woman's breasts and may well have carried out the examination themselves, in the nineteenth century they required women to assist them in their interrogatory duties. Thus in 1794, when Marion Henrysdaughter was suspected of having given birth – a report was circulating that 'milk was running down the said Marion Henrysdaughter's breasts' – Robert Ollason, who was an elder in the Dunrossness kirk session, 'considered it his duty to make further enquiry'. Ollason proceeded to her house accompanied by two other elders and met another when they arrived. The four entered and desired Marion 'to show her breasts, but she gave no answer, pretending to fall in fits'. The following day three elders returned under orders of the minister. Marion's mother 'called out her daughter who showed her breasts but of which the milk flowed plentifully . . .'[38]

Amongst the Shetland cases there are no instances of elders themselves milking women's breasts after 1800. Menstruation, pregnancy, abortion and childbirth were intrinsic to female culture, and until the end of the nineteenth century most births would have been attended by a local midwife, wise-woman or 'howdie'. Men were now content to pay lip service to separate spheres. When Margaret Walterson was reported to have been delivered of an illegitimate child one morning in May 1855, Gilbert Williamson, who was the local schoolmaster and an elder of the Church of Scotland, wasted no time in visiting her accompanied by another elder and two women, one of whom was an occasional midwife. Margaret Walterson was still in bed when they arrived. 'She was not aware of me and the other Elder being in the room as we thought it better to allow the women to interrogate her as if by themselves for fear of agitating her if she knew that we were present. Ann Harrison put the questions to her, some of which suggested by me.'[39] However, elders also used midwives for more than verbal interrogations. It was commonly believed that the only

sure sign that a woman had given birth was if her breasts contained milk.
Elspeth White, a midwife in Lerwick in 1830, was called to examine Janet
Leisk, just eighteen years old, who had reportedly been delivered of a child
a few days previously. News spread quickly around the town. Janet Leisk's
neighbour, upon hearing the rumour, mentioned it to Janet's grandfather
who spoke to Janet's mother, who in turn went to see the elder of the
parish and he sent Elspeth White to Janet's home. The midwife requested
that Janet show her breasts:

> she objected at first to show her breasts but at last consented at her
> mother's request and came forward . . . trembling and crying; that
> on seeing the breasts [Elspeth White] remarked that she did not
> like their appearance, meaning their appearance indicated that the
> said Janet Leisk had recently brought forth a child, upon which her
> mother remarked that she had been wearing tight stays during the
> summer which had bruised her breasts. Declares that she [Elspeth
> White] then tried if there was any milk in them and obtained a small
> quantity by sucking.[40]

Midwives occupied a privileged place in the investigation process, but
the evidence of other female witnesses – women who were themselves
mothers – also assumed importance precisely because childbirth was a
female domain. 'Having had a family myself', remarked Andrina Sinclair
in the case of Agnes Hawick in 1854, 'I was satisfied both from what
she told me of her state and from her appearance that she had been
delivered . . .'[41]

Attempts were made to claim single women's bodies as public property,
especially when they were suspected of being pregnant or having given
birth. Margaret Fraser's body was not only subject to constant observation
and comment by other women – one neighbour exhorted her 'not to
conceal the pregnancy if she was really in that state'[42] – but it was also
subjected to frequent poking and pressing while she complained of nothing
more than a swelling in her belly. One of her neighbours who wished to
test the rumour that Margaret was with child 'felt Margaret's belly and
distinctly was aware of the moving of a child within it'.[43] Another who
suspected the true cause of Margaret's illness visited after Margaret had
given birth:

> felt her breasts and body and was immediately convinced that she
> had been recently delivered not only from the empty feeling of her
> belly and stomach and her body being tied round with a napkin as is
> customary with women after childbirth but also from the appearance
> of blood about her person and other convincing circumstances . . .[44]

This intense interest in a woman's body cannot be explained merely by natural curiosity. Pregnancy and childbirth were surrounded by ritual and social custom designed to support the mother and child. In order to be emotionally prepared for the birth it was necessary that a mother be emotionally and socially 'open' so that she would be able to call on assistance if needed.45 A married woman would submit to public interest in her condition because she knew it was to her benefit. Secrecy and silence were interpreted as potentially dangerous for the life of the child and the social position of the mother. Some believed, for instance, that childbirth was a time when a mother was particularly vulnerable to enchantment by fairies or that newborn babies were at risk of being stolen away by fairies.46 The potential for infanticide may even have been acknowledged. It was more likely, though, that babies were thought to be more at risk from a woman's ignorance at the time of birth. She needed the help of experienced women. A woman who denied her condition shut herself off from the community of women who normally would have facilitated her transformation into a mother. Thus, although it might appear as if midwives and other women sought to expose the suspect, their actions should not necessarily be interpreted as an absence of female solidarity but rather as a means of protecting a woman from herself. Their mode of regulation could be seen as positive in contrast to the actions of session elders who were more interested in punishment than protection. Other women understood the consequences of pregnancy denial. They were also, of course, protecting themselves from being associated with her deed.

By the end of the nineteenth century the privileging of women's knowledge in such cases was slowly on the wane in the face of the increasing acceptance of predominantly male medical and scientific expertise. Prior to this doctors were rare in rural Shetland and would have attended births very seldom. They may have been consulted by pregnant women but, as Jemima Nicolson's case shows, doctors could not be relied upon to give an accurate diagnosis. Jemima consulted doctor Laurence Edmondston in 1858 for a stomach complaint. 'I thought that if I really was in the family way he would have discovered it and would have told me – especially on the occasion when he gripped my person.' Edmondston gave her a tonic, never suspecting she might be pregnant.47 By the 1890s, though, the doctor's knowledge and diagnosis were more often used in court. In 1895 a doctor was called when Mary Dempster, a servant in Lerwick's Royal Hotel, failed to rise in the morning. By the time he arrived she had given birth. 'The doctor asked what ailed her and she said she had not menstruated for three months, that she had often been that way before and that she was now alright. The doctor felt her pulse and looked at her and said "Mary have you not had a miscarriage? She replied "No" . . .' In fact Mary had secreted the child's body in a hole under the toilet cistern where it was soon discovered.[48] A few years later the evidence of Thomas Edmondston Saxby, doctor on the island of Unst, was to be even more damning in the case of Robina Pennant. Robina consulted Saxby when her periods had ceased for two months:

> I asked her if there was no other cause and also whether she knew what I meant by that. She said there was no other cause, that if there had been she would not have come to me . . . Her symptoms indicated pregnancy of about two months. At the time I noted in my day book these facts – it is my habit to make notes on any doubtful or interesting cases . . . I said in a frivolous way that she should get a sweetheart and get married as soon as possible.[49]

Some six months later Saxby was called to see his patient once more and this time he was in no doubt about her condition: 'her abdomen and ankles had swollen . . . the womb could be felt contracting and relaxing . . . other movements like foetal movements could be felt. The stethoscope revealed foetal heart beats 132 per minute'.[50] Still Robina had denied her condition but the stethoscope could tell no lies.

These women maintained the fiction that they were not with child throughout their pregnancy and sometimes after the child's death and, as we have seen, by the end of the century this fiction was becoming increasingly difficult to sustain in the face of more reliable medical diagnosis. However, the denial was not merely a cover or a lie; it expressed that woman's reality. In most cases these women not only created great uncertainty about their condition but, more importantly, they 'denied the child they were carrying any social existence from the outset', and thus they were depriving the child of an identity and refusing a commitment to motherhood.[51] It was this psychological condition that necessitated secrecy and silence and resulted in the death of the child.

The birth and the death of a child

These women gave birth alone, in secret and often in silence. Jemima Nicolson's experience is typical. According to her sister-in-law who lived in the same house in Unst, Jemima had gone to bed earlier than usual that night 'saying that she had got sick from having spent a considerable part of the evening gutting sillocks'.[52] The following morning she lay in bed longer than the rest of the family but 'was up in the course of the day going about her work as usual'.[53] Although Jemima slept in the same room as her brother and sister-in-law, they professed not to have been disturbed during the night. According to Jemima:

> One night about three weeks ago or thereby I was delivered of
> a child in the house of my father Robert Nicolson fisherman at
> Haroldswick . . . but as it was dark I did not see whether it was
> male or female and I think it was dead born as I was not aware of
> any movement or sound. No-one in the family was aware of the
> occurrence except myself. I do not know what time of the night it
> was and I think the whole of the family were asleep. I had gone to
> bed about the usual time along with the rest of the family and had
> fallen asleep and slept for a time, but I do not know for how long.
> I awoke with pain through my body and I got out of bed and was
> standing leaning on the chimney piece when I was delivered of the
> child. I was in the act of sitting down when the child was born. I
> took a shift of my own which was lying close at hand and threw over
> the child which I rolled up in the shift and laid it between the bolster
> and the head of my bed. It lay there three or four days without any
> person being aware of it. I then carried it out and dug a hole in
> the foot of our yard which is situated in the front of the house and
> therein buried the child.[54]

Similarly, Elizabeth Johnson had given birth silently in a room where her master and mistress also slept – 'she made no noise that could waken them'.[55] Margaret Fraser declared that she had 'no pains' when she gave birth.[56] Margaret Thomson also gave birth during the night when the rest of the family were in bed asleep. While she had little pain, the baby 'neither cried nor exhibited any other signs of life'.[57] One woman even maintained that she gave birth while she shared a bed with her sister without waking her. Others gave birth in outhouses, barns, kilns and in the open air.

How could these women give birth with so little fuss? We have already seen how they had detached themselves from the experience of being pregnant. They had not imagined themselves as mothers, they had made no preparations for the birth and therefore they did not experience childbirth in the same way as proud expectant mothers. Giving birth alone, in secret and silently, stood in stark contrast to the normal experience of childbirth when a woman would have been surrounded by other women, when a woman's labour cries were regarded as an aid to delivery and when the birth of a healthy baby would have been greeted with relief and joy.[58] For these women, on the other hand, childbirth was experienced as the getting rid of a burden, the relieving of symptoms which had caused psychological pain. When Margaret Walterson was asked 'what had become of her burden', she replied 'that she had parted with it at the corner of the house early that morning before daylight and that she had turned it away with her foot and that she supposed it had fallen into the loch after which she had turned into the house again'.[59] Interrogated a second time by the church elder, Margaret refused to admit to having delivered a live child 'but seemed to say it was something else – some burden with which she had no previous acquaintance'.[60] Margaret Walterson had already dissociated herself from her child – if she looked at it she was in danger of forming an attachment to it so, like other women in her position, she maintained the fiction that she had created for so many months by telling herself she had merely got rid of an encumbrance.

With a history of denial behind them it made sense to these women to explain what had happened to them as a purging of blood or some other obstruction. Jemima Nicolson explained she had been 'aware while in her bed of the usual change coming on and that she got out of bed and was aware of something like an abortion coming from her but she did not know what became of it and did not see anything'.[61] Gina Skaar, who was found in a bed 'saturated with blood' and with her arms covered with blood up to the elbow, told the midwife that her 'courses had been stopped for 14 months and had come on again'.[62] Mary Dempster told the doctor that she had not menstruated for some months and that she had disposed of nothing more than clotted blood down the closet. It was only when the doctor discovered the afterbirth in a chamber pot that Mary broke down screaming, revealing that she had concealed the child in a hole under the cistern.[63]

The denial narrative constructed by most women helps to explain why the babies died. In the cases considered here there is little evidence of maternal brutality or violence towards the newborn child.[64] Rather, it appears that most died on account of ignorance and fear of the mothers and, in some cases, their accomplices. It was common for women accused of infanticide to state that they had been sure the child was already dead inside them and that the child had thus been still-born. Jane White gave birth on the hillside while she was bringing home her father's cows. She said the child was 'dead-born', the result of two severe falls whilst she was carrying heavy loads of turf. Jane buried the child on the hillside wrapped in a handkerchief.[65] Margaret Thomson also declared that she had experienced a fall 'gripping a cow some weeks previous to the birth and had not felt any life in the child for the lat two or three days before it was born'.[66] However, the heavy physical labour regularly undertaken by Shetland women does not seem to be a legitimate explanation for still-births. In 1917, Dr Saxby who practised on the island of Unst remarked that 'outdoor work on the farm is directly conducive to quick, easy labour', whereas women engaged in sedentary occupations were more likely to experience difficulties.[67]

A more likely cause of death in many instances was neglect of the child in its first moments of life. In 1834 Lillias Umphray asserted that her child was dead-born but two surgeons called to give evidence called attention to Lillias' failure to tie the umbilical cord, which may have caused the child to bleed to death. According to Isaac Cowie, surgeon and accoucheur in Lerwick, 'she might not have been aware of the consequences of not preventing bleeding from the umbilical cord . . . or might not have known the means necessary . . .'[68] Of course ignorance was not an acceptable defence when a woman was being prosecuted for concealment since it was the very act of concealing the pregnancy and failing to call for assistance that condemned a woman.

The arrival of an illegitimate child whose existence had been steadfastly denied for several months seems to have evoked sentiments of shock and fear in the mother and other women associated with her. Of course if a woman had admitted her condition, she would have benefited from the aid and expertise of the female community. It was as if her denial alienated other women who did not wish to be associated with the arrival of an unwanted child. In the summer of 1853 Mary Twatt gave birth to an illegitimate child in her father's house. For some time rumours had circulated that the father of the child was Mary's brother-in-law in whose house she had worked as a servant. This allegation helps to explain the intense interest in Mary's condition but also, perhaps, the reactions of her mother and female neighbours upon the birth of the child. Margaret Twatt heard her daughter cry out in the ben end of the house. She went to attend her and turned the blankets down and 'when she saw what had happened she said "I'll have to go and leave thee" and I [Mary] scarcely knowing what I said replied "Go"'. The blankets were replaced. Some considerable time later Margaret returned and found the child dead. Asked whether the child was born alive, Margaret replied, 'I suppose it was I saw it breathe once, but I gave it no help'. Neither mother nor daughter touched the child until Margaret Twatt wrapped it in cloth and placed it back in the bed where it was left to lie for a day. Neighbours Catherine Moffat, Elizabeth Jamieson and Christina Twatt also heard Mary's screams but none entered the house; the latter who was Mary's aunt refused, saying 'that if they wanted her they would have sent for her'. Barbara Jamieson, another near neighbour, did confront Mary's mother as she was returning from the peathill, saying: 'Maggy there must have been something extraordinary in your house this morning as Mary's cried have alarmed the neighbours. What is the meaning of it?' Barbara had been unable to enter the house as the door had been shut. Margaret Twatt did not reply, whereby Barbara Jamieson remarked, 'friend there can be no secrets from god'.[69] The child was later placed in a box and buried by Mary's father.[70] A similar reluctance to intervene in another case, that of Mary Williamson in 1885, was shown by 53-year-old Agnes Nicolson who had called on Mary's mother to buy a pound of sugar. 'As I passed the byre I saw through the door which was shut a glimmer of a light and heard someone moan bitterly. I was frightened or I would have stopped but I passed on . . .' Not so quickly for her to miss Mary's mother exclaim, 'My Jesus what a terror I have had and now it is ended'.[71]

It is significant that women who killed their babies concealed them – in their beds, about the house and more commonly in outbuildings or in a shallow grave – rather than burying them in consecrated ground. Only one woman, Lillias Umphray, tried to give her baby a consecrated burial by placing it in a hole in Vidlin old churchyard.[72] There are no indications that the children were baptised or that the mothers were concerned that this had not taken place. Across Europe great pains were taken to ensure a child was baptised before it died, and parents of a still-born baby often tried to wake it so that it could be baptised and buried in sacred ground.[73] In the Shetland cases mothers frequently carefully wrapped their dead babies in cloth or whatever came to hand and secreted them until they were found, or until such a time as the mother could find the child a more permanent resting place. Margaret Thomson gave birth in the night. She wrapped the child in clothes and placed it in a chest until the following night when she buried it on a sandy beach nearby. A few days later she removed the child's body and buried it in a shallow grave in a kailyard. Once the child had been discovered and examined, it was buried in the churchyard at Hamnavoe.[74] Similarly, Marion Henrysdaughter kept the body of her dead baby in her bed for a whole day. The following day she secretly buried the child in a hole in a skeo (fish-drying house) and covered it with a flat stone. After an interrogation by the church elder which included showing him her breasts, Marion confessed the child was concealed in the skeo. It was then removed by the alleged father of the child and buried in the churchyard at Dunrossness.[75] Margaret Omond placed her dead child in the furnace of a kiln with 'straw stopt in to conceal it'.[76] Some babies were never found. Gina Skaar was suspected of having thrown the body of her child into the sea where it would have been swept away by the strong tide.[77]

Conclusions

Shetland women who committed infanticide were not deviant women or cold-blooded murderesses. Rather the opposite is the case. These women were desperately trying to avoid condemnation and attempting to conform to the ideal of the good, virtuous woman. Their persistent denial of their condition and the secrecy and silence in which they gave birth indicate that the death of the newborn child was not planned and not carried out with evil intent. These women never imagined themselves as mothers. When the child was born, they often refused to look at it or touch it; it is as if the child did not exist: it did not have a separate identity. Infanticide was the consequence of a socially induced psychological condition. The detachment demonstrated by the failure of these women to acknowledge their condition was probably attributable to a number of causes including abandonment by the father of the child or their experience of sexual assault; the reduced likelihood of marriage as a single mother; the woman's disempowered position in the community both as a marginal worker and an unmarried female; the knowledge that evidence of her condition would probably result in disciplining by the kirk session. We will never know what induced these women to commit this crime. In the nineteenth century, though, in contrast with earlier times, the legal system no longer regarded these women as evil; it treated them sympathetically as victims of circumstance, and the majority were probably able to continue living and working in the community.

But community controls on single women in Shetland were slower to change. The new Enlightenment discourses on virtuous womanhood did not reach Shetland until the second half of the nineteenth century. The church attempted to maintain its grip on deviant sexualities until the 1850s, and thus women under suspicion of child murder were still subject to the observation and intervention of kirk elders and their supporters as a means of maintaining control over all women. In parallel, the female community continued to watch out for its own as a means of protecting women from the censure of the church and from the harm they might do to themselves and the unborn child. Thus, women continued to privilege female interpretations of the body and they maintained a close watch on their sisters as a form of protection for all women. However, if an infanticide was suspected, women's knowledge became a threat rather than a support within a culture of suspicion and control of women's sexuality. It is dangerous to assume that women always supported one another or that female solidarity could overcome institutionalised male power. By 1900, however, Shetland was a different place. The power of the church had declined, medical doctors were more widespread, there were more economic opportunities for women, especially in the herring industry, and transport communications with the Scottish mainland were more frequent. Women did not stop committing infanticide, though there are very few recorded cases in the twentieth century. Those who did could be sure that they would not be subjected to public scrutiny of their bodies and an interrogation of their sexual history. We do not know what happened to Gina Skaar once she had served her prison sentence. One of her supporters expressed the hope that 'something will be done to help her regain her lost status in society'.[78] Certainly, by the end of the century, both popular and official opinion was more inclined to be of the same view.

NOTES

* Research for this chapter was made possible by grants from the British Academy, the Carnegie Trust and the John Robertson Bequest, University of Glasgow.

1. See, for example, Gowing, Laura (1997), 'Secret births and infanticide in 17th century England', *Past and Present* 156, pp. 87–115; Rublack, Ulinka (1999), *The Crimes of Women in Early Modern Germany*, Oxford, Oxford University Press; Rowlands, Alison (1997), '"In great secrecy": the crime of infanticide in Rothenburg ob der Tauber, 1501–1618', *German History* 15:2, pp. 101–21.

2. See Anne-Marie Kilday's chapter in this book.

3. On the disciplinary functions of the session, see Mitchison, Rosalind K. and Leneman, Leah (1989), *Sexuality and Social Control – Scotland 1660–1780*, Oxford, Oxford University Press; and Mitchison, R. and Leneman, L. (1998), *Girls in Trouble. Sexuality and Social Control in Rural Scotland, 1660–1780*. Edinburgh, Scottish Cultural Press.

4. Deborah Symonds lists 347 cases prosecuted in jury trials across Scotland between 1661 and 1821 but there were almost certainly many more women investigated whose cases never resulted in prosecution or who were tried in sheriff courts. Symonds, D. (1997), *Weep Not For Me. Women, Ballads, and Infanticide in Early Modern Scotland*, Pennsylvania, Pennyslvania State University Press, Appendix II.

5. On precognitions as a source, see Crowther, M.A. (1995), 'The criminal precognitions and their value for the historian', *Scottish Archives* 1, pp. 75–84.

6. Kilday notes that 140 women were tried for child murder and concealment of pregnancy in the South-West of Scotland between 1750 and 1815. The absence of research for other parts of the country makes comparisons impossible.

7. See Brown, Callum G. (1998), *Up-Helly-Aa: Custom, Culture and Community in Shetland*, Manchester, Mandolin, pp. 63–75.

8. For a more general discussion of women in Shetland, see Abrams, Lynn (2000), '"The best men in Shetland": women, gender and place in peripheral communities', in Payton, Philip (ed.), *Cornish Studies: Eight*, Exeter, University of Exeter Press, pp. 97–114; and Fryer, Linda G. (1995), '*Knitting by the Fireside and on the Hillside': A History of the Shetland Hand Knitting Industry c. 1600–1950*, Lerwick, The Shetland Times.

9. There are just three cases in the eighteenth century, 29 in the nineteenth and seven in the twentieth.

10. SA (Shetland Archives), SC 12/6/1859/2: judicial declaration of Jemima Nicolson, 19 Feb. 1859.

11. SA, AD 22/2/6/4: Laura Scott, concealment of pregnancy, 8 Oct. 1862.

12. See Symonds, *Weep Not For Me*, pp. 124–5.

13. Edmondston, Arthur (1809), *A View of the Present State of the Zetland Islands*, 2 vols. Edinburgh, James Ballantyne & Co, p.63.

14. SA, SC 12/6/1699/1: Process anent child murder, 1699. I would like to thank

Angus Johnson, archivist, for transcribing the text of this document.

15. On the implementation of this Act, see Anne-Marie Kilday's chapter in this volume. Also Symonds, *Weep Not for Me*, Chapters 5 and 6.
16. SA, AD 22/2/34/40: Gina Skaar, concealment of pregnancy, 10 Feb. 1899.
17. *The Shetland News*, 25 Mar. 1899.
18. *The Shetland News*, 13 May 1899.
19. Quoted in Symonds, *Weep Not for Me*, p. 145.
20. *Ibid.*, pp. 146–7.
21. Ward, Tony (1999), 'The sad subject of infanticide: law, medicine and child murder, 1860–1938', *Social and Legal Studies* 8:2.
22. See www.bbc.co.uk/qed/neo.shtml. Also Gowing, 'Secret births and infanticide', p. 107.
23. See Rublack, *The Crimes of Women*, pp. 172–4. On women's interpretations of the body, see Duden, Barbara (1991), *The Woman Beneath the Skin: a Doctor's Patients in Eighteenth Century Germany*, Cambridge, Mass., Harvard University Press.
24. SA, AD 22/2/4/24: Jemima Nicolson, concealment of pregnancy, 21 Feb. 1859.
25. SA, AD 22/2/3/39: Christina Williamson, concealment of pregnancy, 7 May 1857.
26. SA, AD 22/2/28/5: Margaret Johnston, concealment of pregnancy, 23 Sept. 1893.
27. Ibid.
28. SA, SC 12/6/1815/44: Margaret Fraser, child murder, 27 Sept. 1815.
29. SA, AD 22/2/33/21: Janet Deyell, child murder/concealment of pregnancy, 1 Aug. 1898.
30. Rublack, *Crimes of Women*, p. 175.
31. SA, AD 22/6/1815/44: Margaret Fraser, 27 Sept. 1815.
32. SA, AD 22/2/24/40: Gina Skaar, 10 July 1899.
33. SA, AD 22/2/1/55: Agnes Hawick, child murder or concealment of pregnancy, 25 May 1854.
34. SA, AD 22/2/1/8/2: Mary Twatt, concealment of pregnancy, child murder, incest (precognition of James Twatt) 29 July 1853.
35. Ibid: precognition of Barbara Fraser or Jamieson.
36. SA, AD 22/2/43/29: Williamina Clark, concealment of pregnancy, 13 Mar. 1908.
37. See SA, SC 12/6/1783/8: Margaret Omond, child murder, July 1783. William Mitchell, minister of Tingwall parish: 'I have made the enquiry desired relative to the shocking affair of Margaret Omond . . . now in the Presbytery's opinion guilty of child murder by the Act of William and Mary which I have read several times from the pulpit . . .', 12 July 1873.
38. SA, SC 12/6/1794/17: Marion Henrysdaughter, child murder, 8 Nov. 1794.
39. SA, AD 22/2/2/8: Margaret Mitchell or Walterson, child murder, 23 May 1855.
40. SA, SC 12/6/1830/111: Janet Leisk, child murder, 8 Oct. 1830.
41. SA, AD 22/2/1/55: Agnes Hawick, 25 May 1854.
42. SA, AD 12/6/1815/44: Margaret Fraser, 27 Sept. 1815 (evidence of Catherine Mouat).
43. Ibid. (evidence of Catherine Laing).
44. Ibid. (evidence of Magdalene Moncrieff.

45. See Rowlands, '"In great secrecy"', 106–7. On the rituals surrounding women who had just given birth, see Wilson, Stephen (2000), *The Magical Universe: Everyday Ritual and Magic in Pre-Modern Europe*, London, Hambledon, pp.171–95.

46. 'Women at the time of child-bearing were especially liable to be taken by *hillfolk*, and hence the midwife was generally an expert in the art of preserving her charge from the *trows*', in Spence, John (1899, reprinted 1973), *Shetland Folk-lore*, Johnson and Greig, Lerwick, p.165. See also Henderson, L. and Cowan, E.J. (2001), *Scottish Fairy Belief*, East Linton, Tuckwell Press, pp. 74–6.

47. SA, SC 12/6/1859/2: Jemima Nicolson, concealment of pregnancy, 19 Feb. 1859.

48. SA, AD 22/2/30/50: Mary Dempster, concealment of pregnancy, 4 Oct. 1895.

49. SA, AD 22/2/38/42: Robina Ritch or Pennant, concealment of pregnancy, 14 June 1903.

50. Ibid.

51. See Schulte, Regina (1994), *The Village in Court. Arson, Infanticide and Poaching in the Court Records of Upper Bavaria, 1848–1910*, Cambridge, Cambridge University Press, p. 104.

52. A sillock is the fry of the coalfish.

53. SA, AD 22/2/4/24: Jemima Nicolson, 19. Feb 1859 (precognition of Charlotte Spencer).

54. SA, SC 12/6/1859/2: Jemima Nicolson, judicial declaration, 19 Feb. 1859.

55. SA, SC 12/6/1811/28: Elizabeth Johnson, judicial declaration, 21 May 1811.

56. SA, SC 12/6/1815/44: Margaret Fraser, 8 Sept 1815.

57. SA, SC 12/6/1829/109: Margaret Thomson, judicial declaration, 14 Nov. 1829.

58. On the importance of noise at the birth, see Wilson, *The Magical Universe*, p. 172.

59. SA, AD 22/2/2/8: Margaret Walterson, child murder, 23 May 1855 (evidence of Gilbert Williamson).

60. Ibid. (evidence of Ann Harrison).

61. SA, AD 22/2/4/24: Jemima Nicolson, 21 Feb. 1859 (evidence of James Thomson, sheriff's officer).

62. SA, AD 22/2/34/40: Gina Skaar, precognition, 10 July 1899.

63. SA, AD 22/2/30/50: Mary Dempster, 4 Oct. 1895.

64. The only cases which mention violence towards the child are those of Margaret Fraser whose child was discovered to have a lacerated mouth and a swollen cheek (SA, SC 12/6/1815/44: 1815) and Janet Leisk who allegedly threw the dead body of a child out of the window of her house (SA, SC 12/6/1830/111: 1830).

65. SA, SC 12/6/1840/161: Jane White, child murder, 6 June 1840; SC 12/6/1840/177: Jane White, concealment of pregnancy, 1840.

66. SA, SC 12/6/1829/4: Margaret Thomson, judicial declaration, 14 Nov. 1829.

67. Mackenzie, W.L. (1917), *Report on the Physical Welfare of Mothers and Children. Volume 3 (Scotland)*, Carnegie, Dunfermline, pp. 484–5. See also Cowie, Robert (1874), *Shetland: Descriptive and Historical*, 2nd edition, Edinburgh: 'Among island women complications in the process of parturition

are extremely rare, the very great majority of labours being both natural and speedy'.
68. SA, SC 12/6/1833/110: Lillias Umphray, child murder, 15 Oct. 1833.
69. SA, AD 22/2/1/8/2: Mary Twatt, 1853 (precognition of Barbara Jamieson).
70. SA, AD 22/2/61: Mary Twatt, judicial declaration, 29 Aug. 1853; Margaret Twatt, 2 Aug. 1853.
71. SA, AD 22/2/20/29: Mary Williamson, concealment of pregnancy, 25 Apr. 1885.
72. SA, SC 12/6/1834/47a: Lillias Umphray, 1 Mar. 1834.
73. See Wilson, *The Magical Universe*, pp. 215–6; Schulte, *Village in Court*, p. 106.
74. SA, SC 12/6/1829/109: Margaret Thomson, child murder, judicial declaration, 14 Nov. 1829.
75. SA, SC 12/6/1794/17: Marion Henrysdaughter, judicial declaration, 8 Nov. 1794.
76. SA, SC 12/6/1783/8: Margaret Omond, 3 July 1783.
77. SA, AD 22/2/34/40: Gina Skaar (evidence of William Pole), 10 July 1899.
78. *The Shetland News*, 25 Mar. 1899.

FURTHER READING

Abrams, L. (2000), '"The best men in Shetland": women, gender and place in peripheral communities', in Payton, Philip (ed.), *Cornish Studies: Eight*, Exeter, University of Exeter Press, pp. 97–114.

Duden, B. (1991), *The Woman Beneath the Skin: a Doctor's Patients in Eighteenth Century Germany*, Cambridge, Mass., Harvard University Press.

Fryer, L. G. (1995), '*Knitting by the Fireside and on the Hillside*': A History of the Shetland Hand Knitting Industry c.1600–1950, Lerwick, The Shetland Times.

Gowing, L. (1997), 'Secret births and infanticide in 17th century England', *Past and Present* 156, 87–115.

Henderson, L. and Cowan, E.J. (2001), *Scottish Fairy Belief*, East Linton, Tuckwell Press.

Mitchison, R. K. and Leneman, L. (1989), *Sexuality and Social Control – Scotland, 1660–1780*, Oxford, Oxford University Press.

Mitchison, R. and Leneman, L. (1998), *Girls in Trouble. Sexuality and Social Control in Rural Scotland, 1660–1780.* Edinburgh, Scottish Cultural Press.

Rowlands, A. (1997), '"In great secrecy": the crime of infanticide in Rothenburg ob der Tauber, 1501–1618', *German History* 15:2, pp. 101–21.

Rublack, U. (1999), *The Crimes of Women in Early Modern Germany*, Oxford, Oxford University Press.

Schulte, R. (1994), *The Village in Court. Arson, Infanticide and Poaching in the Court Records of Upper Bavaria, 1848–1910*, Cambridge, Cambridge University Press.

Symonds, D. (1997), *Weep Not For Me. Women, Ballads, and Infanticide in Early Modern Scotland*, Pennsylvania, Pennsylvania State University Press.

Wilson, S. (2000), *The Magical Universe: Everyday Ritual and Magic in Pre-Modern Europe*, London, Hambledon.

INDEX